MODERN ISLAMIC AUTHORITY AND SOCIAL CHANGE

VOLUME 2

MODERN ISLAMIC AUTHORITY AND SOCIAL CHANGE

VOLUME 2

EVOLVING DEBATES IN THE WEST

♦ ♦ ♦

EDITED BY MASOODA BANO

EDINBURGH
University Press

Edinburgh University Press is one of the leading university presses in the U.K. We publish academic books and journals in our selected subject areas across the humanities and social sciences, combining cutting-edge scholarship with high editorial and production values to produce academic works of lasting importance. For more information visit our website: edinburghuniversitypress.com

Edinburgh University Press Ltd
The Tun—Holyrood Road
12 (2f) Jackson's Entry
Edinburgh EH8 8PJ

Typeset in 10/12 Adobe Sabon by
IDSUK (DataConnection) Ltd, and
printed and bound in the United States of America

A CIP record for this book is available from the British Library

ISBN 978 1 4744 3326 6 (hardback)
ISBN 978 1 4744 3328 0 (webready PDF)
ISBN 978 1 4744 3329 7 (epub)

CONTENTS

Preface vii
Note on Transliteration xii
Glossary xiii

Introduction 1
Masooda Bano

Part I Neo-Traditionalists

1. Zaytuna College and the Construction of an American Muslim Identity 39
Nathan Spannaus and Christopher Pooya Razavian

2. The Neo-Traditionalism of Tim Winter 72
Christopher Pooya Razavian

Part II Neo-Legalists

3. From "Islamization of Knowledge" to "American Islam": the International Institute of Islamic Thought (IIIT) 97
Nathan Spannaus

4. Transformative Islamic Reform: Tariq Ramadan and the Center for Islamic Legislation and Ethics (CILE) 123
Nathan Spannaus

Part III Neo-Conservatives

5. Yasir Qadhi and the Development of Reasonable Salafism 155
Christopher Pooya Razavian

6. New Deobandi Institutions in the West 180
Christopher Pooya Razavian and Nathan Spannaus

Notes on the Contributors 211
Index 212

Tables

I.1 Profile of Muslim population in the West 6
1.1 Curriculum of Zaytuna College 59
2.1 Curriculum of CMC 89
6.1 Curriculum of Darul Qasim 185
6.2 Curriculum of Ebrahim College 186
6.3 Curriculum of Darul Uloom New York 189

Map

I.1 Key sites of Islamic knowledge production: the U.S.A. and the U.K. 14

PREFACE

These two volumes are among the first works to be published as part of a five-year project, *Changing Structures of Islamic Authority and Consequences for Social Change: A Transnational Review*, which I initiated in 2014 with the support of a European Research Council (ERC) Start-up Grant: European Union's Seventh Framework Programme (FP7/2007-2013)/ERC grant agreement no. [337108]. These ERC investigator grants, as they are more commonly known, invest in a compelling research idea by allowing the Principal Investigator the time (five years) and resources (close to 1.5 million Euros) to build a team. These volumes are a product of one such team effort.

Since September 11, 2001, Islamic legal and political thought, as well as the socio-economic and political attitudes of Muslims, have been intensively researched. However, the debate on whether it is the text or the context that drives some Muslims to espouse radical ideals remains unsettled. This project stems from a desire to explicitly address this question and map the plurality of Islamic intellectual thought; to see how scholars from within the dominant Islamic traditions engage with modernity; and, equally importantly, to present some decisive findings on what, if any, is the relationship between the socio-economic and political conditions in which the Muslims in question find themselves and their interpretation of the text. Why is it, after all, that intellectual and rationalist inquiry seemed to have flourished best within Muslim societies when they were politically and economically flourishing, and conservative and inward-looking Islamic movements developed strong roots in many Muslim countries under colonial rule, when Muslims were politically and economically marginalized? Historical analysis suggests that context plays a role in how the text is interpreted. As a social scientist interested in the study of societal conditions and Islamic knowledge transmission, mapping the influence of context in both the creation and transmission of Islamic knowledge remains core to my research. My focus in developing this project was thus two-fold: one, to examine how globally influential Islamic scholarly platforms are engaging with change, with a view to mapping the plurality within the tradition; and, two, to situate each tradition within the socio-economic and political conditions in which it evolved, in order to better understand its historical evolution, and consequently to better predict how its current relationship with the state and society may influence its future trajectory.

The impetus for this project, not surprisingly, came from my earlier research. Since 2006 a combination of research fellowships and research grants have enabled me to carry out fieldwork across a number of Muslim contexts. More specifically, I have maintained two long-term fieldwork sites, in Pakistan and northern Nigeria, and a number of semi-permanent ones, where I return periodically for short periods of fieldwork (Egypt, Syria, and Turkey in the Middle East; Bangladesh and India in South Asia; and Saudi Arabia in the Gulf). The details of most of this fieldwork are available in my earlier publications, and in particular in my recently published monograph, *Female Islamic Education Movements: The Re-Democratisation of Islamic Knowledge*, which draws on my fieldwork in three of these sites. In addition, I have had opportunities to conduct interviews within Islamic networks in both Malaysia and Indonesia, thereby gaining reasonable exposure to the East Asian Islamic tradition, although I have chosen not to write about it. Further, since 2012, and particularly as part of this project, I have conducted fieldwork with a number of new Islamic scholarly institutions emerging in the West; I have also taken part in many retreats organized by them. The observations that I make in the introduction to Volume 2 thus draw on this ongoing fieldwork with these institutions in the West.

Comparative accounts are challenging to produce, because they require time, an ability to relate to different contexts, and financial resources. They particularly make area specialists nervous. For comparativists like me, however, the excitement of an academic endeavour rests in identifying any common patterns across the peculiarity of each context; we are often driven to identify the core drivers of institutional change and persistence. While I personally find single-author comparative studies most compelling, it is true that a certain kind of comparative work is best done as a team. Studying the plurality of Sunni Islamic scholarly tradition and embedding the evolution of these competing platforms within their specific societal and historical context not only required a very sound knowledge of Islamic textual sources, but equally it required interdisciplinary expertise; in other words, it required building a team.

In the first two years of this project, I was thus very fortunate to have the assistance of two very bright minds to advance this undertaking: Nathan Spannaus used his training in Islamic intellectual history to trace the evolution of each scholarly platform being studied, and map its relationship with the state and society, while Pooya Razavian, a student of Islamic Studies and also trained in traditional Islamic scholarly tradition in Iran, took the lead on analysis of the Islamic legal debates. I, on the other hand, retained a focus on mapping the contemporary political economy of these institutions. We were also fortunate to have support of Emre Caliskan, a doctoral candidate at Oxford, who brought knowledge of Turkish language to the team. It is this convergence of expertise that is, to me, the core strength of these two volumes; thus Volume 1 not only offers a rare comparison of current debates within the four most influential Sunni Islamic scholarly platforms today; it also presents a more comprehensive analysis of the evolution of each than is normally available in existing publications.

Volume 2 is organized differently from Volume 1; yet it is important to note that the analytical approach and core driving questions are the same. The different organizational structure is actually reflective of the very recent history of the Islamic institutions in the West. Volume 2 focuses on the new institutions emerging in the West that have started to rival the authority of the four institutions covered in Volume 1. Being relatively new, these institutions did not lend themselves to the three-chapter analytical format adopted in Volume 1: in terms of their origin, there were not centuries of history to cover; further, because of being based in the U.K. or the U.S.A., their socio-political context was also less varied than that of the institutions covered in Volume 1. Thus, in Volume 2 I could provide the contextual information on the evolution of all the institutions covered within the introduction, as opposed to dedicating individual chapters to each.

These two volumes are thus not edited volumes in a classical sense, whereby scholars tailor their ongoing research to fit a specific call; instead, they are the product of a team project in which ideas were constantly developed in consultation. While the standard model allows for bringing together the experts in specialist traditions, under the team model the main advantage is that each institution is studied using the same methodological lens and the same conceptual framework. Also, all institutions are subjected to the same starting assumptions or biases (if any). The benefit of this model will, I hope, be easy to appreciate in Volume 1, which systematically compares the four most influential Islamic scholarly platforms in Sunni Islam today; it should prove particularly useful as resource material for teaching.

Here I also wish to address two important issues raised by the reviewers of these two volumes. I address them here rather than in the introduction so as to draw attention to them. First, these two volumes focus on Modern Islamic Authorities within the Sunni scholarly tradition. Thus, they do not claim to map the entire landscape of modern Islamic authority; the most obvious omissions are the leading Islamic scholarly platforms within the Shi'i tradition, Sufi *ṭarīqah*s, and political Islamists such as the Muslim Brotherhood in the Middle East and Jamaat-i-Islami in South Asia. While including examples from these other sources of Islamic authority was desirable, to create space for them within these two volumes was impossible without fundamentally re-orienting the scope of the project. The focus of this project was to study in-depth the most influential Islamic scholarly platforms within the Sunni tradition, and these two volumes have focused narrowly on that. Ideally, we need to develop the same level of in-depth comparative analysis for these other sources

(Shi'i tradition) and forms (Sufi *ṭarīqah*s and political Islam) of Islamic authority to complement these two volumes.

Second, I would like to acknowledge that in the respective introduction to each volume I make some strong assertions. These relate to my reading of how power dynamics are changing *within* the Islamic authority platforms based in Muslim-majority countries covered in Volume 1 as well as *between* them and the new platforms emerging in the West. Further, I make certain assertions about the changing attitudes of young Muslims. I fully recognize that these assertions require further testing. All such arguments are based on the multi-sited fieldwork that I have been conducting since 2006, as explained above; they are based on what I have heard or observed across a number of different contexts. I am therefore as confident of advancing these arguments as a qualitative researcher who feels that they are observing a societal shift in the making can ever be. It could be that, if exposed to further testing through survey-based or other quantitative research methods, some of these observations could be questioned. But I make these assertions precisely in order to motivate such investigations. I am of the view that major socio-economic shifts are under way in Muslim societies and among Muslim diaspora communities in the West, and that these shifts are also going to have major consequences for the transmission of Islamic knowledge in the coming decades and for the power balance between old Islamic authority platforms in Muslim-majority countries and the new ones emerging in the West. My intention here is not to prove that my reading of these developments is correct, given that the change, in my view, is still in the making; it is to inspire further research in this area. In the remaining period of this project, I myself am working with a quantitative researcher and an ethnographer to further test some of the arguments that I put forward.

Finally, I must thank the members of the project advisory committee, who have given (and continue to give) generously of their time and expertise. These include Marcus Banks, John Bowen, Morgan Clarke, Rob Gleave, Stéphane Lacroix, Dietrich Reetz, Francis Robinson, and Malika Zeghal. I remain extremely grateful to them for their support and inspiration; with some of them in particular my debts are very old. As can be expected of an advisory committee consisting of such individuals, I cannot claim to have successfully absorbed all their comments and feedback—however, I have tried my best to do so. Equally, I remain indebted to Muhammad Qasim Zaman, who, from 2011 to 2013, accommodated three meetings with me during my visits to Princeton. (For the last one I had actually arrived unannounced on a Sunday afternoon, encouraged by one of his colleagues that I was bound to find him in his office.) These meetings, which took place before the project started, were instrumental in helping me refine those of my ideas that eventually led to its initiation. I thus remain very grateful for the time that he gave me. I also am indebted to the King Faisal Center for Research and Islamic Studies (KFCRIS) for hosting me during my periods of fieldwork in Saudi Arabia and to Dr. Saud al-Sarhan, KFCRIS's Director, for providing very valuable feedback. My chapter on Saudi Salafism would not have materialized without KFCRIS's support. I will also like to take this opportunity to thank Nicola Ramsey, my editor at Edinburgh University Press, who—despite the length of Volume 1—approached the project with great enthusiasm. I remain indebted to her for her encouragement and support.

Last but not least, I must note the support that Nicola Shepard has provided me during this period. Although mainly appointed to oversee the administrative aspects of the project, she has in practice contributed much more than that.

I have chosen to write a shared Preface to Volume 1 and Volume 2 in the hope that, whichever of the two volumes you may have in your hands now, its scope and contribution will be easy to follow.

Masooda Bano
June 9, 2017
Oxford

NOTE ON TRANSLITERATION

Though addressed to a multi-disciplinary audience, these two volumes follow relatively strict transliteration rules instead of restricting themselves to the use of ʿ to indicate ʿayn and ʾ hamza (the latter being the norm in social science). This decision stems from a desire to be rigorous in referring to Islamic textual sources, legal concepts, and early Muslim jurists and writers. Thus, names of leading Islamic jurists, scholars, or mystics from before the nineteenth century have been transliterated, as have generic Islamic institutional labels such as *dār al-ʿulūm* (house of science). However, when an institution itself maintains a website and publishes an English version of its name, in that case the spellings used by the institution have been adopted: thus Darul Uloom Deoband, as opposed to *Dār al-ʿUlūm* Deoband; or Nadwatul Ulama, as opposed to Nadwat al-ʿUlamāʾ. In the light of the heavy transliteration, all foreign words have been italicized and included in the glossary, so that those readers less conversant with them can easily identify them and consult the glossary. It is hoped that this balance will ensure that the transliteration meets the expectations of Islamic Studies specialists, while the text remains easily accessible to scholars from other disciplines.

GLOSSARY

adab	Islamic norms of behavior and comportment
Ahl al-Sunnah wa al-Jamā'a	the people of the *sunnah* and the community; refers to Sunni Islam
alimiyyah	undergraduate degree awarded at various *dār al-'ulūm*
'aqīdah	Islamic creed or religious beliefs
Dars-i Niẓāmī	a curriculum that originated in South Asia used in traditional Islamic institutions
dār al-ḥarb	"abode of war", the non-Muslim world, the opposite of *dār al-Islām*
dār al-Islām	"abode of Islam", the Muslim world, the opposite of *dār al-ḥarb*
dār al-'ulūm	"house of the sciences", a common title used in South Asia for an Islamic seminary or educational institution
dhimmah	the agreement of protection for non-Muslims living in a Muslim country
faqīh (pl. *fuqahā'*)	an Islamic jurist, an expert in *fiqh*
Fātiḥah	the opening chapter of the Qur'ān
fatwā	a formal but generally non-binding statement on an issue or question related to Islamic law, given by a *muftī* (from Ar. *iftā'*, "to advise")
fiqh	"understanding"; Islamic law or jurisprudence
fiqh al-aqallīyāt	minority *fiqh*, suited for Muslims living in non-Muslim societies
fitnah	temptation, disorder, civil strife
furū'	Islamic positive law (the "branches" of *fiqh*)
ḥadīth	reports describing the words, actions, or habits of Prophet Muhammad

Ḥākimīyah	the rule of God
ḥifẓ	memorization (e.g. of the Qur'ān)
hijāb	head covering for women
hikmah	wisdom
ḥudūd	criminal punishments of scriptural origin
'ibādāt	category of Islamic law related to religious ritual and acts of worship
iftā'	the act of issuing a legal opinion (*fatwā*)
ijāzah	certificate awarded to a student in traditional Islamic studies and enables the student to teach the same texts
ijtihād	the process of legal reasoning in which the jurist applies maximum effort in order derive a ruling
ikhtilāf	disagreement
imām	"one who stands in front", commonly used to one who leads prayer
isnād	chain of narrators
istiḥālah	transformation
jāhilīyah	"ignorance"; often used to describe the "ignorant" way of life of the Arabs before Islam
jalāl	majesty
jamāl	beauty
jihad	to strive, to exert, to fight; legal warfare
kalām	Islamic theology
khayrāt	charity; alms
madhhab	an Islamic legal school of thought (lit. "way")
madrasah	a higher Islamic school
māl	intrinsic value
maqāṣid al-sharī'ah	a methodology of Islamic legal interpretation that focuses on the "objectives" of the *sharī'ah* as guiding principles
maṣlaḥah	the common good
muftī	jurisconsult; a learned scholar in Islamic law, qualified to give *fatwā*
mu'āmalāt	category of Islamic law related to social life and human interactions
mut'ah	time based marriage contract
naskh	abrogation
najis	impure
niqāb	face veil
qaṭ'ī	a classification in Islamic epistemology for knowledge that is certain and definitive
Qur'ān	the Islamic sacred book

Qur'ānic	relating to the Qur'ān
ṣadaqah	charity, alms
al-salaf al-sāliḥ	"pious forebears", the first generations of Muslims
sharī'ah	God's eternal will for humanity that is considered binding. The ideal of Islamic law
shaykh	an honorific title applied to men who have gained religious learning
ṣuḥbah	Friendship, companionship, comradeship
sunnah	Established custom and cumulative tradition based on Prophet Muhammad's example
tajwīd	the art of Qur'ānic recitation
tanzīh	God's transcendence
taqīyah	precautionary dissimulation, denial of religious belief or practice in fear of persecution
taqlīd	following another's position or judgment in Islamic legal or religious matters
taṣawwuf	Sufism, Islamic mysticism
tashbīh	God's immanence
tawḥīd	oneness of God
'ulamā'	religious scholars
ummah	the global Muslim community
uṣūl al-fiqh	Islamic legal theory (the "roots" of fiqh)
al-walā' wa al-barā'	loyalty and disavowal
waḥī	givine revelation
wilāyah	guardianship
wilāyah al-takwīnī	Shi'i belief that with the permission of God the prophets and *imām*s can bring about change within the material world
zakāt	obligatory charity, one of the five pillars of Islam
ẓannī	a classification in Islamic epistemology for knowledge that is probable or conjectural

INTRODUCTION

Masooda Bano

At the turn of the twenty-first century, any suggestion that the authority of traditional centers of learning in Muslim-majority countries could be eclipsed by new Islamic institutions emerging in the West would have appeared so incongruous as to merit no debate: after all, Muslim diaspora communities in the West have from the beginning staffed their newly found mosques with *imāms* from their home countries.[1] Yet, as we will see in this volume, in 2016 such an assertion is easily defensible: increasingly, some of the prominent Islamic scholars today (with followers across the globe, especially among educated Muslims) are born or raised in the Western hemisphere. While Volume 1 mapped the discourses within the four most influential Islamic scholarly platforms in the Muslim-majority countries as they face pressures to adapt to the demands of modern times, this volume maps the weakening of their authority among pockets of second- and third-generation Muslims in the West whose socio-economic and cultural orientation is distinctly different from that of their parents' generation. Better educated than their parents and more socially integrated,[2] many young Muslims are turning for advice to new Islamic scholarly platforms emerging in the West, led by charismatic scholars. To understand the landscape of contemporary Islamic authority, it is important to recognize the growing influence of these institutions emerging in the West. By mapping the ongoing debates within these platforms, the volume illustrates how, despite growing concerns about the radicalization of young Muslims in the West, the current Islamic religious milieu in the West is highly conducive to nurturing an Islamic understanding that, while respecting the core of the Islamic tradition, is also proving adept at guiding young Muslims to be confident members of their respective societies.

Measured purely against the yardstick of traditional Islamic scholarly rigor, the scholars leading these platforms may not appear as grounded as the traditionally trained *'ulamā'* discussed in Volume 1. In fact, all scholars considered in this volume, apart from those from the Deoband tradition, avoid the title of *'ālim* (specialist in Islamic sciences); the most popular honorific used by their followers is that of *shaykh* (a more generic title of respect; a learned man). Most prefer to guide their followers, as we will see, to the work of earlier scholars when it comes to addressing a complex *fiqh* issue, instead of trying to engage in a detailed discussion of Islamic legal theory themselves. Yet these scholars are highly effective in making educated young Muslims in the West, many of whom are leaving the mosques,[3] respect Islamic legal and moral dictates. What explains their appeal? The answer to this rests in understanding how a legal or moral code, if it is to stay binding, has to demonstrate social relevance: these scholars are able to operationalize Islamic legal and ethical principles for the young Muslims; they are able to act as a bridge between Islamic and Western philosophical and legal traditions. In other words, the main strength of these new Islamic scholarly platforms emerging in the West rests in the ability of the scholars leading them to combine their *tacit* knowledge of the modern reality with the Islamic moral and legal framework.

Scholars writing about the importance of knowledge in social theory have emphasized the need to differentiate between various categories of knowledge. An important distinction is maintained between knowledge acquired through direct experience (*tacit or lay knowledge*) and knowledge that is acquired through a formal learning process (*communicable or specialist knowledge*). Introduced by Michael Polanyi, the concept of tacit knowledge has had popular appeal because of its implicit suggestion that "*we can know more than we can tell*", as much human learning happens unconsciously through being part of a given environment, context, and culture.[4] The key to appreciating the importance of the new Islamic scholarly platforms emerging in the West rests in recognising the role of tacit knowledge in enabling a scholar to relate the Islamic legal and moral framework to the reality as understood by his followers.

The scholars leading these new initiatives have invested heavily in acquiring specialist knowledge of traditional Islamic sciences; most have dedicated many years to studying with traditional scholars in Muslim-majority countries. Their ability to demonstrate sound knowledge of these sciences is by all counts critical to establishing their authority. Their main appeal to educated young Muslims, however, rests not in their attempts to write complex treatises on Islamic *fiqh*; instead their influence stems from their ability to combine that specialized Islamic knowledge with their personal everyday experience of being a modern-educated Western Muslim who is exposed to the same opportunities, temptations, and challenges as they are. Coming mainly from middle-income and educated families, these scholars have a very different socio-economic and educational profile (and consequently different experiences, tastes, and sensibilities) from most of the traditionally trained *'ulamā'* in the institutions profiled in Volume 1. These scholars are keen to combine Islamic and Western knowledge to enable young Muslims to see the links between their everyday life choices and the Islamic legal and moral framework. It is this ability to bridge the gap between Islamic and modern forms of knowledge, rather than necessarily a very fine command of traditional *fiqh* debates, that is central to the growing appeal of the scholars profiled in this volume, because this is precisely the ability that many traditionally trained *'ulamā'* have lacked since the colonial period.[5]

As is well recorded, the colonial period led to the displacement by Western educational institutions of *madrasahs* as the primary platform for imparting knowledge. The result was two-fold: one, *madrasah* education lost its socio-economic relevance, and a marked separation developed between Islamic and modern sciences; two, Muslim social elites deserted the *madrasahs* in favour of Western educational institutions.[6] Since the colonial period, *madrasahs* in all Muslim-majority countries have catered primarily to students from lower-income families; these very students then go on to become future teachers and *'ulamā'*.[7] The result is that the everyday realities and experiences of the Islamic scholars being trained through *madrasah* platforms are totally different from those of Muslims from upper-middle-income and affluent classes who, on the other hand, shape the socio-economic institutions. This has led to bifurcated mental models among Muslims, whereby Islam remains very important as a personal belief system, and in this arena *'ulamā'* continue to command respect, but in social, economic, and political matters, Islamic law or moral code, and *'ulamā'* who claim specialist expertise in it, are seen as irrelevant.[8]

The real contribution of these new Islamic scholars in the West is that they are reversing this isolation of Islamic and modern knowledge (some consciously, others unknowingly), for two reasons. First, these scholars are keen to draw parallels between Islamic moral, legal, and philosophical concepts and those concepts that have become globally influential under Western influence. These scholars take the dominant Western realities and then explain them within an Islamic framework, not necessarily by participating in complex *fiqh* debates (although they do use some core concepts or make reference to the work of a specialist), but by resolving the apparent intellectual tension between Islam and modern social reality. Being able to engage equally effectively with both the modern and Islamic modes of knowledge and thinking, these scholars are particularly effective in operationalizing the Islamic moral and legal framework for young and socially integrated Muslims in the West who want to balance the demands of their faith with being active members of their societies. Second, because they themselves come from middle-income social strata, they have tacit knowledge of the reality as experienced by their followers, and thus can relate to their concerns more meaningfully.

Here it is also very important to note that the key to the growing popularity of the institutions profiled in this volume is that, even though they are actively trying to connect Islamic and Western philosophical concepts and debates, they are not aspiring to create a "modern" or "enlightened" Islam, unlike the post-colonial secular political and military élites, who wanted Islamic dictates to fit the Western moral and legal framework.[9] Instead, the potential of these initiatives to become the leading voice of Islam in the coming decades rests in their keenness to stay true to Islamic legal dictates while also deploying the methodological creativity allowed in classical Islamic *fiqh* (jurisprudence) to keep abreast of contemporary realities. Thus, while encouraging reasoned debate and trying to build synergy between many Western and Islamic concepts and ethics, unlike the modernists, these scholars do not agree with abandoning or reforming aspects of Islamic *fiqh* that are seen to be inconsistent with Western modernity or liberal theory; instead, their focus is on learning to respect the core of Islamic *fiqh* while being confident enough to reason and debate and find creative responses to questions whose answers are either unsettled or require fresh reasoning in the light of the changed context. This balance between being loyal to tradition and staying responsive to modern changes is not easily struck (as we also saw in Volume 1); yet we will see how the deliberations taking place on the platforms covered in this volume are highly promising.

It is precisely because of their commitment to strive for such a balance that I contend that these institutions are to play an important role in the way that Islam is understood and lived by *affluent* Muslim communities around the globe. The emphasis on "affluent" is noteworthy; as we will see, it is material affluence, rather than nationality or ethnicity, that best explains the growing appeal of these institutions, both within the diaspora Muslim communities in the West and among more educated youth in Muslim-majority countries. It is the young, educated, and civilization-sensitive Muslims (who regard Islam not just as a rigid theological or legal framework but as a rich philosophical, cultural, and legalistic tradition) who are most visible among the followers of the institutions in question. Admittedly, such an assertion about the profile of their followers needs to be supported by survey data. For now, I base this claim on the prolonged fieldwork that I have been conducting with some of the institutions considered in this volume, through participation in their retreats, conferences, and seminars, and interviews with their members (see Preface). The followers whom I have interviewed almost always come from more economically prosperous, educated, and socially progressive sections of society, whether from within the Muslim diaspora communities in the West or from Muslim-majority counties. Their influence on Muslim social elites around the globe is, therefore, growing—and driving this expansion are the globalized sensibilities of economically well-to-do Muslims, who are increasingly part of the global value system and culture mapped in some detail in Volume 1.

Thus, while many studies show that the planners of militant attacks come from educated and upper-middle-income classes,[10] this volume reinforces the conclusion from Volume 1 that profiles of individual militants should not distract us from the fact that economic prosperity and democratic strengthening in Muslim societies are the best antidotes to militant Islam. As studies have shown, among the ideologically driven, it is not individual grievances but societal injustices or perceived marginalization of the communities to which those individuals belong that more often than not help to create sympathy for radical movements.[11] Many, however, are driven not by ideology or economics but (as we are increasingly finding in cases of recent attacks in Western cities) by perverse incentives: a sense of adventure, frustrated aspirations, or simple criminal and deviant behavior.[12] In order to appreciate the significance of these new scholarly platforms in the West for shaping the Islam of the future, it is important to start by profiling the Muslim diaspora communities in the West and tracing the evolution of Islamic knowledge-transmission platforms within them.

Muslims and Islamic Knowledge Transmission in the West

While it is true that Islam spread rapidly to new territories within the first century of its emergence, it arguably became a truly global religion in the second half of the twentieth century, with Muslim communities of notable sizes emerging in Western Europe and North America, and to some degree even in Australia and New Zealand.[13] In 2010, there were an estimated 44 million Muslims in Europe, constituting 5.9 percent of the total population;[14] in the U.S.A., the total number of Muslims is estimated to be 3.3 million. At 0.8 percent of the total population the American Muslims constitute a much smaller share of the citizenry, yet their presence is equally pronounced. The profile of Muslim immigrant populations, however, varies both within Europe and between Europe and North America. Within Europe, the Muslim immigrant populations, barring a few exceptions, have strong links to the host country's colonial past. In the U.K., the South Asian migrants, particularly from Pakistan and Bangladesh, constitute the most visible Muslim community, followed by Arabs and Africans.[15] In France, Algerians and Moroccans have strong roots, as do Turks. In Germany, the Muslim immigrants are predominantly of Turkish origin, while Spain and Italy have comparatively smaller pockets of Muslim populations (see Table I.1).

These migratory trends, which developed from the middle of the twentieth century, were mainly a product of growing demands for labor in the fast-industrializing economy of Europe: not surprisingly, port cities and industrial towns developed the most densely populated Muslim neighborhoods.[16] The first generation of European Muslims who filled this demand for labor came overwhelmingly from low-income rural communities in their home countries, and they were the least endowed with the attributes—such as language, cultural exposure, or education—known to facilitate economic prosperity and cultural integration among migrant communities. Overwhelmingly Muslim neighborhoods, such as the Savile neighborhood in Dewsbury in the United Kingdom or Molenbeek in Brussels in Belgium,[17] which are today almost closed enclaves nurturing a parallel culture within their host communities, are products of these migratory origins. For these communities, ill-equipped to

Table I.1 Profile of Muslim population in the West

Country	**Muslim Population (No).**	**Muslim population (% share of population)**	**Key countries of origin**
Europe and U.K.			
Germany	4,760,000	5.8	Turkey
France	4,710,000	7.5	Algeria, Morocco, Tunisia
United Kingdom	2,960,000	4.8	Pakistan, India, Bangladesh
Italy	2,220,000	3.7	Libya, Eritrea, Somalia
Bulgaria	1,020,000	13.7	Turkey
Netherlands	1,000,000	6.0	Turkey, Morocco
Spain	980,000	2.1	Mixed (Algeria, Morocco, Nigeria, Pakistan, etc.)
Belgium	630,000	5.9	Tukey, Morocco
Greece	610,000	5.3	Turkey
Austria	450,000	5.4	Turkey, Bosnia
Sweden	430,000	4.6	Middle East, Iraq, Iran
Cyprus	280,000	25.3	Turkey
Denmark	230,000	4.1	Mixed
Romania	70,000	0.3	Mixed
Slovenia	70,000	3.6	Bosnia
Croatia	60,000	1.4	Mixed
Ireland	50,000	1.1	South Asia, Turkey
Finland	40,000	0.8	Mixed
Portugal	30,000	0.3	Mixed
Luxembourg	10,000	2.3	Mixed
North America			
United States (2015)	3, 300,000	1	Whites (28%), African-American (35%), Asians (18%), Hispanic (18%)
Canada (2011)	940,000	2.8	Mixed (Pakistan, Iran, Lebanon, Afghanistan, Somalia, Morocco, etc.)

Source: Pew Research Centre (2010 estimates)

integrate with the host communities or secure white-collar jobs, the economic marginalization of the first generation of immigrants has persisted until the present day.[18] In the United Kingdom, for example, only 25 percent of the Muslim population is engaged in economic activity—the lowest level within all religious groups—and fewer Muslims are in the top three professional occupations than members of any other faith community.[19] Successive waves of migration in the 1980s and subsequently in the present century have, however, attracted a more mixed pool of immigrants: globalization has increased opportunities for formal-sector employment, at least for individuals with technical skills.[20]

In the United States, on the other hand, the Muslim migration pattern has historically been different, and so is the socio-economic profile of the Muslim communities. Unlike Europe, the United States restricted immigration opportunities for all but the relatively better-educated and professional individuals. This has led to distinctly different patterns of integration, whereby most Muslims have been happy to be part of the American melting pot.[21] Muslims in the United States, on the whole, live in more ethnically and religiously mixed neighborhoods and are economically better off than their counterparts in the U.K. and Europe.[22] The United States also nurtures a distinct Black Muslim culture, owing much to the legacy of Malcolm X.[23] The two communities have traditionally had weak links, owing to their different socio-economic profiles. The Black American Muslims often come from lower-income backgrounds and neighborhoods than the immigrant communities;[24] prisons, in particular, proved a fertile ground for conversions among Blacks.[25] This economic divide is visible in many states and cities—Chicago being a good example—with the result that mosque culture varies strongly, depending on neighborhood characteristics. Recent initiatives, such as Zaytuna College (covered in this volume), which is led by two extremely prominent American Muslim converts—one black and the other white—are, however, demonstrating the potential to bridge this divide.

Across Europe, including the United Kingdom, and the United States, in order to preserve their Islamic beliefs and practices the first generation of Muslim immigrants found it essential to sponsor an *imām* (Islamic scholar) from their home communities to staff the local mosque.[26] The *imām*'s services were needed both to conduct the essential prayer rituals and to provide Islamic education for the young. Given the propensity within the first generation of immigrants to settle in ethnically homogeneous neighborhoods, the mosques in the United Kingdom and the rest of Europe have emerged mostly on ethnic and linguistic lines, each catering to the needs of the community that established and financed it.[27] In the United States the experience was similar, although, because neighborhoods are more mixed, the worshippers and the *imāms* in the mosques have a more ethnically mixed profile.[28] This heavy reliance on *imāms* from Muslim-majority countries has meant that dominant Islamic scholarly traditions have expanded successfully into the Western context. The four traditional centers of Islamic learning covered in Volume 1—al-Azhar, Diyanet, Deoband, and Saudi Salafism—were thus, not surprisingly, able to expand their influence to the Muslim diaspora in the West. *Imāms* trained in these four institutions lead many of the mosques across the United States, the United Kingdom, and other parts of Europe.[29] Some, as we will see, have also established important satellite institutions in the West.

While the Muslim communities in all European countries are influenced by all four of the traditions cited above, the extent of the influence of a particular institution in each country is proportional to the ethnic make-up of its Muslim diaspora community. Within Western Europe, Germany, the Netherlands, and France, which have large numbers of Turkish immigrants, Diyanet provides *imāms* to staff most Turkish mosques.[30] However, some Turkish communities, such as *Suleymancis*, *Millî Görüş*, and *Fethullah Gülen*, historically suspicious of Diyanet's secular outlook, have preferred to have their own *imāms;* the *Gülen* movement, since being implicated in the failed 2016 Turkish military coup, is, however, increasingly under pressure. Similarly, the presence of large numbers of *maghrebi* immigrants, mainly from Morocco, has meant that *imāms* trained in Moroccan religious institutions staff many European mosques sponsored by Moroccan communities; as John Bowen notes in his analysis of the French Islamic discourse, a mosque like the one in Fez will serve the needs of most French Muslims.[31] Morocco's Hassan II Foundation has also played a role in facilitating such links. However, within this community, the influence of al-Azhar University graduates has also been significant.

Within the United Kingdom, on the other hand, the large numbers of South Asian immigrants have ensured the domination of Deobandi Islam and its related missionary movement, Tableegi Jamaat. Unlike Diyanet and al-Azhar, the Deoband movement extended its influence within diaspora communities not solely through the supply of *imāms* or its graduates, but also by establishing a number of *madrasahs* in the United Kingdom and the United States. The Darul Uloom Deoband in Bury (established in 1975) and the one in Dewsbury (established in 1982, and also acting as the headquarters of Tableegi Jamaat in Europe) serve as important platforms for the teaching and training of *imāms* in the Deoband tradition in the West, as do their counterparts in New York and Buffalo. Although various other denominations in Sunni as well as Shi'i Islam have a visible presence in Europe[32] and the United States, these four traditions remain the most influential. Within South Asian communities, the main competition posed to Deoband comes from Barelvis, Jamaat-i-Islami, and more recently Minhaj ul Quran; the latter has a particularly expansive network in the Netherlands.[33]

More recently, however, three developments have facilitated the emergence of new Islamic scholarly platforms in the West. The first is the changing profile of the second- and third-generation Muslims, especially in the United Kingdom and other countries in Europe. While in the United States the first generation itself prospered economically and thereby was more integrated into the mainstream of society,[34] in the United Kingdom and Europe in general similar improvements are visible in pockets of second- and third-generation Muslims.[35] Access to higher education, employment in the formal sector, and growing up in a Western cultural framework are changing the subjectivities of many young Muslims, compared with their parents' generation.[36] It is thus not surprising that media reports indicate a decline in youth participation in mosque activities staffed by overseas *imāms*.[37]

Second, while September 11 has exposed Muslims to negative media publicity that has inflamed Islamophobia, these developments have also had an unexpected positive outcome: that of initiating critical self-reflection among many young Muslims. A few may have become radicalized since September 11, but others have been motivated to study Islamic texts to assess for themselves the validity of different claims attributed to Islam. This process of reflection and retrospection has led them to explore a range of Islamic education platforms and to search for scholars who can make sense of both Islam and the reality of their life in the Western world. The relative economic prosperity of the second- and third-generation Muslims compared with their parents' generation, and the increased self-reflection triggered by the events of September 11, has thus led to a generation of young Western Muslims who are reluctant to learn their Islam from an *imām* who does not share their background (often not even their language), and with whom they struggle to associate. The language in itself becomes a major barrier to establishing meaningful dialogue, and the *imām*'s lack of modern education and totally different cultural exposure further fails to engender respect.[38]

Third, especially in the United States, a visible community of Western converts has emerged. Many of these have embraced Islam not because of radical or reactionary tendencies, which at times are attributed to Western converts,[39] but in response to their inner calling. Many have a strong Christian background and are from educated middle-income families. Their embrace of Islam is thus not reactionary but a result of deep reflection on matters of theology. This volume shows how highly influential Muslim scholars in the West are emerging from within this expanding pool of converts. Many among them spend considerable time in the Muslim world, learning the basic texts; on their return, the knowledge acquired at the traditional centers of learning provides the legitimacy that leads to leadership positions within Muslim communities. The mixed origins of these converts enable them to choose a moderate path that, while being true to the core elements of the Islamic *fiqh,* is not hostile to Western tradition. Two of the most influential scholars among young Western Muslims—Humza Yusuf and Tim Winter (Abdal Hakim Murad)—share precisely this profile.

These recent developments, we will see, have spurred new Islamic initiatives in the West, with visible followings among educated young Muslims around the globe. Equally important is to note how the scholarly platforms emerging in North America are actually extremely dynamic. This reflects the difference in the economic profile of American Muslims. In the United States, most new Islamic educational and propagation platforms actually charge quite heavily for their services:[40] an affluent Muslim community, such as the one in America, which can pay for the use of these services, and can also donate generously,[41] is an essential prerequisite for these initiatives to thrive. Before looking at these initiatives, it is important to understand how Western states have tried to regulate Islamic education platforms and practices, and how these efforts have had little or no success.

Indigenizing Islam in the West: From Above

If September 11 has led to self-reflection among Muslim youth in the West, this period is also noticeable for the increased efforts by European governments to regulate or complement more effectively the mosque-based Islamic education platforms that have over the years multiplied among migrant Muslim populations. From the 1990s onwards, most European states began to recognize the need to better regulate the Islamic education sphere that was evolving within their Muslim communities. This led to increased efforts to establish state-led consultations, to form Muslim councils that would enable states to negotiate with different Islamic groups on one platform, and to establish commissions to represent the Muslim faith.[42] Prior to that, European states largely had a hands-off approach toward regulating Islamic education; Jonathan Laurence notes how until quite recently this was a task left to the foreign embassies of Muslim countries, which led to the domination of what he calls "Embassy Islam."[43] Since September 11, these efforts have acquired more immediate importance.

Studying the relationship between state and mosques in Belgium, France, Germany, Italy, the Netherlands, Spain, and the United Kingdom, Laurence notes, "State–mosque relations are of vital importance because these institutional links with religious communities prepare the ground for long-term political integration."[44] Mosques are important not just for children's education (a service that, as some studies have shown, is not as widely used as is often perceived, with many children dropping out before completing the course[45]), but for the wider networking opportunities that they provide for proselytizing groups such as Tableegi Jamaat, Salafis, and Hizb-ut-Tahrir.[46] Since September 11, European governments have initiated programmes to cultivate better links with the mosques; they have also argued for an increased role for Islamic councils, established in some form by all European countries. The governments have encouraged these councils, such as the Muslim Council of Britain (MCB),[47] to bring members of opposing Muslim groups together on one platform, because this helps them to regulate Islamic discourse. As Laurence notes: "State policies toward Islam between 1990 and 2010 have consisted of governments soliciting assurances directly from a broad range of Muslim groups in order to bring them into a regime of religious recognition for Islam, and doing so without significantly altering European state–church institutions."[48] These councils, he concludes, have helped to break the monopoly of "Embassy Islam."

But government efforts have not been confined to the mosques and the councils. In recent years many governments have initiated new programmes aimed at eradicating radical strands of Islam, driven by the realization that "either we train our Muslims to become global citizens, who live in a democratic, pluralist society, or on the contrary, the Islamists win, and take over those Muslim European constituencies."[49] Consequently, many European states have been involved in a protracted dialogue with the leaders of Muslim communities concerning the need to reform the existing models of Islamic education provision, which are viewed as promoting values that contradict the Western liberal tradition.[50] Some have initiated parallel programmes. The Netherlands, for instance, made it obligatory for *imāms* arriving from foreign lands to attend a compulsory cultural-orientation programme;[51] Germany has moved toward establishing University Chairs in Islamic Theology.[52] These efforts aim to initiate a more indigenized debate on Islam within European mosques and other Islamic platforms in Europe, and are seen as critical to circumventing the reliance on *imāms* imported from Muslim-majority countries. The move toward promoting locally trained *imāms*, or making it compulsory for *imāms* coming from overseas to attend introductory programmes on the culture of the host country, is hoped to make mosques conducive to integrating Muslims within Europe and reducing channels for the radicalization of Muslim youth. These attempts reflect a recognition by European states that those who control the centers of Islamic teaching and get to interpret Islamic texts for the public exercise significant influence on the actions of believers.

In many ways, these efforts by British and other European governments to reform Islamic educational institutions and make their teaching compliant with the demands of Western modernity share much with the initiatives in post-colonial Muslim states where Westernized elites were keen to reform Islam and the Islamic educational platforms to promote a more modern vision of society. The outcomes of these efforts led by European governments are also the same: they are largely failing. The governments' failure to design effective programmes that can win support from moderate and conservative Muslims alike results both from their lack of credibility (as non-Muslim states, the reforms that are initiated are perceived to be motivated by vested interests) and from a genuine inability to decipher what an Islamic intellectual reform project should look like for it not to appear as just another attempt at secularizing Islam.

Compared with these state-led efforts, new Islamic scholarly platforms emerging in the West are much more successful in establishing a debate in favor of indigenizing Islam in the West. Bruinessen and Allievei note how Bassam Tibi and Tariq Ramadan have both proposed the concept of "Euro-Islam," although with differing emphases.[53] They note that both of these scholars have also implied that "the way Europe Muslims are reshaping the relationship between Islam and society will bear upon the future of Islam in the Muslim-majority world as well."[54] Tibi's and Ramadan's predictions are indeed proving to be correct. The emergence of more educated second- and third-generation Muslims in Europe and the United States, combined with the attention that Islam has received on the global stage since September 11, while nudging some Muslim youth toward radical Islam, have made others think more actively about their religion and propelled them to seek the intellectual or deeply spiritual dimensions of Islam. While much attention has been paid to the influence on young Muslims of Ibn Taymīyah (associated with militant Islam in popular media),[55] evidence of growing interest in the works of al-Ghazālī, Ibn 'Arabī, and Jalāl ad-Dīn Muhammad Rūmī[56] among young Muslims has been ignored.

This volume covers institutions that are responding to the changed profiles and tastes of the second- and third-generation Muslim youth in the West and are also becoming increasingly popular among the educated and affluent sections of society in Muslim-majority countries. Some of these trends are entirely home-grown in the West; others are extensions of institutions covered in Volume 1, but for them to be included in this volume they had to be proving more reflective and adaptive to the changing context than the parent institution.

Indigenizing Islam in the West: From Below

Before introducing the institutions covered in this volume, a word on their selection is in order. The genesis of this volume rests in the interviews that I conducted in the summer of 2012 with the aim of understanding the sources of Islamic knowledge for young educated British and European Muslims. Who are they going to for religious advice, whether in person or via the Internet? The triggers for these interviews were a couple of media reports in the British press that argued that many young educated Muslims, finding it difficult to relate to the *imāms* from overseas, are leaving the mosques. Anecdotal in nature, the arguments advanced in these media accounts were nonetheless convincing, as they pointed toward shifts in the subjectivities of young Western Muslims akin to what I was witnessing in Muslim-majority countries (see Volume 1). These interviews very quickly revealed that in Europe (Germany, France, the Netherlands, and the United Kingdom) and the United States young educated Muslims were impressed by a similar profile of scholars, and the most popular Islamic scholars and platforms were actually based in the United States: Humza Yusuf emerged as the most popular figure in each country. The scholars identified also mostly had some institutional base of their own through which they were trying to embed their scholarship. This second element was a particularly important factor in their selection for inclusion in this volume, because if centers of Islamic learning in the Muslim-majority countries are to be rivaled, they have to be rivaled by institutions that can grow and survive beyond the lifetime of a single scholar.

These interviews made clear that institutions that are trying to develop new methodologies to merge the distinct philosophical as well as pedagogical approaches associated with Western versus Islamic scholarly tradition were the ones that had most traction among the economically mobile and integrated young Muslim population. The popularity of scholars leading these institutions was visible in the packed halls that greeted their public appearances; in their extensive web presence, whereby not only are their speeches made available on YouTube, but most get thousands of hits;[57] and in their full diaries, which as a result of ever-growing requests for lectures and public appearances are increasingly maintained by professional secretaries. The methodological approaches advocated by these different scholars vary, but a central contribution of this volume is to highlight how the new initiatives that they are inspiring can be meaningfully grouped in three categories: *neo-traditionalism*, *neo-legalism*, and *neo-conservatism*. Further, while all the scholars profiled in this volume are arguing for finding the moderate path that can enable Muslims to stay loyal to Islamic moral and legal codes while staying productively engaged with modern-day realities, each one is conscious that its proposed approach should first and foremost be tailored to the needs of his immediate community. Thus, the need to create an "American Islam," a "British Islam," or a "European Islam" that is responsive to the unique conditions faced by Muslims in these societies is a recurrent theme in the discourse of these scholars.

This volume covers the most prominent institutions representative of each of the three trends identified above. The fact that the selected institutions are mainly based in the United States and the United Kingdom was not the result of a conscious decision; it is reflective of the absence of comparably influential new Muslim institutions in other European contexts. This is not to say that interesting educational initiatives are not emerging in Europe.

New and interesting institutions in other European contexts do indeed exist; one important example is that of Alqueria de Rosales. Located in the mountains north of Granada in southern Spain, Alqueria de Rosales is one of the first *madrasah*s in contemporary Spain, having been established almost twenty years ago.[58] This educational and cultural initiative is led by a small group of Spanish converts who are working toward reviving the rich intellectual tradition associated with the Islamic heritage of Andalusia. While the Foundation aims to move toward establishing more formal education programmes, it currently provides one- to two-week retreats, of which the most popular focuses on the work of al-Ghazālī. These retreats bring together Muslims from all walks of life, from the West as well as Muslim-majority countries. The 2012 and 2014 retreats in which I participated attracted not only a large number of young, second-generation Muslims from the United Kingdom, the Netherlands, and Spain, but also a number of young students

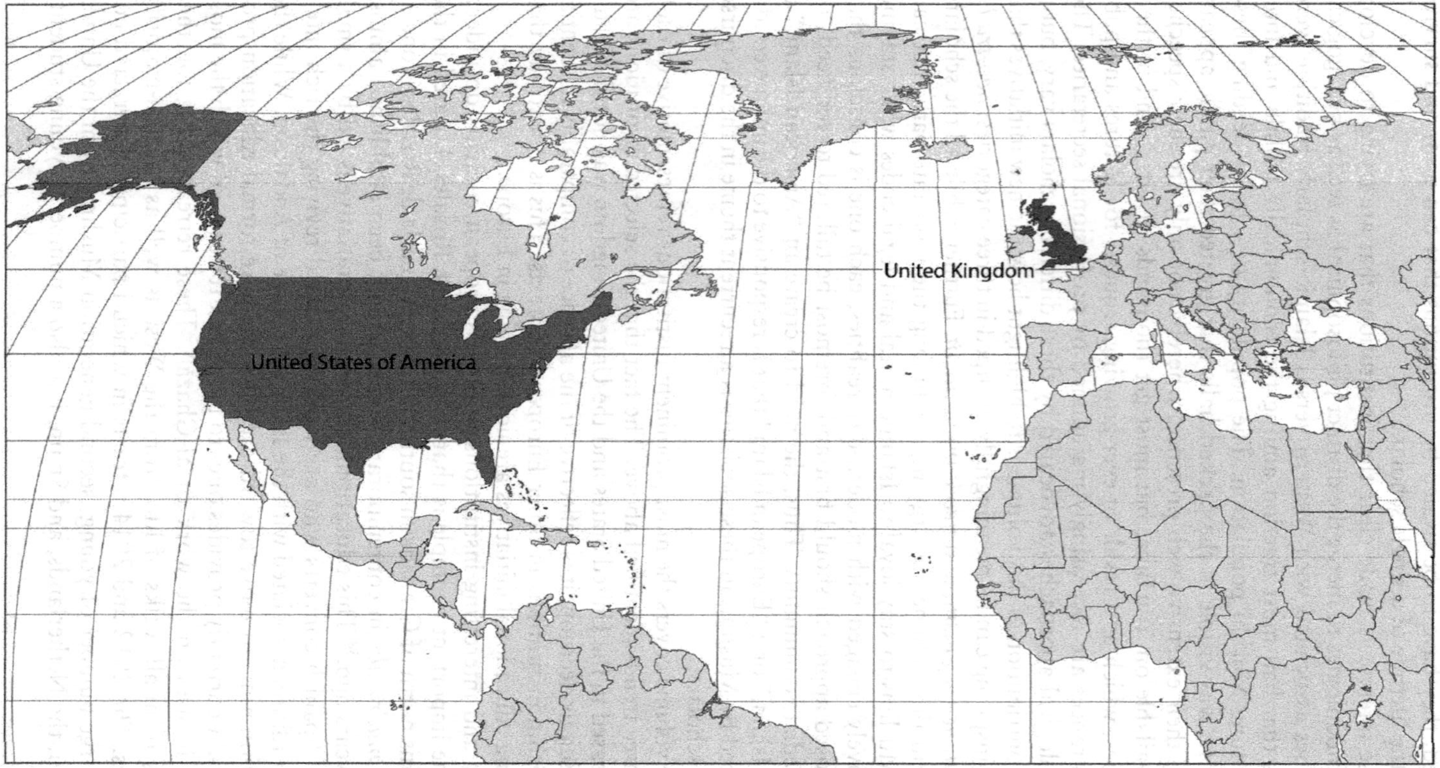

Map I.1 Key sites of Islamic knowledge production: the U.S.A. and the U.K.

and professionals from Egypt, Pakistan, and other Muslim countries. It is thus at one level a very influential institutional platform for Islamic learning emerging in Europe. However, it is yet to fully develop a strong educational programme of its own; its retreats draw heavily on visiting scholars from the United Kingdom and the United States, in particular Tim Winter and Dr. Umar Faruq Abd-Allah, respectively.

Thus, new Islamic scholarly platforms are evolving in the other European contexts,[59] but most are yet to gain visibility beyond their surrounding communities. The scholars based in the United Kingdom and the United States have the advantage of working in English, which makes their lectures and writings globally accessible. It is therefore no surprise that it was the young British and European Muslims whom I interviewed across the United Kingdom and mainland Europe who made me first recognize the strong following of Humza Yusuf. Further, as is the case with *Rosales,* many European institutions are evolving but need more time to consolidate their work before they gain visible influence. Finally, most of the new initiatives within Germany, France, and the Netherlands are still mosque-based, whereby *imāms* trained from within the second or third generation of immigrant Muslims are adopting new approaches;[60] their impact is, however, quite localized. The institutions analyzed in this volume are constantly trying to strike the right balance between staying loyal to the Islamic tradition yet being responsive to the needs of modern times. This, as we have seen in Volume 1, is the central challenge for all Islamic authorities.

Neo-traditionalism

Neo-traditionalism is an approach that interprets the Islamic scholarly tradition as being inherently adept at coping with change and diversity; its focus is on reviving a respect for rich Islamic scholarly tradition as preserved by the four Sunni *madhhabs*, while simultaneously cultivating an appreciation for *taṣawwuf* (Islamic mysticism) through working on "cleansing of the heart." Learning the *adab* (Islamic norms of behavior) and being in the *Ṣuḥba* (companionship) of the scholars is central to this approach. The focus remains on inculcating a deep faith in God through the teaching of the *'aqīdah* (creed), cultivating a commitment to fulfilling Islamic ritual practices, and, most importantly, guiding students to experience both the philosophical and mystical aspects of *taṣawwuf.* Thus, Rūmī and Ibn 'Arabī, the former representing the more mystical aspects of Sufism and the latter linked to the most philosophical strands, are both important to this tradition, as is al-Ghazālī. This approach is noticeable for its emphasis on diversity and spirituality; it is also explicitly opposed to Wahhabism, which it sees as posing a threat to a true understanding of Islam. The neo-traditionalist approach thus aims to combine rationality, spirituality, and Islamic legal tradition.

This approach, which is very close in spirit to Turkish and al-Azhari readings of the Islamic tradition (see Volume 1), and is proving highly popular among young, university-going Muslims in the West, is associated in particular with a growing pool of Western converts who are taking prominent teaching roles within the Muslim communities in the West. The most prominent of these are Humza Yusuf in the United States and Tim Winter in the United Kingdom. Equally respectful of the Islamic and Christian traditions, they show how Islam can actually help to address many challenges posed by Western modernity, such as excessive materialism and individual isolation; their critiques of modernity are very much in line with those associated with Western philosophers such as Charles Taylor.[61] Both have also moved toward establishing institutions that can help to spread their conception of the authentic Islamic tradition: Zaytuna College in Berkeley, California (U.S.A.) and Cambridge Muslim College, Cambridge (U.K.).

Zaytuna College is the first Islamic liberal arts college in the United States; it was established in Berkeley in 2009 by Humza Yusuf, Imam Zaid Shakir, and Hatem Bazian. The goal is to provide an Islamic education model "rooted in the Western liberal arts tradition," which can enable the student to "pursue a life of thought and reflection."[62] The stated agenda of this College is to "indigenize Islam in the West."[63] Proud equally of their Western heritage and their Islamic identity, these scholars argue that Islam is no stranger to the Western tradition. In their view, historically both traditions learned from each other; they argue that there is a need for Muslims to revive the authentic Islamic tradition that is capable of engaging productively with modernity, rather than reacting to it. Further, they argue that Muslims in the West have the resources, the educational opportunities, and the social context most suited to support such a reform.

The College offers a bachelor degree in Islamic Studies, based on its own integrated curriculum that provides a serious grounding in foundational Islamic texts as well as in those from the Western philosophical tradition. Its degrees are open to both men and women and are designed to train students to become "Muslim community and religious leaders, succeeding in graduate and professional schools, entering into public service, and becoming inspiring Islamic Studies teachers in rapidly expanding networks of Muslim schools in Northern American and elsewhere in the Western world."[64] The founders of the College are proving very effective in mobilizing resources. Many of its students receive financial support, and the College recently acquired a new building in a very central area of Berkeley, next to the University of California, Berkeley campus. Through Humza Yusuf the College is also linked to many other influential Islamic learning initiatives that are proving equally popular among young, educated, and socially progressive Muslims, and through them increasingly also their parents: *Rihla*, Sacred Caravan, and Sandala Productions.[65]

The comparable institution in the United Kingdom is Cambridge Muslim College (CMC). Established in 2002 by three trustees of the Muslim Academic Trust—Yusuf Islam (the famous British convert singer-songwriter Cat Stevens), Shaykh Tijani Gahbiche, and Tim Winter—this College is mainly the brainchild of Tim Winter. At CMC one of the main initiatives is dedicated to teaching graduates from British Islamic seminaries, namely the *dār al-'ulūms*, in order to augment their religious learning with a liberal arts training. The goal is to have these students better understand the realities of contemporary British society so that they can better serve their communities. The College has launched a four-year Islamic Studies programme, starting in 2016.[66] The CMC is thus making slow but steady progress toward its goal of becoming "a recognised centre of excellence offering a B.A. and M.A. in Islamic Studies, taught by a team of Islamic scholars in conjunction and collaboration with the expertise available at the University of Cambridge."[67]

Neo-legalism

This second approach is equally focused on enabling Islam to enrich Western modernity, guided by the conviction that Islam can in fact provide a moral framework capable of overcoming many challenges faced by the West; however, its proposed methodology is totally different from that of the neo-traditionalists. Here the emphasis on *ṣuḥba* as well as *taṣawwuf* is entirely absent. Instead, the focus is purely on finding answers to contemporary challenges by attempting to bridge the gap between Islamic law, contemporary realities, and modern sciences. The International Institute of Islamic Thought (IIIT), an institute in a suburb of Washington, D.C., has played the most important part in leading this project.[68] Having many prominent Muslim scholars on its board of directors, the institute represents one of the earliest efforts in the West to develop methodological tools to adjust Islamic laws to contemporary needs. The institute's mission statement emphasizes its dedication to "revival and reform of Islamic thought and its methodology in order to enable the *Ummah* to deal effectively with present challenges, and contribute to the progress of human civilization in ways that will give it a meaning and a direction derived from divine guidance. The realization of such a position will help the *Ummah* regain its intellectual and cultural identity and re-affirm its presence as a dynamic civilization."[69] The case of IIIT is particularly useful in illustrating how efforts to bridge the gulf between Islam and modern knowledge have faced serious challenges and have more often than not converged on using *maqāṣid al-sharī'ah* (principles of the *sharī'ah*) as the most useful reconciliatory tool. By emphasizing the need to focus on the underlying purposes of *sharī'ah*, instead of following specific legal dictates, *maqāṣid al-sharī'ah* allows for reinterpretation of the orthodox Islamic texts and laws in the light of contemporary needs, and it has major implications for what could be considered just in Islamic law.

The other related initiative fitting this category is the Centre for Islamic Legislation and Ethics (CILE), funded by the Qatar Foundation.[70] Launched in 2012, the Centre is led by Professor Tariq Ramadan, who, alongside Humza Yusuf, is one of the most influential contemporary Islamic thinkers, widely popular among young Muslims in the West, and who, although initially writing extensively about the need for European Muslims to carve out a distinctive European Islam, is today increasingly confident that the Islamic discourse emerging in the West has resonance with Muslims around the globe, due to young Muslims' shared experiences. The Centre aims to initiate an intellectual discourse within Islam that will make it possible to find real-life answers to the needs of Muslims in Europe, as well as those in Muslim-majority countries, while staying true to the spirit of *sharī'ah*. Himself a professor at the University of Oxford, at the Centre Ramadan is leading a major programme that brings the scholars of the *fiqh* together with scholars of the context, to enable the two sides to discuss the modern challenges in line with Islamic ethics. Some of the themes under research include gender, economy, medicine and bioethics, and the environment.[71]

Neo-conservatism

While the institutions representing the above two approaches have evolved primarily on their own, the third category relates to institutions that are an extension of the two most conservative Islamic scholarly platforms covered in Volume 1, namely Deoband and Saudi Salafism, but the scholars leading them are keen to make their tradition relate to modern challenges. The two Deobandi institutions covered in this section—Ebrahim College in the United Kingdom and Darul Qasim in the United States—show how some graduates of *dār al-'ulūm*s are moving on to advocate adjustments from within the Deobandi tradition. Darul Qasim, which operates out of Chicago, is worthy of attention because it is a unique effort from within the Deobandi tradition to encourage a more pluralistic study of Islam. Unlike the traditional Deobandi focus on *taqlīd* of *Ḥanafī madhhab* (see Volume 1, Part III), Darul Qasim is developing a curriculum that allows the student to study any of the four Sunni *madhhab*s in its attempt to allow for plurality of thought within Islamic learning.[72] At the same time, the *madrasah* retains the traditional Deobandi commitment to mastering the core Islamic texts in detail. Similarly, Ebrahim College in the United Kingdom is an attempt by graduates of traditional Deobandi *dār al-'ulūm*s in the United Kingdom to encourage a more socially embedded reading of Islamic texts, which will enable young Muslims to better relate to their British identity.

Within the Saudi Salafi tradition, the work of Yasir Qadhi at AlMaghrib Institute, operating out of New York, is noticeable for similar versatility. The goal of AlMaghrib, founded in 2002, "is to make learning Islam in a quality fashion as easy as possible."[73] The Institute is keen to explore "how could we teach you Islam in a way that was fun, social, quality, spiritual, and oh yeah, academic?"[74] AlMaghrib focuses on conducting seminars all over the world, including the United States, Canada, the United Kingdom, Australia, and even a few Gulf States such as Kuwait and the United Arab Emirates. These seminars and classes aim to tackle some of the most difficult and controversial topics head-on, whether the rise of militant atheism, or the evolution issue, the existence of evil, political allegiances, rebellion against dictators, secular feminism, the conflict between citizenship and the support for armed forces that are pressing forward with their own agenda regardless, and so much more.[75]

The institute also offers a bachelor's degree, and although the degree is not yet accredited, teaching takes place in four departments: Islamic Theology and Ethics, Islamic Law and Legal Theory, Qur'ānic and Ḥadīth Sciences, and Islamic History and Homiletics. Yasir Qadhi's defence of same-sex marriage laws in America, his approach to liberal citizenship, and his views about Islamic law are alien to many mainstream Salafis. In order to argue for new interpretations, he uses various conservative historical *fatwā*s, such as the ban on the printing press, to highlight the negative effect that conservative *fatwā*s can have on Muslim life. The case of Yasir Qadhi in particular shows how by ignoring the *madhhab*s Salafism can, on the one hand, lead to highly conservative social rulings (see Volume 1, Part II), while, on the other, the same Salafi methodology can be used to convince Muslims in the West to respect the secular constitution of the country of which they are nationals.

Thus, one of the striking features of these initiatives is that they have all come to appreciate the importance of developing an Islamic discourse that is primarily formulated in response to the immediate social context. Hence, all these institutions are talking about developing a Western Islam, or a European Islam, or a British Islam, or an American Islam. This emphasis in itself reflects the importance that these platforms are placing on making Islamic discourse relate to the everyday reality of young people. None is arguing for abandoning what is broadly viewed as the core of Islamic *fiqh*, but all are in agreement that Islamic legal and scholarly tradition requires them to engage in reasoned debate to find answers that are consistent with the spirit of the Sharī'ah and also are optimal responses to the needs of the time. The findings here are thus very much in line with John Bowen's analysis of the Islamic platforms in the United Kingdom and France: concerning Sharī'ah Councils in the United Kingdom, he similarly argues that they are trying to strike a balance between being Muslim and being British, and like their French counterparts are trying to adjust to their local context.[76] The difference is that while Bowen looked at individual mosque-based preachers in France and the Sharī'ah Councils in the United Kingdom, this volume has established similar arguments for the new Islamic learning centers emerging in the United Kingdom, other parts of Europe, and the United States. Further, unlike the proponents of the Sharī'ah Councils, the scholars leading these new initiatives increasingly respect the secular state and argue that Muslims are required by Islamic law to respect the laws of the land in which they live.

While working toward a similar end, namely that of helping Western Muslims to live by Islamic norms and yet be productive members of their societies, each of the three approaches outlined above offers a distinct methodology in order to reach that end. The chapters in this volume thus help to answer the question: what are the profiles and histories of these institutions and those of the scholars who have initiated them? What tools of methodological reasoning are they using to adapt Islamic legal and moral dictates with realities faced by young Muslims in the West? Which Islamic scholars or texts do they draw upon to justify their proposed methodology of reform? How do these scholars compare with the *'ulamā'* in orthodox centers of Islamic authority? What does their call for "indigenization of Islam in the West" mean in practice? Will it make the integration of Muslims in the West easier?

Relating Islamic *Fiqh*: Core Conceptual and Methodological Tools

A review of the writings, lectures, and speeches of the scholars whose work is profiled in this volume reveals that they are not producing a dense corps of Islamic legal treatises elaborating on complex aspects of Islamic *fiqh*. Instead, they seem to be particularly adept at selectively drawing on key concepts from the Islamic legal, moral, and philosophical tradition and applying it to contemporary issues in a way that defends their particular line of reasoning on a given subject. The neo-traditionalists in addition prefer to direct their students to works of earlier scholars, university-based academics, or prominent jurists or scholars in the Muslim-majority countries so that those interested in the deeper textual debates can obtain the relevant information. The neo-conservatives do less of such cross-referencing to the work of other scholars, but they also justify adapting specific Islamic legal principles by drawing on selected concepts from the Islamic scholarly tradition. Only in the case of neo-legalists can we trace a conscious effort to develop a new methodology of Islamic legal derivation for contemporary times; initially referred to as *tawḥīd*ic epistemology, the resulting scholarship eventually became subsumed under the broader banner of *maqāṣid al-sharī'ah*.

Thus, each of the three categories of institutions covered in this volume have slightly distinct positions on how best to relate Islamic legal and moral dictates to one's immediate realities; however, all three are combining their specialist knowledge of Islamic sciences with the knowledge of Western scholarly tradition and the tacit knowledge derived from being educated, middle-class, Western Muslims.

Fiqh al-wāqi', Fiqh al-aqallīyāt, Maqāṣid al-sharī'ah

As in the case of the institutions profiled in Volume 1, even among the new Islamic scholarly platforms emerging in the West, *fiqh al-wāqi'* (*fiqh of reality*) is proving to be the most popular concept, along with *fiqh al-aqallīyāt* and *maqāṣid al-sharī'ah*, to justify adapting Islamic legal debates to modern realities. All three concepts help to emphasize that modernity has brought about significant changes, compared with the contexts in which traditional laws were originally derived, and that we need to understand the spirit of the law so that the letter of the law can be better applied to these changing circumstances. The neo-traditionalists in particular refer to this body of *fiqh* scholarship to defend their reasoning. However, they do not themselves engage in deeper conceptual debates on defining *fiqh al-wāqiʿ*, *fiqh al-aqallīyāt*, or *maqāṣid al-sharīʿah*; instead, they often reference the writings of traditionally trained scholars in Muslim-majority countries who are writing detailed commentaries on these concepts and methods. Humza Yusuf, for example, frequently refers to the work of Bin Bayyah (see Volume 1, Chapter 3). These scholars instead channel their own efforts toward the application of these rulings to everyday questions.

Humza Yusuf, for instance, presents a defence of Muslims' need to respect the laws of a secular state by drawing on the work of a Malaysian scholar Muhammad Naguib al-Attas, who draws a distinction between "secularization" and the "secular" state; secularization, he argues, tries to overthrow all that is religious, although it is possible for a secular state to uphold religion. Drawing on this discussion, Humza Yusuf argues that an Islamic state is "neither wholly theocratic nor wholly secular," and that a Muslim state calling itself secular does not necessarily have to work against religion.[77] Secular politics is therefore not necessarily problematic from a Muslim perspective, as it does not necessarily have to deny religious values and virtues in politics and human affairs. Instead, he argues that a secular state can operate well without a religious grounding, even in a way that is Islamic. Developing such a line of reasoning enables Humza Yusuf to contend that secular states such as Finland and Sweden have such a high degree of social justice that Muslims can consider these states exemplary, comparable to the rule of the legendary Saladin. He argues that good governance does not rely on religion, but on a government's commitment to basic morality, common decency, and social justice. In terms of his method of reasoning, he thus draws on the writings of respected Islamic legal scholars to establish the essence of a given Islamic moral and legal principle; however, he then devotes much greater attention to its application to concrete examples.

Similarly, Tim Winter consistently tries to show the relevance of an Islamic legal dictate by relating it to recent research and thinking in Western academia. Winter's essay entitled "Boys will be Boys" presents a good example of his method of reasoning. Winter argues that many debates about gender among Muslim intellectuals are limited to the classical issues of *fiqh*. While he does not deny the great importance of understanding the *fiqhi* debates on these issues, he argues that this approach has been too apologetic. What he wishes to do is "construct a language of gender which offers not a defence or mitigation of current Muslim attitudes and establishments, but a credible strategy for resolving dilemmas which the Western thinkers and commentators around us are now meticulously examining."[78] In the essay, Winter tries to move past a dichotomy where Muslims are trying to defend their positions on gender difference to a Western audience, and instead enters into a dialogue with the new gender paradigm being debated in Western academic circles. This is precisely why Winter begins his article with a consideration of Germaine Greer's *The Whole Woman* as her work personifies the "ways in which the social and also scientific context of Western gender discourse has shifted over this period."[79]

Islamization of Knowledge, Tawḥīdic Epistemology, Maqāṣid al-sharīʻah

The neo-legalistic scholars, as noted in the previous section, have made comparatively more conscious efforts to develop new methodological tools to relate the essence of Islamic *fiqh* to modern realities. The International Institute of Islamic Thought (IIIT) set out to reformulate modern sciences on an Islamic basis—to give them a "*tawḥīd*ic" orientation. The belief that modern sciences as currently constituted are not compatible with an Islamic way of thinking, and that we need to develop scholarship and research that would adapt Western academic disciplines to Islam was the central driving force behind the work of its scholars. The alternative in view of its leadership was continuity of a hopelessly divided Muslim mind-set. The development of an entirely new way of thinking, a full *tawḥīd*ic episteme, became IIIT's main goal whereby the advances and contributions of modern sciences had to be understood, mastered, and then adapted to fit into an Islamic framework. However, when—despite concentrated efforts—the Islamization of knowledge project could not deliver any tangible results, IIIT chose to narrow its focus to the development of *maqāṣid al-sharīʻah* and *fiqh al-aqallīyāt* (minority *fiqh*)[80]— the two approaches that by the late 1990s were gaining traction across different groups.

The neo-legalists (IIIT's leadership and Tariq Ramadan included), unlike the neo-traditionalists, do not agree that the methodologies developed by the four Sunni *madhhabs* are adequate to reconcile the current gap between the Islamic tradition and modern sciences or the present-day realities. Tariq Ramadan maintains that the Islamic legal tradition's current predicament stems from its inability to adapt sufficiently or satisfactorily to the seismic transformations associated with modernity. In his view, the traditionalists' adherence to their *madhhab* precludes the sufficient use of reason; rather, their continued reliance on legal norms laid out in medieval texts prevents efforts to amend those norms to fit contemporary circumstances. He instead argues for *Salafi Reformism*, which he maintains can combine both reason and loyalty to Islamic *fiqh*: "the Text still remains the source, but reason, applied according to the rules of deduction and inference (*qawaid al-istinbat*), enjoys significant latitude for interpretation and elaboration through the exercise of *ijtihad*."[81]

IIIT has in particular invested heavily in supporting research and publications on *maqāṣid al-sharīʻah* and how it should be applied. Jasser Auda, previously a researcher associated with IIIT London and now a scholar with the

Qatar Foundation, has made major contributions in this field. Unlike many scholars, who view the *maqāṣid* as a broad moral framework, Auda relates them to very technical aspects of legal theory (*uṣūl al-fiqh*). He advocates applying the *maqāṣid* theory as a way of dealing with conflicting scriptural evidence in legal reasoning. Instead of weighing varying pieces of evidence according to different textual, hermeneutical, or derivative criteria, as is the case in classical *fiqh*, Auda argues for viewing the evidence through the lens of the different types of *maqāṣid*. Such an approach, he contends, is more comprehensive, allowing for a wider range of scriptural evidence to be incorporated into legal reasoning.[82]

While IIIT's efforts remain focused on publishing research in these areas, Tariq Ramadan is trying to develop a modern Islamic legal and ethical framework through the work ongoing at the Centre for Islamic Legislation and Ethics (CILE). By bringing together specialists in *fiqh* with specialists in the modern sciences, he is trying to develop an Islamic ethical and legal framework that is more responsive to contemporary realities and advances in other sciences. As we will see in Chapter 4, encouraging the *'ulamā'* and the scholars in modern sciences to develop a common vocabulary is not without its challenge; however, the neo-legalists are committed to finding some answers.

Reasonable Citizen, Reasonable Pluralism (ikhtilāf)*, and Responsible Citizen*

Finally, a review of the writings being produced by the neo-conservatives reveals that these scholars in fact rely heavily on an ad hoc use of concepts from the traditional Islamic legal scholarship to justify their positions. While the neo-traditionalists normally refer to a particular body of Islamic scholarship, or the work of a scholar from the classical period, to justify their position, the neo-conservatives instead often pick only on a specific concept, instead of a particular genre of scholarship, from the Islamic legal tradition, to help them to justify their position. This can be expected of Yasir Qadhi, who, given his Salafi orientation, feels less bound by traditional *fiqh* scholarship, prioritizing direct engagement with Qur'ān and *ḥadīth* instead. Interestingly, however, the two Deobandi platforms discussed in this volume, although committed to *taqlīd* of Deobandi scholarly tradition, also defend their positions by selective use of Islamic concepts, instead of quoting specialist writings of earlier Deobandi scholars.

Arguing that Muslims today are facing problems that have no solutions in the classical texts, Yasir Qadhi argues that we need a type of scholarship that is in tune with the lived experience of the people. Otherwise, he believes, people will simply ignore the *fatwā*s of the scholars and live life as they see fit. The way he proposes to do this is by talking about Islamic moral and legal guidelines in a language that his university-educated Western Muslim followers can relate to. This is illustrated by the way he relates to the concept of "reasonable citizen" in Western theory with a defence of respect for secular law. Relating the concept of "reasonable citizen" to the Islamic moral framework, Qadhi argues that citizens are considered reasonable when they view one another as being free and equal, and when they believe in the criterion of reciprocity. The criterion of reciprocity requires that citizens offer one another fair terms of co-operation, and they agree to act on those terms even if it comes at a cost in a particular situation given that other citizens also act on those terms.[83] Reasonable citizens, therefore, understand that each individual has his or her own comprehensive doctrine of beliefs, and they do not believe that it is legitimate to impose one's comprehensive beliefs on others. Developing this line of reasoning, he concludes that for Muslims living in the West it should not be difficult to ignore apostasy and homosexuality. He also defends the criterion of reciprocity by arguing that Muslims should be willing to support rights for other minority groups because those rights can be used in favour of Muslims as well, even if that particular right comes at a cost to Islamic values.

Like Yasir Qadhi, Ad Duha from Ebrahim College in London profiled in Chapter 6 argues that reasonable pluralism is the best protection for Western Muslims who aspire to live by their beliefs. As Razavian elaborates in Chapter 6, the term "reasonable pluralism" was popularized by the political philosopher John Rawls. Ad Duha echoes similar views by invoking the Islamic concept of *ikhtilāf* (disagreement). The issue of *ikhtilāf* has a long history within Islamic thought, and Ad Duha's usage of the term brings this history to the fore. Through the use of the concept of *ikhtilāf*, Ad Duha is able to make an argument for reasonable pluralism without necessarily having to detail its philosophical premises. Similar to Rawls' argument, the concept of *ikhtilāf* assumes that reasonable people will develop differing opinions about issues of religious law. This issue of *ikhtilāf* is significant for Ad Duha in his discussion on voting, which tends to spark tense debates within Muslim communities in the U.K. By arguing that voting is an issue of *ikhtilāf*, whereby some scholars say that it is permissible and others say that it is not, Ad Duha concludes that there is no single ruling for all people. Therefore, it is not permissible to judge others on the basis of criteria that one has accepted oneself but that others have not accepted. Ad Duha extends this concept of reasonable pluralism to defend the obligation to respect the rights of non-Muslims, too: although one may disagree with their religious viewpoints, it is not moral to coerce them to adhere to Islamic beliefs or actions.

In a similar kind of way, Hafiz Amin, the head of Darul Qasim also profiled in Chapter 6, puts forward the concept of "responsible citizen," which is very close to Qadhi's use of "reasonable citizen." In a public statement intended to offer Muslims a general guideline on how to deal with cases of sexual harassment, the institutional leadership argues that all Muslims have a general duty to command good and forbid evil (*al-'amr bi al-ma'rūf wa al-naḥy 'an al-munkar*). It then quotes the *hadīth* in which the Prophet says: "Each one of you are shepherds and each one of you is responsible for your (own) flock." The statement links this notion of forbidding evil to the notion of citizenship, arguing that Muslims are required to be responsible citizens. The way that one becomes a responsible citizen is through enacting the principle of forbidding evil. Thus, if one witnesses an evil act, one should try to stop that act by one's own hand, or by speech, or by condemning the said act in one's heart. But, it also made very clear that, while in a Muslim-majority country it is the duty of the state to enact Islamic law and administer punishment, and it is the combination of forbidding evil and the administration of justice through the state that "absolves the whole Muslim community from its moral and legal obligation in such matters," the use of physical means to stop the evil act "is limited to what is allowed by the law of the land." If the state does not allow it, it is not permissible. Although this statement is focused on only one particular incident, it highlights how Darul Qasim views the relationship between Muslims and the law of non-Muslim-majority countries: Muslims should try to stop sinful actions but they should not do anything that would be against the law; nor should they hinder the process of justice.

Thus, we see that in the West the scholars gaining attention are not necessarily engaging in deep debates on *fiqh* (although they have to be able to show enough familiarity with relevant concepts); instead, their appeal rests in their ability to relate those Islamic concepts to Western philosophical and legal traditions. Since the university-educated Muslims who constitute their primary audience are more literate in the Western philosophical and intellectual tradition, efforts at popularising specific Islamic legal concepts yield better results when linked to modern concepts. Thus, the debate on *ikhtilāf* may not trigger the curiosity of a young Western-educated Muslim in its own right, but when explicitly linked to the notion of tolerance and responsible citizenship in Western legal or moral theory, it becomes both intellectually interesting and easily relatable. It is the ability of these scholars to relate Islamic moral and legal ethics to modern everyday realities and modes of thinking in a language that is familiar to the young educated Muslims in the West that explains their real appeal.

A Few Sociological Observations

While the chapters in this volume are primarily devoted to mapping the thoughts, ideas, and reasoning of the scholars who are gaining popularity in the West, especially among the younger generation of Muslims, this section briefly identifies some important sociological factors, which can help us better appreciate the basis of their appeal. These observations are based on my own fieldwork with many of these institutions whereby I have carried out interviews with these scholars as well as their followers and have also participated in many of their teaching activities. Here I outline some of the important factors that we need to study and investigate further if we are to fully understand the impact that these new scholarly platforms are to have on shaping the future face of Islam and on the authority of traditional Islamic scholarly platforms profiled in Volume 1.

Building Bridges

An important aspect of these initiatives is that while advocating distinct methodological approaches they are much more open to mutual consultation and dialogue than is the norm today among the Islamic learning platforms in Muslim-majority countries. Scholars from these platforms routinely converge on similar platforms, such as the annual convention of the Islamic Society of North America (ISNA), which attracts up to 5,000 participants each year.[84] Humza Yusuf, Zaid Shakir, and Tariq Ramadan[85] are normally among the most prominent speakers at the ISNA convention and are invited to speak at all the major plenary sessions. Their appearance on these shared platforms is partly a result of the centrality of some of these non-mosque and non-*madrasah* platforms in the West to the establishment of Islamic authority.[86]

However, these institutions also make one-on-one contacts. Zaid Shakir from Zaytuna College was, for example, invited to speak at Ebrahim College in London in early 2016,[87] although the two institutions are associated with two very different traditions. At the same time, these institutions and scholars are closely connected to the traditional centers of learning in the Muslim-majority countries. In fact, until these institutions themselves start to produce solid cadres of well-trained Islamic scholars, they will remain reliant on sending their own students to traditional centers of learning in Muslim-majority countries to gain command of the Arabic language and the most important foundational texts. The importance of these institutions rests in cultivating an interest among the young, educated, and socially progressive Muslims to engage with Islam in a way that allows for reasoned debate and is responsive to the realities of their life; their ability to ground the students in deeper Islamic texts will evolve only gradually.

Bringing Parents In and Developing Global Following

The second important feature of the attempts by these scholars to indigenize Islam in the West is their insistence that the Islamic ethic is in fact consistent with the true European and American tradition; this in particular is the case with the neo-traditionalists. Western societies are seen to have deviated from their true values, and Islam is argued to have the ability to enrich these societies. More recently, however, many of these scholars have begun to suggest that the Islamic discourse evolving in the West is equally relevant to the Muslim-majority countries: due to globalization, they argue, educated and socially progressive youth across the world share similar sensibilities. This new-found confidence is the result of the growing numbers of followers that they attract in these countries. Tariq Ramadan, Humza Yusuf, and Tim Winter: all three have expressed similar thoughts.[88] The evidence of their growing influence is also visible in the increasingly mixed age profile of their followers. They are now attracting not just second- and third-generation Muslims, but increasingly also their parents. Interviews that I have conducted across the generational divide show that most followers from the older generation became involved in these platforms through their children.

The Importance of Muslims in the United States

The cross-institutional analysis also shows that within the West the United States is proving to be the most fertile ground for the emergence of some of the most promising Islamic education platforms. While four out of the six institutions profiled in this volume are based in the United States, it is more important to note that the United States has in addition many more institutions that could fit within these three categories. For example, Nouman Ali Khan's *Bayyinah* is another important example of the neo-conservative category, and *Ta'leef Collective* is an influential example from the ranks of neo-traditionalists.[89] This vibrant Islamic scholarly milieu in the United States has much to do with the economic affluence of American Muslims. The evidence for this is the high fees charged by some of these platforms and retreats led by neo-traditionalist scholars, which are attended not just by members of the affluent Muslim diaspora in the West but increasingly also by affluent Muslims from all across the Muslim world (Pakistan, Malaysia, Indonesia, Saudi Arabia, Egypt, etc.). The United States also is home to a much larger number of white converts involved in educational endeavors than is the case in the United Kingdom and the rest of Europe.[90]

What is most important about these white converts is that they have made it "cool" to be Muslim.[91] Profiles like those of Humza Yusuf and Tim Winter are making it acceptable in the eyes of young Muslims to become an Islamic scholar. They promote a strong sense of a counter-cultural way of life that is different from the norm but is not violently opposed to Western values; rather, it engages deeply with the Western philosophical tradition and shows that Islam can enrich it by bringing in the metaphysical elements. This is encouraging some young boys and girls from progressive Muslim families to consider becoming *imāms*, as is evident in the profiles of the students of Zaytuna.[92] In the Muslim world, it is still not possible to appear "cool" while becoming an *imām*: the incentives in fact are reversed, as elite status in most Muslim post-colonial societies continues to be linked to being Western.[93] For young educated Muslims in the West, on the other hand, this new face of Islam in fact is more hip because most recognize that trying to be Western is often counterproductive, as one can never be "exactly like them."[94] Their ability to bring these Muslims from elite families to study of Islam is what makes their future potential even more promising.

Where To for Muslim-majority Countries?

As these new institutions evolve, the institutions in the Muslim world will face growing challenges to their authority; for the immediate future they will, however, continue to attract the most ambitious graduates of the new centers in the West who want to pursue specialist study of Islamic texts. But, even after these new institutions have developed more rigorous Islamic Studies and Arabic-language programmes of their own, certain features of the Muslim-majority countries will continue to give the institutions based therein an advantage. First, their students are more able to devote their energies to full-time Islamic education than those in the West; memorization does play an important role in Islamic scholarly tradition, and larger family sizes in the Muslim-majority countries make it easier for some families to dedicate a child to the *hifz* (Qur'ānic memorization) process and pursuit of higher Islamic Studies.[95]

Second, living in a Muslim-majority country can arguably help to sustain faith, as the reminders of Islam in everyday life are more frequent and immediate. As one of my Syrian Canadian respondents who I had met in Istanbul had noted: "In the United States one has to search for a mosque; here in my immediate neighborhood there are five mosques. I am spoilt for choice. This ease of access to the mosques or general embedding in the broader Islamic culture does help sustain the faith, as you need to make less effort to incorporate religious practice in everyday life." But the signs are that ultimately these advantages enjoyed by the Muslim-majority countries will fade away if the religious discourse emerging from the Islamic institutions that they nurture does not appeal to the mind and spirit of the modern-educated, socially progressive Muslims.

Islamic Authority and Responsiveness to Reality

The fact that new Islamic scholarly platforms have emerged among Muslims in the diaspora is consistent with the central contention of these two volumes, which is that religious authority has to be able to demonstrate an ability to be reasonable and responsive to the demands of the changing times, while respecting the core of the tradition. These new platforms are thus a classic example of internal reform, which, as discussed by Francis Robinson and Qasim Zaman in great detail, has been an essential feature of the Islamic scholarly tradition.[96] Responding to the realities of the young Muslims in the West, these institutions are drawing on the space available within the traditional Islamic *fiqh* to argue in favor of a secular constitution and to advise their Muslim followers to respect the constitution of the land in which they live. The reasoning presented by the scholars cited in this volume provides strong evidence to critique those readings of Islamic authority that argue that it is not creativity but mere "mimicking of the past"[97] that is essential to understanding the workings of Islamic authority.

Instead, this volume shows that the institutions that are gaining a stronghold among the educated and socially progressive Muslims in the West, as well as in Muslim-majority countries, are those that are adept at respecting the core of the tradition while knowing what aspects of the tradition can be constantly debated to ensure that the tradition on the whole stays responsive to contemporary realities. Thus, while the core of the *ʿaqīdah* (creed) and *ibādāt* (ritual practices) stays untouched, Islamic *fiqh* affecting everyday socio-economic and political issues is left open to reasoned debate within the parameters set by the Islamic scholarly tradition. This scope for flexibility and creativity within the Islamic tradition has been central to its successful embedding over the centuries across different cultures; acknowledging this dynamic aspect of Islamic scholarly tradition should by no means be interpreted as "deception."[98]

Yet, as we will see in this volume, the creative energy and reasoning within the Islamic scholarly platforms profiled in this volume is by no means leading to a complete replication of Western modernity and a consequent erosion of Islamic civilizational identity. Rather, what we are seeing is a growing tendency among young educated Muslims to reflect on the achievements but also the limitations of Western modernity, and its component parts. This is allowing young Muslims to pick and choose and create alternative visions of modernity, rather than simply accepting Western modernity and the related changes in the socio-economic order as an inevitable reality for all societies and communities. This is particularly so because most young Muslims in the West are growing up in families where religion is still a powerful force; the contrasts that they see between their home environment and the secular order outside it facilitates comparisons of all kinds. While the liberty and freedom of the secular tradition appeals to most, the excessive individualism and lack of spirituality create an appreciation for the tradition among the same. The result is thus a heightened desire to find a balance between individual freedom and respect for tradition—a struggle that is equally alive in the scholarship of many Western philosophers writing on the subject of modernity.[99]

While Western media coverage understandably remains focused on the violent attacks being perpetrated in the name of Islam, the reality is that Western societies are also in fact nurturing platforms for the emergence of the most promising Islamic scholarly movements. In some way, both the scholarly and the militant Islamic movements present a critique of Western modernity, but while the former is confident of Islam's ability to draw the best from Western modernity and in fact be in a position to contribute to it, the latter lacks that confidence and resorts to violence as the only expression of critique available to it. That the West is today the ground for the emergence of the most violent (namely ISIS) and at the same time the most promising trends (profiled in this volume) in the future of Islamic thought and practice is thus a fascinating puzzle, the answer to which must be explored by undertaking a detailed study of the socio-economic background of the young Muslims gravitating toward these two opposing trends. For now, this volume aims to give the reader a taste of the rich milieu of Islamic scholarly debates evolving in the West, and to show how they are indicative of young Muslims' desires to integrate more effectively in the West and be productive members of their societies, while respecting the core of their faith.

Notes

1. Sophie Gilliat-Ray, *Muslims in Britain: An Introduction* (Cambridge–New York: Cambridge University Press, 2010); Martin van Bruinessen and Stefano Allievi, eds, *Producing Islamic Knowledge: Transmission and Dissemination in Western Europe* (London–New York: Routledge, 2013); Akbar Ahmed, *Journey into America: The Challenge of Islam* (Washington, D.C.: Brookings Institution Press, 2011).
2. MCB, *British Muslims in Numbers: A Demographic, Socio-economic and Health Profile of Muslims in Britain drawing on the 2011 Census* (London: The Muslim Council of Britain, 2015).
3. MCB, ibid.
4. Michael Polanyi, *The Tacit Dimension* (Chicago–London: University of Chicago Press, 2009).
5. For fascinating insights into the changed socio-economic profile of the Islamic scholarly classes after the colonial encounter in two different contexts, see Thomas Pierret, *Religion and State in Syria: The Sunni Ulama from Coup to Revolution* (Cambridge–New York: Cambridge University Press, 2013); Francis Robinson, *The Ulama of Farangi Mahall and Islamic Culture in South Asia* (London: Hurst, 2001).
6. Francis Robinson, *Islam and Muslim History in South Asia* (Oxford–New Delhi: Oxford University Press, 2003); Robert W. Hefner and Muhammad Qasim Zaman, eds, *Schooling Islam: The Culture and Politics of Modern Muslim Education* (Princeton: Princeton University Press, 2007).
7. Studies from different Muslim societies show the low socio-economic profile of the *madrasah* students and teachers and the mosque *imāms*; see Masooda Bano, *The Rational Believer: Choices and Decisions in the Madrasas of Pakistan* (Ithaca: Cornell University Press, 2012).
8. Most Muslim countries today follow modern constitutions inherited from their former colonial rulers, rather than following Islamic *shari'ah* law. Case studies illustrating the limited application of *shari'ah* in most Muslim countries can be found in Robert W. Hefner, ed., *Shari'a Politics: Islamic Law and Society in the Modern World* (Bloomington: Indiana University Press, 2011).
9. Most post-colonial Muslim elites inherited such a world view; examples include Mustafa Kemal Atatürk in Turkey, Gamal Abdel Nasser in Egypt, and General Ayub Khan in Pakistan. This mind-set still persists, as is evident in General Musharraf's attempt to create *Enlightened Islam* as President of Pakistan (1999–2008), and General Abdel Fattah el-Sisi's pledge to bring about a religious revolution in Egypt.

10. Diego Gambetta and Steffen Hertog, *Engineers of Jihad: The Curious Connection between Violent Extremism and Education* (Princeton: Princeton University Press, 2016).
11. Masooda Bano, *The Rational Believer*; in particular, see Chapter 8.
12. For a review of the debate between Gilles Kepel and Olivier Roy (two leading French academics and specialists on Islam) on why French Muslims join groups such as ISIS, and why this debate is becoming increasingly acrimonious, see Adam Nossiter, "'That Ignoramus': 2 French Scholars of Radical Islam Turn Bitter Rivals," *The New York Times*, July 12, 2016, accessed August 15, 2016, http://www.nytimes.com/2016/07/13/world/europe/france-radical-islam.html. Kepel places more blame on context and ideological indoctrination; Roy, on the other hand, increasingly argues for recognizing individual propensities in those who are radicalized.
13. James Bell et al., "The World's Muslims: Religion, Politics and Society," *The Pew Forum on Religion & Public Life Report* (Washington, D.C., 2013), accessed August 15, 2016, http://www.pewforum.org/2013/04/30/the-worlds-muslims-religion-politics-society-overview/.
14. Bell et al., "World's Muslims."
15. Tahir Abbas, ed., *Muslim Britain: Communities under Pressure* (London–New York: Zed Books, 2005).
16. Robert S. Leiken, *Europe's Angry Muslims* (Oxford–New York: Oxford University Press, 2012); John R. Bowen, *Can Islam Be French? Pluralism and Pragmatism in a Secularist State* (Princeton: Princeton University Press, 2011).
17. Leiken, *Europe's Angry Muslims*; Christina Capatides, "Molenbeek and Schaerbeek: A Tale of Two Tragedies," *CBS News*, April 11, 2016, accessed June 23, 2016, http://www.cbsnews.com/news/molenbeek-and-schaerbeek-brussels-belgium-a-tale-of-two-terror-tragedies/.
18. Abbas, *Muslim Britain*.
19. Tahir Abbas, "British South Asian Muslims: State and Multicultural Society," in Abbas, *Muslim Britain*, 3–17.
20. International Monetary Fund, "Globalization: Threat or Opportunity?" *IMF Issues Brief* 2000 (corrected 2002), accessed August 15, 2016, https://www.imf.org/external/np/exr/ib/2000/041200to.htm.
21. Ahmed, *Journey into America*; Zareena Grewal, *Islam is a Foreign Country: American Muslims and the Global Crisis of Authority* (New York: New York University Press, 2013).
22. Pew Research Center, "Muslim Americans: Middle Class and Mostly Mainstream," Pew Research Center Report 2007, accessed August 15, 2016, http://www.pewresearch.org/2007/05/22/muslim-americans-middle-class-and-mostly-mainstream/.
23. Grewal, *Islam is a Foreign Country*.
24. "Muslim-American Demographics Reveal a Diverse Group That Rejects Categorization," *The Huffington Post*, March 26, 2014, accessed August 15, 2016, http://www.huffingtonpost.com/2014/03/26/muslim-american-demographics_n_5027866.html.
25. Carol Brown, "Prisons are Breeding Grounds for Jihadists," *American Thinker*, December 5, 2014, accessed August 13, 2016, http://www.americanthinker.com/articles/2014/12/prisons_are_breeding_grounds_for_jihadists.html; "Black Muslims, the NOI and American Prisons . . .," *Prison Culture*, July 16, 2012, accessed August 13, 2016, http://www.usprisonculture.com/blog/2012/07/16/black-muslims-and-american-prisons/.

26. van Bruinessen and Allievi, *Producing Islamic Knowledge*; Jonathan Laurence, *The Emancipation of Europe's Muslims: The State's Role in Minority Integration* (Princeton: Princeton University Press, 2012).
27. van Bruinessen and Allievi, *Producing Islamic Knowledge*.
28. Ahmed, *Journey into America*; Zareena Grewal, *Islam is a Foreign Country*.
29. van Bruinessen and Allievi, *Producing Islamic Knowledge*; Ahmed, *Journey into America*.
30. Thijl Sunier, Nico Landman, et al., "Diyanet: The Turkish Directorate for Religious Affairs in a Changing Environment," *VU University Amsterdam and Utrecht University Research Report*, 2011, accessed August 18, 2016, http://www.fsw.vu.nl/en/Images/Diyanet_report_2011_tcm250-421402.pdf.
31. Bowen, *Can Islam be French?*
32. Brigitte Maréchal, "Mosques, Organisations, and Leadership," in *Muslims in the Enlarged Europe: Religion and Society*, eds Brigitte Marechal et al. (Leiden–Boston: Brill, 2003), 79–150; Brigitte Maréchal, "Modalities of Islamic Instruction," in ibid., 19–77. These and other chapters in this volume present a highly useful account of the organization of Islamic education in different countries of Europe and how reliance on *imāms* invited from overseas to staff mosques in Europe remains a serious concern for the four Western European states (France, Germany, the Netherlands, and the U.K.) that have sizeable Muslim populations.
33. M. Amer Morgahi, "An Emerging European Islam: The Case of Minhajul Qur'an in the Netherlands," in *Producing Islamic Knowledge*, eds van Bruinessen and Allievi, 47–64.
34. Pew Research Center, "Muslim Americans."
35. Abbas, ed., *Muslim Britain*.
36. Linda Herrera and Asef Bayat, eds, *Being Young and Muslim: New Cultural Politics in the Global South and North* (Oxford–New York: Oxford University Press, 2010).
37. Umm Raiyaan, "Why Are New Muslims Leaving Islam?," *Islam21c*, August 7, 2012, accessed August 17, 2016, http://www.islam21c.com/islamic-thought/5823-why-are-new-muslims-leaving-islam/; Ahmed Eid, "UnMosqued: Why Are Young Muslims Leaving American Mosques?," *The Huffington Post*, December 17, 2013, accessed August 17, 2016, http://www.huffingtonpost.com/ahmed-eid/young-american-muslims_b_4109256.html; Andrew Anthony, "Losing Their Religion: The Hidden Crisis of Faith among Britain's Young Muslims," *The Guardian*, May 17, 2015, accessed August 17, 2016, https://www.theguardian.com/global/2015/may/17/losing-their-religion-british-ex-muslims-non-believers-hidden-crisis-faith.
38. These issues came up repeatedly in the interviews that I have conducted with young Muslims in the United Kingdom, Europe, and the United States.
39. Leon Moosavi, "Are Converts More Likely to be Extremists than Other Muslims?," *The Guardian*, May 24, 2013, accessed August 17, 2016, https://www.theguardian.com/commentisfree/belief/2013/may/24/islam-converts-woolwich-attackers-extremists; Beenish Ahmed, "Why Converts to Islam are so Susceptible to Becoming Terrorists," *ThinkProgress*, February 3, 2016, accessed August 17, 2016, https://thinkprogress.org/why-converts-to-islam-are-so-susceptible-to-becoming-terrorists-118582cfa179.
40. The Zaytuna tuition fee for the academic year 2016/17 is US$19,000, plus US$10,000 is required to cover housing costs: Zaytuna College, "Admissions,"

accessed August 15, 2016, https://www.zaytuna.edu/admissions/; participation in the three-week Rihla retreat costs more than US$3,000 per person: Deen Intensive Foundation, "The Rihla Program," accessed August 15, 2016, http://www.deenintensive.com/the-rihla-program/; joining the ten-day ʿumrah program with Sacred Caravan similarly costs close to $4,000 per person: Sacred Caravan, "The 2016 Sacred Caravan Umrah Program," accessed August 15, 2016, http://sacredcaravan.wufoo.com/forms/z1aornk918rw72v/.

41. All these institutions also run active fundraising campaigns using all media to advertise. During Ramadan, these efforts intensify: routine e-mail messages are circulated on their mailing lists, asking people to donate generously and reminding them of the importance and benefits of giving *zakāt*, *sadaqah*, and *khayrat*.
42. Laurence, *The Emancipation of Europe's Muslims*, 133.
43. Ibid.
44. Ibid.
45. Ibid.
46. van Bruinessen and Allievi, *Producing Islamic Knowledge*.
47. MCB was founded in 1997; details of its activities can be found at its official website, *The Muslim Council of Britain*, accessed August 15, 2016, http://www.mcb.org.uk/.
48. Laurence, *The Emancipation of Europe's Muslims*, 244.
49. Gilles Kepel quoted in Laurence, *The Emancipation of Europe's Muslims*, 11.
50. Brigitte Maréchal, "Modalities of Islamic Instruction," in *Muslims in the Enlarged Europe*.
51. Matthew Bowlby and Benjamin van Impelen, "The Imam Training Debate: The Future of Religion for Dutch Muslims," *Humanity in Action*, accessed August 13, 2016, http://www.humanityinaction.org/knowledgebase/190-the-imam-training-debate-the-future-of-religion-for-dutch-muslims.
52. Isabelle de Pommereau, "German Universities Move to Train Next Generation of Imams," *Christian Science Monitor*, May 19, 2012, accessed August 13, 2016, http://islam.ru/en/content/story/german-universities-move-train-next-generation-imams.
53. van Bruinessen and Allievi, *Producing Islamic Knowledge*.
54. Ibid.
55. For a review of such assertions and their critique, see Yahya Michot, *The Father of Islamic Radicalism? Muslims under Non-Muslim Rule* (Oxford: Interface Publications, 2006).
56. An increasing number of al-Ghazālī's works are now available in English. There is also an increase in scholarly books, seminars, and study workshops focused on the study of al-Ghazālī's thought. His image is also often invoked in popular media to highlight the more philosophical and mystical dimensions of Islam: *Al-Ghazali: The Alchemist of Happiness*, directed by Ovidio Salazar (DVD) (Matmedia Productions, 2004), a film on al-Ghazālī, is one example.
57. For example, Humza Yusuf's lecture entitled "This is the Muhammad You Call a Terrorist" shows 55,844 hits (*YouTube*, February 23, 2009, accessed August 17, 2016, https://www.youtube.com/watch?v=ySCNYLL4NWQ).
58. For information about Alqueria de Rosales's activities, see its official website, accessed August 15, 2016, http://alqueriaderosales.org/.
59. Bowen, *Can Islam be French?*; Esra Özyürek, *Being German, Becoming Muslim: Race, Religion, and Conversion in the New Europe* (Princeton: Princeton University Press, 2014).

60. Ibid.
61. Charles Taylor, *A Secular Age* (Cambridge, M.A.: Harvard University Press, 2007).
62. Zaytuna College, "About, Our Mission," accessed 13 August 2016, https://www.zaytuna.edu/about/our_mission/.
63. Ibid.
64. Ibid.
65. *Deen Intensive Foundation*, accessed August 17, 2016, http://www.deenintensive.com/; *Sacred Caravan*, accessed August 17, 2016, http://www.sacredcaravan.com/; *Sandala*, accessed August 17, 2016, https://sandala.org/.
66. Cambridge Muslim College, "Four-Year Programme," accessed 15 August 2016, http://www.cambridgemuslimcollege.org/programmes/four-yp/.
67. Ibid.
68. See the *International Institute of Islamic Thought (IIIT)* website, accessed August 15, 2016, http://www.iiit.org/.
69. Ibid.
70. See the *CILE–Research Center for Islamic Legislation and Ethics* website, accessed August 15, 2016, http://www.cilecenter.org/.
71. Ibid.
72. Interview with Shaykh Mohammed Amin Kholwadia, Chicago, August 2014.
73. "Our Seminars," *AlMaghrib Institute*, accessed August 15, 2016, http://almaghrib.org/seminars.
74. Ibid.
75. "No Doubt (God, Religion and Politics in the Modern World) [Seminar Profile]," *AlMaghrib Institute*, accessed May 21, 2016, http://almaghrib.org/seminars/islamic-theology/no-doubt#info.
76. Bowen, *Can Islam Be French?*; Bowen, *On British Islam.*
77. Muhammad Naguib Al-Attas, *Prolegomena to the Metaphysics of Islam: An Exposition of the Fundamental Elements of the Worldview of Islam* (Kuala Lumpur: International Institute of Islamic Thought and Civilization, 1995), 29.
78. Timothy Winter, "Boys Will Be Boys," masud.co.uk, accessed January 29, 2015, http://masud.co.uk/ISLAM/ahm/boys.htm.
79. Ibid.
80. International Institute of Islamic Thought, "Research Grants."
81. Ibid., 28–29, also 22.
82. Jasser Auda, "A *Maqāṣidī* Approach to Contemporary Application of the *Sharīʿah*," *Intellectual Discourse* 19 (2011), 193–217.
83. Ibid, 446.
84. See the website of the *Islamic Society of North America (ISNA)*, accessed August 15, 2016, http://www.isna.net/.
85. At the 2012 ISNA convention held in Washington, D.C. in August, which I attended, Tariq Ramadan presented his CILE project to a packed hall and highlighted how the methodological tools his team is trying to develop will make Islam answer real-life concerns faced by young Muslims who want to be part of the West while staying true to their Islamic faith.
86. See *Reviving the Islamic Spirit* in Canada, accessed August 17, 2016, http://risconvention.com/.
87. "Visiting Scholar–Imam Zaid Shakir (Zaytuna College USA)," *Ebrahim College*, August 26, 2014, accessed August 17, 2016, https://ebrahimcollege.org.uk/visiting-scholar-imam-zaid-shakir-zaytuna-college-usa/.

88. In their recent speeches and writings.
89. See their respective websites at: *Bayyinah*, accessed August 15, 2016, http://bayyinah.com/; *Ta'leef Collective*, accessed August 15, 2016, http://taleefcollective.org.
90. An observation based on my own fieldwork.
91. This reference was made by Dr. Umar Faruq Abd-Allah in a seminar he gave in Medina, when leading the 2016 Sacred Caravan 'umrah trip in place of Humza Yusuf, April 2016.
92. Jack Jenkins, "What It's Like to Attend America's First Accredited Muslim College," *ThinkProgress*, April 18, 2016, accessed August 17, 2016, https://thinkprogress.org/what-its-like-to-attend-america-s-first-accredited-muslim-college-e129701dbed6#.5wkg0xlnn.
93. Ammara Maqsood, "'Buying Modern': Muslim Subjectivity, the West and Patterns of Islamic Consumption in Lahore, Pakistan," *Cultural Studies* 28 (2014), 184–207.
94. A common response during my interviews.
95. Masooda Bano, *The Rational Believer: Choices and Decisions in the Madrasas of Pakistan* (Ithaca: Cornell University Press, 2012), Chapter 4.
96. Francis Robinson, "Islamic Reform and Modernities in South Asia," *Modern Asian Studies* 42 (2008), 259–81; Muhammad Qasim Zaman, *Modern Islamic Thought in a Radical Age: Religious Authority and Internal Criticism* (Cambridge: Cambridge University Press, 2012).
97. Hussein Ali Agrama, *Questioning Secularism: Islam, Sovereignty, and the Rule of Law in Modern Egypt* (Chicago: University of Chicago Press, 2012); see discussion in the Introduction to Volume 1.
98. Ibid.
99. Charles Taylor, *A Secular Age*; for a review of others Western thinkers sharing similar critiques of Western modernity, see Roxanne L. Euben, *Enemy in the Mirror: Islamic Fundamentalism and the Limits of Modern Rationalism* (Princeton: Princeton University Press, 1997).

PART I

♦ ♦ ♦

NEO-TRADITIONALISTS

This part illustrates the growing appeal of a specific approach to the revival of the Islamic spiritual tradition, as exemplified by the popularity of Humza Yusuf in the U.S.A. and Tim Winter (Abdal Hakim Murad) in the U.K. Both emphasize the need not just for studying Islam but for living it in everyday life, actively trying to purify the inner self. Both encourage followers to seek the *ṣuḥba* (companionship) of spiritual scholars while retaining a heavy focus on respect for the four *madhhab*s. Chapter 1 focuses on the scholarship and practice of Humza Yusuf, looking at how his influence on young American Muslims is being institutionalised through Zaytuna College, the first Islamic Liberal Arts College in the U.S.A. Chapter 2 looks at the scholarship of Tim Winter, with a particular focus on the Cambridge Muslim College. Under his intellectual guidance, the college has developed a one-year course for graduates of British *dār al-ʿulūm*s, enabling them to relate their study of *sharīʿah* with the realities of the society in which they live.

CHAPTER
1

ZAYTUNA COLLEGE AND THE CONSTRUCTION OF AN AMERICAN MUSLIM IDENTITY

Nathan Spannaus and Christopher Pooya Razavian

Zaytuna College, a Muslim liberal arts college located in Berkeley, California, is unique among Islamic institutions. It is simultaneously a Muslim institute of higher education and one that aspires to find a place in American academia. These two aspects, the American and the Islamic, are what quintessentially shape Zaytuna, including its function and its religious outlook.

Hamza Yusuf, a white American convert to Islam, founded it in 1996 as Zaytuna Institute—named after the famous Tunisian madrasa—in nearby Hayward, California, with the help of Hesham Alalusi, a businessman and philanthropist from Iraq who had settled in California. A physical building was established in 1998, and the early years of Zaytuna were devoted to offering classes and lectures to the Muslim community in the San Francisco Bay Area. As Yusuf and the institution grew in prominence it attracted a number of Muslim activists and educators to its programmes, and the scope of its activities grew. An *imām* training programme was inaugurated in 2004, and in 2008 the transition to a four-year liberal arts curriculum began, with a move into its current buildings in Berkeley and Zaytuna College's first graduating class beginning in 2010.

Zaytuna College, under the leadership of Yusuf and Imam Zaid Shakir, a black American convert and Muslim scholar, is oriented toward the spread of knowledge of Islam and Islamic tradition, self-consciously within an American context. As a Muslim institution led by American Muslims, it seeks to create a space for Muslims and Islam within the religious and educational landscape of America. Its leaders' Americanness, as native converts, plays a large role in Zaytuna's acclimation of Islam to the American setting, a setting in which both Yusuf and Shakir are at home.

Hamza Yusuf

Hamza Yusuf was born Mark Hanson in Washington state in 1958. His family moved to northern California soon after, and he spent his childhood in Berkeley. His family was Christian—his father Irish Catholic and his mother Greek Orthodox—and he received education in both traditions as a child.

Yusuf converted to Islam in 1977, after a period of religious reflection that followed being seriously injured in a car accident. He became acquainted with some members of the Shādhilīyah Sufi order in California, who encouraged him toward Sufism. He quit college and moved to England to the *shaykh* of their sub-order, a white convert named Abd AlQadir as-Sufi (*né* Ian Dallas) who lived in Norwich. (Later, Yusuf, who would decisively break with as-Sufi in 1984, says merely that he fell in with a group of Muslims he describes as "spiritual," omitting any mention of the Shādhilīyah.) According to Yusuf, he sought a more serious approach to the religion, and he began studying Arabic, when he met a certain Shaykh Abdullah Ali Mahmoud from Sharjah in the United Arab Emirates. Mahmoud arranged for Yusuf to attend classes at the Islamic Institute of Al-Ayn in the U.A.E. Yusuf would spend five years in the U.A.E, studying at the Islamic Institute. He eventually mastered Arabic and parts of the Qur᾽ān well enough that he began serving as muezzin and later *imām* in a small mosque in Al-Ayn. In addition to the Islamic Institute, whose level of instruction he says was low, Yusuf studied privately with more traditional scholars, first Abdullah Ould Siddiq, a native of Mauritania and then-*muftī* of Abu Dhabi, through whom Yusuf became acquainted with other West African Mālikī scholars in the U.A.E., including Sheikh Abdullah bin Bayyah.[1]

In 1984, Yusuf left the U.A.E. for Mauritania to study with Murabit al-Hajj Muhammad Fahfu in his *madrasah* on the edge of the Sahara. He spent three years studying there, an experience that he has called transformative. He was motivated to find Murabit al-Hajj by the regard in which he is held among West Africans, and Yusuf claims to have seen visions of both him and his wife Maryam in dreams prior to arriving in Mauritania. Once there, Yusuf was exposed to methods of instruction that were far older than what he had experienced prior. Learning was done through memorization and recitation of texts, utilizing a wooden plank called a *lawh* as a writing surface with charcoal as the implement. Teaching was done face-to-face with the teacher, usually on an individual basis or in very small numbers. Yusuf has repeatedly emphasized the traditional character of the education there, untainted by outside, modern influence. Likewise, he has spoken very highly of the spiritual environment at Murabit al-Hajj's madrasa and the moral component of the teaching.[2]

Spirituality and morality are important focal points for Yusuf's understanding of Islam. He talks frequently in his speeches about living as a Muslim and about the need for incorporating Islam into one's life as more of an attitude or approach than a matter of dogma or ritual— about the latter Yusuf accepts some degree of flexibility.[3] He also mentions compassion as an important part of Islam. He enrolled in nursing school upon returning to California in 1988–9, while also studying homeopathic medicine. He worked for several years in the cardiac unit of a hospital. At this time, he began serving as *imām* in different mosques around the Bay Area. He soon had made a name for himself as a teacher and a lecturer, and he was invited to speak at the Islamic Society of North America conference in 1993.

At this time, Yusuf also moved away from his medical work toward religious activities. He enrolled in a bachelor's degree programme in comparative religion at San José State University (he would graduate in 1997), and in 1994 he helped start the Rihla programme, short retreats built around religious study, later to become part of the Deen Intensive Foundation, which promotes a "traditional" Islamic education in a "traditional" Islamic environment, with an emphasis on piety and spirituality as well as restrictions on students' dress and use of technology. (It has been remarked that the Rihlas are an attempt to recreate Yusuf's experience in Mauritania for an American audience.) Teaching was done in small groups, with students sitting on the ground in front of teachers (called *shaykh*s). Each student had to declare a *madhhab*, according to which classes were divided.[4]

Zaytuna was founded in 1996, the closeness of which to the beginning of the Rihlas is not coincidental; Zaytuna was established, at least initially, to be a more permanent version of the Rihlas' religious atmosphere and emphasis on spiritual and moral engagement. Many of the same regulations that exist on the Rihla, particularly in terms of dress code, were enforced in Zaytuna's classrooms, and teachers encouraged certain behaviors outside of the classroom, like avoiding television or unhealthy food.[5]

After September 11, Yusuf's public profile, on the rise among Muslims since the early 1990s, grew rapidly. He was selected by President George W. Bush to serve as the Muslim representative for an interfaith dinner at the White House in late September 2001, and numerous similar appearances followed over the next few years.[6] The combination of Yusuf's whiteness, Americanness, bilingual facility in Arabic and English, Islamic education, familiarity with American culture and—perhaps most importantly—religious moderation has made him a prominent symbol of an American Islam, for Muslims and non-Muslims alike.[7] It was at this time that Yusuf began downplaying and omitting past critical comments regarding American foreign policy that he had made, which elicited complaints among Muslims of hypocrisy. Likewise, a statement made in October 2001 that Muslim extremists should leave the West "if they are going to rant and rave about [it]" drew considerable anger among Western Muslims.[8]

Yusuf has amended some of his comments from 2001 to 2002. Other than his increased prominence, his activities have changed little since the late 1990s. He still travels frequently to teach and give lectures, and he still participates in the Rihla programme. He has become advisor to more institutions and governments, while making connections with institutions of higher education, namely Stanford University's programme in Islamic Studies and the Graduate Theological Seminary in Berkeley. Yusuf has also joined the board of Bin Bayyah's Global Center for Renewal and Guidance, formed in 2012, an organization aimed at promoting a moderate form of Islam and making Islamic authority more coherent and less fragmented in order to counter and exclude extremism.[9]

Of the figures to whom Yusuf is connected, Bin Bayyah may exert the most influence on his thinking. Yusuf frequently mentions his old teacher in glowing terms, and while he doesn't issue *fatwā*s himself, he does consult with Bin Bayyah on complex questions and pass along the latter's *fatwā*s to people who come to him for advice. It is not clear, however, if this is an indication of Yusuf's allegiance to Bin Bayyah, or rather merely that Bin Bayyah is particularly concerned about these issues and can—and is willing to—speak to them easily. Bin Bayyah works primarily on matters of *fiqh* and has published a book on *fiqh al-aqallīyāt* (jurisprudence of minorities), so the type of questions of practice that Yusuf receives from American Muslims are a definite focus for him. (See the detailed discussion of Bin Bayyah in Volume 1, Chapter 3.)

In addition to Bin Bayyah, Yusuf has been influenced by other global Muslim figures, notably the Malaysian intellectual Naquib al-Attas, a major proponent of the Islamization of knowledge project. Indeed, despite his personal closeness to Bin Bayyah, Yusuf seems much less concerned about particular matters of law or belief than about educational practice and spirituality.

Yet Yusuf does not focus on specific points of dogma or religious ideology, but rather the breadth of the Islamic scholarly tradition, which is deeply important to him, and he has taken steps to maintain elements of it among his students and within his teaching (as aspects of Zaytuna's curriculum reflect). This is more a matter of approach than a particular position. To wit, Yusuf was educated in the Mālikī school, and the *madhhab* paradigm holds obvious significance for him, but he does not promote Mālikism in any particular way. Instead, Yusuf seeks to propagate and preserve the scholarly tradition as a means of resisting current extremist or ideological uses of Islam, which are common but, according to him, at odds with the vast expanse of Islamic history. He states plainly that "Islam is misperceived by the Muslims,"[10] and by regaining their own intellectual heritage, Muslims can reassert the cultural and intellectual vitality of Islam. (Sadek Hamid has grouped Yusuf and Zaid Shakir into what he terms the "Traditional Islam network," which also includes Nuh Keller, Timothy Winter/Abdal Hakim Murad, and Bin Bayyah.[11])

The goal is the creation of what can be called an "integral" Islam that reflects not only aspects of behavior and comportment (as puritanical Salafis may assert) but inner and intellectual attachment to Islamic faith as well. For Yusuf, it is inner devotion that leads to proper moral behavior, and this is best cultivated through knowledge and education.[12]

This stance contributes to Yusuf's negative view of mainstream education, both in America and the Islamic world. According to him, this approach to education abandons the spiritual component of the individual, creating graduates with narrowly focused skills and abilities but no moral foundation. Such critiques are part of the impetus behind Zaytuna, and in addition he has founded the Kinza Academy with his sister, Nabilah (also a convert), an organization dedicated to supporting home-schooling among Muslims to counteract the shortcomings of the American primary educational system.[13]

Yusuf's emphasis on spirituality and inward morality is without doubt Sufi-inspired, and he himself remains affiliated with the Shādhilīyah order, although to what degree is unclear, and he takes pains to avoid talking specifically about Sufism in order to avoid stepping into any controversial issues surrounding it.[14]

Imam Zaid Shakir

Born Ricky Mitchell in Berkeley in 1956, Zaid Shakir converted to Islam in 1977. The similarities with Hamza Yusuf's early life, however, are limited to these superficial details. While Yusuf comes from an affluent background, Shakir's childhood was spent in relative poverty. His family—six siblings and a single mother—moved around when he was young. He grew up in Georgia and Connecticut, in addition to California. Following his mother's death in 1975, he left community college and enlisted in the United States Air Force in 1976.

Shakir began moving away from his Baptist upbringing as a teenager, and he explored different religious and ideological perspectives, including for a time transcendental meditation and communism. He says that those two influenced him the most, and he has combined them in his understanding of Islam, as spiritual awareness mixed with social activism. He converted, he says, after a long period of reflection while he was in the Air Force.[15]

After leaving the military, Shakir decided to pursue an education. He received a bachelor's degree in International Relations in 1983, and then enrolled in and completed a master's degree programme in political science at Rutgers, The State University of New Jersey. Particularly while at Rutgers, Shakir combined his studies with political and social activism. He led the drive for divestment from South Africa at Rutgers to protest Apartheid, and he helped found the local New Brunswick Islamic Center. He spent a year in Cairo studying Arabic after graduating from Rutgers, and then he took a teaching position in political science and Middle East studies at Southern Connecticut State University.

Shakir continued his activism and became more involved in Islamic organizations. He helped establish the Masjid al-Islam in New Haven, Connecticut, serving as its first *imām*, and he co-founded the Tri-State Muslim Education

Initiative and the Connecticut Muslim Coordinating Committee. He also served as student chaplain at Yale University and worked in chaplaincy training at Yale Medical School. He attracted more attention from national Islamic organizations, and he participated in the first Rihla meeting in 1994 with Hamza Yusuf and others.[16]

Also in 1994, Shakir went abroad to further his Islamic education. He enrolled in the Islamic Studies programme at Abu Nur Institute in Damascus, studying Qur'ān, *ḥadīth*, *fiqh*, and theology. Abu Nur Institute was part of the larger Abu Nur religious network, under the leadership of the Grand Mufti of Syria, Ahmad Kaftaru (1912–2004). In addition to his position as Grand Mufti, Kaftaru was also head of a sub-order of the Naqshbandi-Khālidīyah begun by his father, and Abu Nur mosques and schools were designed to promote a Sufi-inspired approach to Islam in order to counteract the influence of the Muslim Brotherhood and Saudi Salafism within Syria as well as abroad. (Although not funded by the Syrian government, the Abu Nur network was supported by the state for this purpose; Abu Nur Institute was in fact founded in 1982 in the midst of an Islamist uprising within the country.)[17] Shakir graduated in—it seems—the spring of 2001, when he returned to his duties as imām in New Haven.

In 2003, Shakir moved back to California to join the faculty of Zaytuna Institute. He helped develop the graduate seminary programme, which began in 2004 and served as a venue for developing the pedagogical approach that would be employed in the undergraduate liberal arts curriculum used by Zaytuna College, of which Shakir served as co-founder in 2008.[18]

Throughout his career, Shakir has been extensively engaged in different forms of social and economic activism that stand apart in some ways from his role as Islamic leader. In addition to his anti-Apartheid work, during the 1990s he spearheaded community revitalization projects and anti-drug campaigns in and around New Haven, and he has been a leader in a multi-year relief project to eradicate malaria in West Africa. In 2009, he co-founded United for Change, an organization devoted to bringing the range of Islamic organizations and groups in North America together for social activism that has engaged in anti-malaria, anti-violence, and anti-poverty efforts.[19] Just in 2013–14, Shakir participated in rallies across the United States against police brutality and climate change.

This element of social activism marks the greatest distinction between Shakir's and Yusuf's views. (Geneive Abdo contrasts the two by labeling Shakir an activist and Yusuf an intellectual.[20]) The latter's focus on spirituality and cultivating personal morality in Muslims through education emphasizes an inner dimension that is central to his approach to Islam. Yusuf frequently discusses the role of the heart in spirituality and piety, and he stresses that knowledge of the religion helps strengthen and purify the believer's heart.[21]

Shakir, on the other hand, shows greater concern for outward expressions of piety, manifested in struggles for justice and equality. As shown in his activist ventures, this approach is not limited to Islam or Muslims—in fact, quite the opposite. In an article on human rights and Islam from 2003, he criticizes a widespread view among Muslims that associates human rights with the *sharīʿah*, arguing that such a claim is not only meaningless to non-Muslims (and therefore politically ineffective), but also ignores the universal aspects of the *sharīʿah* that promote the safety, prosperity, and well-being of all people.[22] Indeed, for Shakir, Islam and being a Muslim means working to improve one's society substantively, without limiting one's efforts strictly to Muslims or "Muslim" concerns.

There is considerable overlap between Shakir's and Yusuf's respective stances, to be sure, but the difference in emphasis on outward and inward action is notable. The combination of the two approaches is important to understanding Zaytuna as an institution. Yusuf's views on the spiritual elements of traditional Islamic education and its benefits for the individual believer are apparent in the curriculum as well as some of the rules placed on students. Shakir's focus on the outward manifestation of Islam within society is apparent in the function of Zaytuna itself. Shakir joined the faculty as part of its efforts to begin training American *imāms*, which were seen as sorely needed to serve the Muslim community. For Shakir, this was a way to strengthen Muslims' place within American society, while the need for *American imāms* was in large part driven by the need for Muslims in America to be less isolated and more broadly active.[23] Only by establishing lasting Muslim institutions—like Zaytuna—can Muslims effect positive change. As Shakir himself puts it, "Unless we build strong credible institutions, we cannot impact society and bring about benefit to all within."[24]

The American focus in Shakir's views is apparent. Even ostensibly global events, such as the Danish cartoon controversy, he approaches from the perspective of their impact on the American context.[25] In many ways, Shakir is following the long-established model of politically and socially active black American religious leaders, who have used their religious institutions and organizations as a platform to issue religiously inspired—but not overwhelmingly religious or exclusionary—critiques of American economics, culture, society, and politics.

American Muslim Identity

Shakir's focus on the American setting may manifest itself in particular ways, but it is not unique to him. Rather, the primary goal of Zaytuna, its raison d'être as an institution, is the articulation of an American Muslim identity, a model of Muslimness suited to the American/Western environment. (The original motto of Zaytuna Institute was "Where Islam meets America," and this serves as a concise encapsulation of its aim.[26]) Such an identity, at home in America and not at odds with, or divorced from, the broader society, is seen as a necessity by a number of Muslim leaders. Winter, a British Muslim convert and Cambridge academic, has argued that immigrant Muslims in America must better acclimate themselves to their new home and integrate into American society.[27] These claims have been echoed by Sherman Jackson, a black American Muslim and professor, who has written that black American Muslims, by virtue of the fact that they are undoubtedly American culturally and socially, should act as guides for immigrant Muslims in balancing Islamic norms with American life.[28] In a 2013 speech at a Zaytuna-sponsored conference, Jackson argued that Muslims in America need to determine what is essential and what is inessential in their faith, so as to make "principled comprises" with their religion in order to "meet society where it is."[29]

Both Winter and Jackson are informally associated with Zaytuna, and their views mirror Zaytuna's aim. This goal is not primarily ideological, in the sense of incubating a particular way of thinking, but rather it is concerned with finding a mode of *being* Muslim within American society. As such, it is broadly ecumenical, accepting of a number of varying Islamic orientations as a matter of pragmatism. Zaid Shakir has told audiences to "use their common sense" rather than needlessly adhere to rigid dogma, pointing out that America "is not Saudi Arabia."[30] But it is also a matter of conviction; Zaytuna's leaders, Hamza Yusuf chief among them, have frequently and vocally argued against factionalism and discord within the American Muslim community.[31] Such an approach is suited to the broad diversity among American Muslims, as well as an acknowledgment that a coherent form of Muslimness established within American society does not yet exist.[32] Indeed, Yusuf preaches that Muslims must work to craft an Islamic tradition that is indigenous to the West—"that is *here*," he says—using a language of Islam that is at home in this setting.[33]

Zaytuna was founded in pursuit of this goal.[34] Yusuf states that it is intended to fill the gap of Muslim higher education in America, which already has religiously oriented education for numerous other faiths.[35] Shakir likewise argues that such institutions are needed to allow the American Muslim community to flourish and mature within the context of the global *ummah*: "You have an American Muslim culture emerging, which is very important, because then you can get a unique understanding of the religion that would allow the American Muslim to take his or her rightful place amongst the various Muslim communities of the world."[36]

The formation of an American Muslim identity requires forging a congruence of sorts between the two elements and must, if successful, comprise both. In order to do that, Muslims must understand both. This point is strongly emphasized in the Zaytuna College *Catalog*: that students should learn the Islamic and Western cultural traditions, and to be conversant in both, is repeatedly expressed, and it has played a large role in determining the college's curriculum.[37] Yusuf and Shakir also pepper their speeches with references stretching far beyond Islamic tradition, including points of American literature, history, politics, and pop culture.

Zaytuna's efforts to forge this hybrid identity are complicated and influenced by common concerns—among Muslims and non-Muslims alike—about the compatibility of "American" and "Muslim" as categories, concerns that Zaytuna's founders and faculty are keen on allaying. They frequently express admiration for aspects of American society and key American values—tolerance and diversity among them—and emphasize the parallels between the two. Zaid Shakir has said that he sees no incongruity between Islam and American democracy.[38] He, however, was widely criticized in the American media for a 2006 interview in *The New York Times* in which he said that he hoped America would become a Muslim country.[39] Yusuf, who has been subject to similar, if less strident criticisms for perceived anti-American positions, has stated that America, as the leading power in the world, should serve as "a beacon of humanity," promoting the best of American society globally.[40] The religious acceptance that Yusuf sees in America has prompted him to argue that it is easier to be Muslim there than in many Muslim countries.[41]

Importantly, Zaytuna does not downplay its Americanness, whether in terms of the faculty, itself as an institution, or indeed its student body. Most of its teachers are native converts, deeply steeped in American culture and society. Similarly, virtually all Zaytuna students are either American-born or long-time permanent residents. Many have expressed feeling fully American, without tension with their religious identity.[42] And the college itself has organized events aimed at explicitly aligning with Americanness. It has put on programmes emphasizing Muslims' allegiance and loyalty to America (which, not incidentally, were also used to fundraise), and its first convocation ceremony in 2010 featured an address by Virginia Gray Henry, a descendent of Revolutionary War hero Patrick Henry and a Muslim convert. After her speech, Yusuf stated that her "auspicious" presence there signified the connection between the American Revolution and Zaytuna, which, he states, is part of that revolution's drive for liberty.[43]

A similar point of emphasis for Zaytuna is the ways in which American society can benefit from Muslims' contributions. Members of the Zaytuna community frequently talk about Muslims' unique perspective on America and what they can offer intellectually, and the College *Catalog* states that one of the school's academic goals is "connect[ing] Islamic thought to broader public conversations in the West."[44] These efforts at serving society require stable and functioning institutions, a gap that Zaytuna is intended to fill.

On the flipside of these concerns from mainstream society are questions of the Islamic suitability of an explicitly *American* Muslim institution that circulate among Muslims wary that Zaytuna's embrace of its Americanness undermines its religious legitimacy. This scrutiny has fallen particularly upon Yusuf, who has been criticized for everything from his association with the Bush administration following September 11 (he was labeled Bush's "pet Muslim" or "Hamza Useless" by some) to public appearances in which he hasn't worn a kufi hat.[45] Blunting these criticisms, the Zaytuna leadership unfailingly emphasizes the "traditional" character of their project; their efforts to create an American Muslim identity do not entail changing the religion itself, but merely expressing its essence in an American idiom.[46] Yusuf uses the metaphor of water in a vessel to describe the relationship between Islam and cultural setting: different vessels will give the water different colors, but the water itself remains the same.[47]

Complicating the issue are the frequent but erroneous characterizations in the American media of Yusuf (who receives the overwhelming majority of the attention) and Zaytuna as "reformist" or "progressive," based seemingly on little more than their embrace of Americanness and rejection of violence.[48] In fact, Zaytuna is decidedly conservative—in the strict sense of the word—in orientation and outlook. Indeed, its authority is constructed upon its continuation of, and conformity to, the established (Sunni) Islamic tradition, to the exclusion of any substantive alteration thereof (discussed below). This position is expressed most clearly in Yusuf's debate with the Islamic legal reformer Tariq Ramadan from 2008.[49] Positions, views, and methodologies established and maintained by scholars within the Islamic past are considered necessarily authoritative, and thus accepted as valid (if not compelling) within Zaytuna. This is the reasoning behind some of its uncommon pedagogical practices, in particular memorization, which was a central method of learning in the pre-modern Islamic scholarly tradition but is generally abandoned today.[50] This acceptance includes a number of positions that are at odds with broader trends within American society, such as negative attitudes toward women's religious roles and homosexuality, to say nothing of rules on male–female interactions distinct from the norm of American college campuses.[51] For instance, Shakir wrote a response to a 2005 event in which a woman (American convert Amina Wadud) led a mixed-gender Friday prayer service, stating that the practice had been widely rejected by scholars over the centuries; as such, it has no basis in Islamic history or tradition, and he therefore could not condone it.[52]

Such a marked upholding of tradition engenders a feeling of Islamic legitimacy, even among those who may disagree. And though it perhaps goes without saying, religious legitimacy is of paramount importance to Zaytuna. Not only does it allow the institution to operate and attract students and followers, but it also facilitates conversation and engagement with other sectors of the Muslim community. External engagement is a major theme for Zaytuna,[53] as it seeks to influence Muslim practice in America and elsewhere.

Anti-secularization

Central to Zaytuna's project is the cultivation and promotion of Islamic piety and personal religiosity. As noted above, this does not rely on a particular ideological stance, but rather revolves around a broad rejection of, and campaign against, individual irreligiosity in the guise of secularization.

This is not, it should be pointed out, a rejection of *all* forms of secularization or even secular society, but rather a specific a-religious orientation. In support of this position, Yusuf cites the work of a Malaysian scholar, Muhammad Naguib Al-Attas, who draws a distinction between "secularisation" and the "secular" state. He states that it is possible for a secular state to uphold religion, while secularization tries to overthrow all that is religious. He argues that there has been a confusion among Muslims that pits a secular state against a theocratic state, stating instead that an Islamic state is "neither wholly theocratic nor wholly secular," and that a Muslim state calling itself secular does not necessarily have to work against religion.[54] Secular politics is therefore not necessarily problematic from a Muslim perspective, as, al-Attas writes, it "does not necessarily have to divest nature of spiritual meaning [and] does not necessarily have to deny religious values and virtues in politics and human affairs."[55]

Indeed, Yusuf stands firmly against the use of Islam for political movements or as a political ideology, in particular Islamism. He argues that Muslims should be looking toward spiritual development, which has been ignored by Islamist movements. While Islamists see themselves as opposing secularism, Yusuf views Islamism as a part of the trend toward a lack of morality and meaning in society.

In a series of lectures on William Chittick's book *The Vision of Islam*, Yusuf comments that the concept of an Islamic state is similar to Zionism in its transformation of Judaism into a political ideology. He equates the concept of the Islamic state with coercing people to believe in Islam, which he considers impossible: "An Islamic state is the idea that you can force people to be good Muslims which is a completely insane idea. It has never existed and it will never exist. If you think religion can be legislated by a government you are completely deluded."[56] Elsewhere he writes:

> Islam is not an ideology, political or otherwise. It is a revelation from God that explains and reminds people of their duties toward their Creator in honoring and worshipping God with gratitude for the gift of life and all the concomitants of that gift, and of their duties toward their fellow creatures as unique and protected creations of God . . . Politics involves making sure the mail gets out, allotting appropriate monies for public works, and ensuring the security of a people from internal or external threats; all of these can be done without recourse to any specific religious tradition.[57]

Instead, secular states can operate well without a religious grounding, even in a way that is Islamic. Yusuf argues that secular states such as Finland and Sweden have such a high degree of social justice that Muslims should consider these states exemplary, comparing them favorably to the time of the legendary Ṣalāḥ al-Dīn and unfavorably to contemporary Egypt as an oppressive dictatorship.[58] For him, good governance does not rely on religion, but rather on basic morality, common decency, and a commitment to social justice within a government.

It is ensured by the individuals in charge of important tasks, which requires honesty, transparency, and vetting, all ideals that can be attained through a secular state. There is no need for a religious ideology.[59]

By contrast, secularization, the stripping away of religious morality in both societies and individuals, is viewed as a distinct danger, and Zaytuna's rejection of it verges on the categorical. This represents the most basic and fundamental aspect in the construction of Zaytuna's claim to Islamic authority. Although its main objective is the formation of an American Muslim identity, its primary message is the importance of religious consciousness and personal (religious) morality, in direct opposition to secularization.

Yusuf is particularly vocal in his critique of what he calls the secular mindset, and he connects it to a wide range of social, cultural, economic, and even environmental and medical problems. This mindset, he argues, is divorced from any sort of moral purpose, and it leads people to live their lives in the same manner. Moral purpose, he states, provides meaning for people's lives, and he decries what he sees as the meaninglessness of modern society, the lack of a higher purpose to things like politics, business, the military, science, and even modern philosophy.[60]

Many contemporary problems can therefore be ultimately attributed to secularization, as people without moral grounding act in ways that have no real meaning and serve no real benefit—or are harmful—because they do not consider the value or consequences of their actions. This is reflected in people acting or conducting themselves for what can be labeled "base" reasons, to fulfill simple needs and desires, without any "higher" considerations. Yusuf often uses the analogy that people are becoming like jellyfish—brainless, spineless beings that eat and reproduce and do nothing other than spread in pursuit of both. That the pollution of the oceans has, he states, created an environment in which only the jellyfish thrives is for Yusuf a perfect encapsulation of how modern society is most conducive to mindless consumption.[61] Although things like eating, making money, or having sex are obviously basic parts of life, to do them aimlessly or without meaning (in other words, to do them just to do them) is to operate without moral purpose or grounding.

Resisting secularization thus requires a different mindset, one that is grounded in moral consciousness, where one's actions are considered in light of a distinctly moral framework. Yusuf and—it seems accurate to add—Zaytuna take an ecumenical stance toward this mindset. Yusuf, for instance, includes references in his speeches to moral thinking from a wide range of sources, from Japanese samurai to prehistoric Native Americans, and he has told non-Muslim audiences that they must follow whatever "tradition" they come from, explicitly in order to resist the mindlessness and purposelessness wrought by secularization.[62]

The same is true among Muslims. Zaytuna, as noted, is broadly accepting of different Islamic orientations, and while it has a particular approach to the religion that forms the basis of its educational and community activities (see below), it seems that spreading that approach is less important to resisting secularization. The American Muslim identity that Zaytuna wishes to shape is, more than anything else, not secular, nor is it "culturally Islamic." Rather, it involves a constant consciousness and awareness of one's actions in light of the moral norms of Islam. To *be* a Muslim, then, by this understanding, is to *think* as a Muslim, within one's daily life, and then act accordingly.

Spirituality

This consciousness—thinking as a Muslim—ultimately comes from inner piety, which is fostered through spirituality. Spirituality, in turn, allows for greater awareness of moral purpose, bolstering one's religious consciousness. So linked, spirituality and morality are important focal points for Yusuf's understanding of Islam. He talks frequently in his speeches about living as a Muslim, the need for incorporating Islam into one's life as a matter of attitude more than a matter of dogma or ritual. Likewise, he discusses the role of the heart in spirituality and piety, and he stresses that knowledge of the religion helps strengthen and purify the believer's heart.[63]

This approach has its basis in Sufism, the influence of which is apparent in Zaytuna's project. Yusuf makes frequent mention of the famous medieval Sufis Ahmad Zarruq and Abū Ḥāmid al-Ghazālī (among others), both of whom put forward an understanding of Sufism that focused on morality and the connection between a Muslim's knowledge and understanding and inner piety, and how that translated into correct action. Ghazālī in particular is famed for his *Iḥyā' al-'Ulūm al-Dīn* (Revival of the Religious Sciences), which argues for the link between religious knowledge and moral and spiritual growth. Ghazālī is listed as a member of Zaytuna's "Perennial faculty," and Yusuf himself has translated and commented upon the *Iḥyā'*, which clearly has had a tremendous impact upon him.[64] Likewise, Shakir considers charitable activism and inner spirituality to be linked.[65]

This Sufi-inspired spirituality, which provides the underlying foundation for Zaytuna's resistance to secularization, is based on a consciousness and awareness of morality and requires mindfulness of correct action. Spirituality cultivates this mindfulness. As Shakir states, the Sufi practice of *dhikr* (a form of formalized pious recitation) helps focus the mind and bring out spirituality from within.[66] Without mindfulness, any "Islamic" behavior carried out lacks purpose or awareness on the Muslim's part, rendering it as empty as a "secular" act. Indeed, Yusuf states that "Islam without spirituality is a shell," and spirituality is a necessary part of a fully Islamic way of acting and being.[67]

Accordingly, cultivating spirituality is built into Zaytuna. One student has said that the faculty work to bring out "spiritual wholeness" within their students.[68] Yusuf in particular emphasizes the necessity for spirituality growth as part of education (considering it an essential part of traditional Islamic schooling), but he also sees it within the liberal arts approach, which itself serves to encourage mindfulness and moral purpose. Not surprisingly, Zaytuna views this aspect of itself as contributing to the broader society; in the College *Catalog* it states that the moral and spiritual objectives of its pedagogical approach may "go a long way toward infusing faith into civil society, thereby enhancing the commonweal."[69]

Adab

Introducing spirituality into education is for Yusuf the solution to what he sees as Muslims' current crisis of knowledge. Yusuf takes this idea from al-Attas, who, as part of his work toward the Islamization of knowledge project has deeply criticized secular (or secularized) knowledge as lacking in morality. Accordingly, Muslims' crisis comes from their general unawareness of the threat posed by secularization. Citing the definition given in Harvey Cox's *The Secular City*, al-Attas attempts to show secularization's moral dangers to his Muslim audience. According to Cox, it is

> the loosing of the world from religious and quasi-religious understandings of itself, the dispelling of all closed world-views, the breaking of all supernatural myths and sacred symbols . . . the "defatalization of history", the discovery by man that he has been left with the world on his hands, that he can no longer blame fortune or the furies for what he does with it . . .; [it is] man turning his attention away from worlds beyond and toward this world and this time.[70]

From Cox, al-Attas understands the end goal of secularization as moral and value relativism, which he believes can be resisted by combining spirituality with knowledge, a process he labels as *adab*.

Zaytuna has adopted this attitude from al-Attas. It is written on its website that the college's learning goals:

> have been identified in the Arabic term adab, eloquently expressed by the contemporary Muslim philosopher, Professor Naquib al-Attas: "The fundamental element inherent in the concept of education in Islam is the inculcation of adab (*tae fu*)." The term contains a complex set of meanings that includes decency, comportment, decorum, etiquette, manners, morals, propriety, and humaneness.[71]

Moreover, the importance of *adab* has been expressed as an acronym reflecting Zaytuna's educational principles:

> As an acronym, ADAB reminds us of not just the end of education—a human being with adab—but also the means to it: Acquiring the tools of learning;

Demonstrating high moral character; Analyzing subjects in relation to each other; and Building community through service.[72]

By focusing on *adab* as an essential quality and goal of education, Zaytuna seeks to infuse the knowledge it imparts with meaning, such that it is not simply practical and factual, but also moral. Knowledge that serves no higher purpose beyond itself is, for Yusuf, dangerous in its ability to lead people into amoral thinking and acting without meaning or benefit. He criticizes some forms of modern science, for instance, for treating human beings and their relationships as simple problems to be measured and solved, which renders them mere "accidents" (in the philosophical sense), whose existence is neither special nor inherently meaningful.[73] Education is meant to encompass both knowledge and morality while also instilling a necessary sense of purpose.

Knowledge

Of these three—morality, purpose, and knowledge—the first two are comprised by *adab*, but knowledge stands as an issue apart. It is undoubtedly connected with *adab* within Islamic tradition, through the link between religious knowledge (expressed variously in the concepts *'ilm*, *īmān*, *taṣdīq*, and *islām*) and norms of correct behavior. As Ira Lapidus describes it, "They all point to the relationship between knowledge and action—to the inward flux of intellect, judgment, and emotion in relation to outward expression in speech, gesture, ritual and action—as the key to the very nature of man's being and his relationship to God."[74] But knowledge in the contemporary period has become more problematic, particularly for Muslims. While they can understand *adab* and the necessity of purpose and morality in learning as Islamic virtues, or indeed derived from Islam, knowledge itself has in many ways lost its connection with the religion. As a further part of the crisis of knowledge that he identifies, Al-Attas argues that the amazement of Muslims at the scientific progress of the West has led them to secularization and a disregard for their own traditional teachings.[75] This has meant that the Islamic worldview has been supplanted by the secular worldview, which is now disseminated by the current Muslim leadership.

Moreover, in the rush to embrace modern, secular knowledge, older forms of Islamic knowledge and Islamic learning have been abandoned. Yusuf has lamented this situation, with the attendant loss of the traditional centers of Muslim education as part of the modernization of the Muslim world. The problems stemming from this loss have been two-fold. First, Muslims have replaced their own knowledge with foreign forms without critical engagement: "So in the Muslim world we have adopted alien worldviews. These are not the worldviews of our own tradition. They have been given to us by people that have come to certain conclusions about the world."[76] Instead of indigenous,

Islamic knowledge, Muslims now strive after the exclusionary episteme of "a materialistic hegemonic civilisation, that does not note, that does not acknowledge other forms of knowledge," the true nature of which Muslims do not understand.[77]

Second, the pervasive spread of secular knowledge has left Muslims without leaders who are intellectually and religiously equipped to guide the community. As al-Attas writes, the introduction of secular knowledge is caused by three interrelated conditions:

1. Confusion and error in knowledge, creating the condition for:
2. The loss of adab within the Community. The condition arising out of (1) and (2) is:
3. The rise of leaders who are not qualified for valid leadership of the Muslim Community, who do not possess the high moral, intellectual and spiritual standards required for Islamic leadership, who perpetuate the condition in (1) above and ensure the continued control of affairs of the Community by leaders like them who dominate all fields.[78]

Yusuf's criticisms of Islamic religious authorities globally mirror al-Attas' argument, and he decries the state of Muslim leaders and their lack of proper knowledge and *adab*.[79]

Defining Tradition

The response to the crisis of knowledge is a renewed focus on the Islamic scholarly tradition in all its breadth. In an article written shortly after September 11 Yusuf contends that one of the main reasons that Muslims are facing the current dilemma is that they have lost touch with this tradition and its forms of knowledge:

> Our real situation is this: we Muslims have lost theologically sound understanding [*sic*] of our teaching. Islam has been hijacked by a discourse of anger and the rhetoric of rage. We have allowed for too long our minbars to become bully pulpits in which people with often recognisable psychopathology use anger—a very powerful emotion—to rile Muslims up, only to leave them feeling bitter and spiteful towards people who in the most part are completely unaware of the conditions in the Muslim world, or the oppressive assaults of some Western countries on Muslim peoples. We have lost our bearings because we have lost our theology. We have almost no theologians in the entire Muslim world. The study of *kalaam*, once the hallmark of our intellectual tradition, has been reduced to memorizing 144 lines of al-Jawhara and a good commentary to study it, at best.[80]

Yusuf embrace of the scholarly tradition is noteworthy, and it plays a central role in Zaytuna's religious function. As an institution, Zaytuna can be labeled "neo-traditionalist" in its combination of traditionalist methodology with modern sensibilities.[81] Neo-traditionalists believe that tradition will undergo a process of change in order to fit with modern social circumstances, but these changes are made possible due to mechanisms and processes extant within the tradition itself.

Importantly, scholars working at Zaytuna identify themselves with this label, notably Shaykh Abdullah ibn Hamid Ali, a full-time faculty member and specialist in Islamic Law who has undertaken a traditional Islamic seminary education at Al-Qarawiyin University in Fes, Morocco.[82] On his personal website Ali responds to a question asked by one the readers as to why he describes himself as neo-traditionalist. He begins by describing what is traditional about his approach: he adheres to the four Sunni legal schools, he follows the Ash'arī and Maturīdī doctrines, and he practices text-based Sufism. In addition, he believes that traditional knowledge is passed down through personal contact with living teachers.[83]

After having secured the "traditional" aspects of his beliefs, Ali begins to expand on the "neo-." He argues that authentic traditional thought "can only be known and practiced by those who have not been influenced by modern thinking."[84] Given that that we have all been influenced by modernity, it is not possible to reconstruct tradition as it was.

However, neo-traditionalism is not just about the inability to reconstruct authentic tradition, but it is also about the recognition that tradition is at times impractical. Ali lists a few examples as to how it is simply not always feasible to adhere to well-known rulings of the classical schools of law:

> For example, today it is impossible to adhere to a classical school of fiqh—taking only from the standard opinions (mashhur) in every issue, especially in Western countries. Imagine demanding that monetary transactions be carried out in the way they should be in the Shafi'i or Hanbali Schools in America or the UK. Or imagine telling people in those countries that praying Jumu'a is not valid because they don't fulfill the Hanafi condition of there being a sultan to initiate it; or a Maliki's (and others) insistence that it must be performed in a single central masjid; or the insistence of all of them that the khutba must be performed entirely in Arabic even if those attending can't understand a single word (among other issues).[85]

The question remains as to how Ali is able to still claim that he is in any sense "traditional" even though he agrees to the adjustments cited above. A clue may be given at the very end of the article where he states that "the case might be that the "tradition" is simply dynamic and adjusts accordingly with the vicissitudes of time in those areas that are generally considered to be mutable."[86]

The concept of mutability, or *taghayyur*, is a concept that itself is grounded in traditional Islamic thought. Simply put, Islamic scholars have always had to deal with the problem of societal change, although not to the extent that has been brought about with modernity. One of the concepts that has developed in jurisprudence to tackle the concept of social change is the idea that some parts of Islamic thought are immutable, *thābit*, and some parts are mutable, *mutaghayyir*. Ali has written a small article regarding atheism and freedom of conscience, in which he describes the concepts of immutable and mutable injunctions.[87] He argues that "practically all Islamic legal injunctions have a mutable character"[88] and that, ultimately, laws regarding apostasy need to be reformed. This concept of stasis and mutability is repeated both by Bin Bayyah and Hamza Yusuf.

Renovation, not Reform

The neo-traditionalists at Zaytuna do not see themselves as reformers, but rather as renovators of an established tradition. Hamza Yusuf tries to show the difference between these two approaches in his Oxford debate with Tariq Ramadan. He begins by stating that he has a problem with the term "reform," and that following his teacher Bin Bayyah, he prefers the term "renovation" because it is closer to the idea of *tajdīd*.[89] He states that the idea of reformation includes a complete restructuring, whereas he believes that the foundations of the house of Islam are solid even though there are areas that require renovation.[90] Yusuf also argues that this process of renovation has been going on for centuries, and that the Muslims of the nineteenth century would not recognize the Muslims of today.

Yusuf contends that Islam has all the tools necessary for renovation, and he states that Islam is a vast tradition with a diverse range of opinions that modern scholars are able to pull from.[91] He gives an example regarding women leading prayer. He argues that even this issue has been debated by classical scholars such as ibn Taymīyah, and that even ibn Taymīyah allowed women to lead prayer in particular circumstances and in particular formats.[92] Yusuf argues that unfortunately this vast tradition is overlooked by many contemporary scholars.[93] Critics of Yusuf have tried to state that they have not found any such opinion among ibn Taymīyah's works.

Yusuf consistently refers back to his teacher Shaykh Abdullah Bin Bayyah when speaking about renovation. Bin Bayyah has been an influential figure at Zaytuna College and has had a close affiliation with the college and the community for more than a decade. Nearly all public appearances of Bin Bayyah in the West are accompanied by Hamza Yusuf's translations, and he was one of the guests of honor at Zaytuna's first graduation ceremony.

There are two facets of Bin Bayyah's works that are of interest to Zaytuna College. The first is his approach to the Islamic law, labelled *fiqh al-wāqi'* (jurisprudence of reality). The second is his work on Muslims living as minorities in non-Muslim countries. The overarching connection between the two topics is the importance that is given to context. Bin Bayyah offers an approach that takes into consideration the ever-changing contexts in which Muslims live. Whether this context is modernity or living in a non-Muslim country, this approach highlights the real circumstances in which Muslims find themselves and how they have changed from the settings in which traditional laws were derived. Strict adherence to the law, therefore, can at times go against the spirit of the law. (Examples of this can already be seen in the works of Shaykh Ali cited above.)

In a recent speech Bin Bayyah presented his conception of *fiqh al-wāqiʿ*.[94] As usual, he was accompanied by Yusuf, who provided an English translation along with extra explanations. The jurisprudence of reality is a modern framework that will help to systematize reform within traditional Sunni schools of thought. The emphasis on "reality" is to understand the spirit of the law so that the letter of the law can be better applied in changing circumstances. One specific example is with the concepts of *dār al-islām* and *dār al-ḥarb*. Bin Bayyah argues that we now live in a multicultural world that requires new rulings, rather than the earlier, dichotomous view of the world.[95]

This same understanding of context can be applied to Muslims living in non-Muslim countries. In a 1999 lecture delivered to Zaytuna Institute, Bin Bayyah stressed to the audience that "your circumstances here are not normal circumstances by any means. You are in very unusual circumstances, and because of that, there are certain things that the *sharīʿah* allows that it does not allow in times and places where those circumstances do not exist."[96] Thus, he acknowledges the possibility—to say nothing of the necessity—for the adaptation of Islamic norms to fit differing societies and environments.

Centrality of *Madhhab*s

Zaytuna's neo-traditionalist character and outlook have most conspicuously placed it at odds with forms of Salafi thought, which Yusuf in particular has unequivocally criticized and warned Muslims against. While speaking in Malaysia in 2014, he described the dangers of Salafism and repeatedly called Malaysian Muslims to remain in the path of Shāfiʿī *madhhab*. When asked what type of lectures a Muslim should listen to he replied that one should follow one of the four *madhhab*s, stating that people should be wary of various claims to Sunni legitimacy: "but we should be able to say that we know for certain who was *ahl-sunnah wa al-jamāʿa* in the past. And we should try to be as close to them, and *ahl-sunnah* of the past for over a thousand years followed one of the four *madhhabs*."[97]

Unlike Salafis, Yusuf (and by extension Zaytuna College) views the Islamic tradition in a holistic manner.[98] This view underpins Yusuf's approach to authentic Islamic identity, which is itself based on prescriptive knowledge:

a Muslim today should know what Islamic tradition contained, historically, at least in all its breadth (if not its depth), in order to know how to conduct themselves in a normatively Islamic way. We can see this reflected in Zaytuna's curriculum, which comprises the major academic subjects from the tradition, and that—quite tellingly—students must follow *in toto*, with limited allowance to pick and choose which subjects they pursue instead of others.[99] Rather, students are expected to achieve some degree of mastery over all of them.

Zaytuna's curriculum is a mix of a traditional Islamic curriculum and the Great Books approach to liberal arts. The Great Books was a concept originally put forward by Martimer J. Alder (d. 2001) and Robert Maynard Hutchins (d. 1977), both professors at The University of Chicago (where the latter served as long-time president) and popular public intellectuals.[100] In 1952 they published a fifty-four-volume set through *Encyclopaedia Britannica* called the "Great Books of the Western World." It was a fad in the 1950s that eventually lost its popularity.

The idea behind the Great Books was that engaging with them would lead to a liberal education and help to establish a democratic culture, in which everyone who knew these books could participate in the "Great Conversation."[101] For Alder and Hutchins, a real education was a liberal arts education. Sharing similar influences, John Erskine (d. 1951), a professor at Columbia University had at about the same time developed an honors course based on the Great Books idea. Hamza Yusuf, born Mark Hanson, is named after Mark Van Doren (d. 1972) one of the professors who taught this course at Columbia.[102]

The Zaytuna College *Catalog* begins by referencing this Great Books tradition; it quotes Hutchins' classic essay "The Great Conversation": "No man was educated unless he was acquainted with the masterpieces of his tradition."[103] The catalog further notes: "Zaytuna curriculum takes this claim to heart."[104] The curriculum for the 2015/16 academic year is presented in Table 1.1.

The curriculum follows the Great Books method by keeping influential books at the center of the course. Thus, for example, the course on formal logic is centered on Aristotle's *Organon*, logic in the Islamic tradition is centered on Imām Athīr al-Dīn al-Abharī's (d.1265) *Īsāghūjī*, and the course on Qur'ānic sciences is centered on *al-Itqān fī 'Ulūm al-Qur'ān* by Jalāl al-Dīn al-Suyūṭī (d. 1505).[105] (The curriculum, however, does not specify a book for many of the courses.)

The prescriptive nature of the Zaytuna curriculum offers an excellent encapsulation of Yusuf's neo-traditionalism. For him, Islamic tradition should be accepted and embraced in all its aspects by Muslims as an essential part of Muslim identity. By contrast, to pick and choose, either by ignoring particular elements of the tradition or by rejecting it altogether is almost necessarily to fall into religious error.[106] The tradition thus serves as a safeguard against mistaken beliefs and practices, which only works if taken in its entirety, rather than piecemeal.

Table 1.1 Curriculum of Zaytuna College

	Year 1	Year 2	Year 3	Year 4
Fall Semester	• Arabic Grammar 1 (5 units) • Islamic Law 1: Purification and Prayer • Freshman Seminar • Creedal Theology • Introduction to the *Qur'ān*	• Arabic Grammar and Texts 1 (4 units) • Prophetic Tradition • The Rise and Fall of Civilizations • Mathematics (4 units with lab) • Logic in the Islamic Tradition	• Arabic Text Study 1 • Islamic History • The Soul and the Cosmos • Islamic Legal Philosophy • Economics • Senior Thesis: Research Methods Seminar (1 unit)	• Arabic Rhetoric and Literature • Ethics • Islamic Law: Family • Islamic Law: Inheritance • Comparative Theology • Senior Thesis: Writing (1 unit)
Spring Semester	• Arabic Grammar 2 (5 units) • Islamic Law 2: Alms, Fasting, and Pilgrimage • Formal Logic • Rhetoric • Prophetic Biography	• Arabic Grammar and Texts 2 (4 units) • Qur'ānic Sciences • Material Logic • U.S. History • Astronomy (4 units with lab)	• Arabic Text Study 2 • History of Science • Natural Theology • Principles of Islamic Jurisprudence • Philosophy • Senior Thesis: Research (1 unit)	• Senior Arabic Seminar • Politics • Islamic Law: Commercial • Constitutional Law • Contemporary Muslim Thought • Senior Thesis: Completion (1 unit)

Source: Zaytuna College website

Zaytuna, accordingly, is built around instilling knowledge of the tradition in students through "a holistic approach to life and learning."[107] Indeed, Yusuf's emphasis on treating the tradition as a necessary, coherent whole extends beyond content to the very method of instruction. He espouses the benefits of oral recitation and memorization as part of traditional Islamic learning,[108] and as a result his own scholarly works are primarily given in oral form, published as audio or video recordings. Moreover, most of these works are organized as commentaries, which were the main genre of Islamic tradition, combining oral instruction with the transmission of an important text.[109]

Islam and Western Values

Yusuf presents the tradition as both intellectually fertile and encompassing a degree of diversity. It is this neo-traditionalist approach to Islam that helps members of Zaytuna blend Western and Islamic values. By being able to look at core values within both traditions they are able to find points of overlap and agreement. Nearly a year after the events of September 11, Yusuf argued that there was a progressive side to Islam and that Islam and Western values can fit together. He made this argument by looking at the core values of both traditions:

> We Muslims are unpersuaded by many triumphalist claims made for the west, but are happy with its core values. As a westerner, the child of civil rights and anti-war activists, I embraced Islam not in abandonment of my core values, drawn almost entirely from the progressive tradition, but as an affirmation of them. I have since studied Islamic law for 10 years with traditionally trained scholars, and while some particulars in medieval legal texts have troubled me, never have the universals come into conflict with anything my progressive Californian mother taught me. Instead, I have marveled at how most of what western society claims as its own highest ideals are deeply rooted in Islamic tradition.[110]

Although often in a less polemical fashion, Yusuf frequently makes explicit connections between Islamic tradition and Western culture (as well as others), pointing out overlapping values and morals. Doing so is an essential aspect of crafting an American Muslim identity, of course, and the arts provide one of the major areas for Yusuf to draw such links.

Literature in particular is a common focal point. It is a central part of the history of Islamic arts; poetry served as one of the major modes of expression within Islamic tradition, and in many respects it is *the* Islamic form of art. Yusuf describes Muhammad's appreciation for poetry and its place in the very beginnings of Islam.[111] Similarly, he points out that the prophetic companions appreciated and wrote poetry—he calls them "poet warriors"—and understood its broader importance within life.[112] He states that God gave man words so that they can express themselves and what is in their hearts, and the Arabs prized poetic language and its ability to speak the truth.[113]

Yusuf argues that this—speaking the truth of one's heart—is the inherent purpose of poetry, and something that is necessary for people to continue to do. This is particularly important for Muslims, he says, as they are commanded by God to speak the truth and must use poetry against the pretty but empty words of modern culture. Writing poetry that is true and appreciating poetry from the past are ways of resisting the corrupting influence of things like advertising, which uses poetic language to spread lies rather than the truth.[114]

Yusuf points to many examples of Muslim poets from the past whose work remains important and informative. Indeed, Yusuf himself has translated several works of Sufi poetry into English in order to spread their moral and spiritual message.[115] But Yusuf's appreciation for poetry is not limited strictly to Muslim poets. He expresses admiration for poets of the Western canon such as Shakespeare and Homer, and in particular the Romantics, whose focus on culture and the inner human spirit overlaps significantly with Yusuf's goal of encouraging inner morality and wisdom. One of the classroom videos from Zaytuna shows Yusuf leading a discussion of the poem *Ozymandias* by the English Romantic Percy Bysshe Shelley (1792–1822). Yusuf states that the poem was one of his favorites as a young man, and he walks the students through the meanings of the lines and phrases one by one, in the manner of a commentary.

Literature in general serves Yusuf's goal of cultivating spiritual awareness and moral being. He writes that great books "encourage introspection and inspire positive change."[116] The Romantics of course pushed back through their art against the disillusionment and impersonalization of mechanized modernity, an attitude that shares much with Yusuf's. Tellingly, he interprets Shelley's poem as a metaphor for the work of an artist surviving the deeds of a great ruler, reinforcing his belief that acts of spiritual or aesthetic purpose are greater than the acquisition or exercise of power.[117] He praises Jane Austen's (1775–1817) *Sense and Sensibility*, as a "beautiful study of two ways of being in the world. Marriane [*sic*] is the precursor to the modern, egocentric, fun-filled, tradition-scoffing "individual." Elinor is the wonderful, dutiful, stoic, and giving caretaker of hearts. By the end of the novel, the two have discovered themselves and risen above the trials and torments of life on earth."[118] Similarly, he recommends two novels by Fyodor Dostoyevsky (1821–81): *Notes from the Underground* and *The Brothers Karamazov*. Both of these works are philosophical in nature, dealing with interconnected issues of religion, morality, individualism, society, and culture. The latter in particular encapsulates many of Yusuf's main points of emphasis. It is a novel about three brothers—one going through life listless and without purpose, one a convinced atheist and materialist, and one a naïve but devout Christian—and the shifting emotional and intellectual relationships between them within the context of a rapidly modernizing culture.[119]

Literature for Yusuf represents a type of culture that is not dominated by black-and-white thinking, but allows for the expression of ambiguity, ambivalence, and unpopular truths, reinforcing his neo-traditionalist stance against Salafism's more Manichean approach.

Positioning itself as neo-traditionalist, Zaytuna can both rely on the diversity (to a degree) of the historical Islamic tradition and appeal to contemporary circumstances as necessitating adaptation, thereby allowing for a degree of flexibility and pragmatism into its religious orientation, which is certainly advantageous in the American context. Indeed, Zaytuna as an institution is itself neo-traditionalist in this way, through its combination of traditional forms of Islamic knowledge and American liberal arts education. As its catalog states, the college "aims to educate and prepare morally committed professional, intellectual, and spiritual leaders who are grounded in the Islamic scholarly tradition and conversant with the cultural currents and critical ideas shaping modern society."[120]

The minority setting within America also allows Zaytuna the proverbial "luxury of opposition," where it can critique aspects of American society as well as foreign expressions of Islam while avoiding taking too-controversial positions of its own. Issues related to gender are illustrative of this fact. As noted above, Shakir disagreed with female-led prayer, but did so in a way that separated himself from that stance; he stated that it had no basis in tradition and therefore was not something he could approve, even as he acknowledged the pious impulse behind the desire to lead prayer.[121] Yusuf has used Islamic tradition to simultaneously critique the modern push for gender equality as going too far (denying the biological differences between the sexes and ultimately harming women) and to denounce mistreatment and injustices against women in Muslim societies, which he attributes to both poverty and the widespread misunderstanding of religious texts.[122] Similarly, Yusuf has called wearing the *ḥijāb* an obligation, but also argued that it should not be used to marginalize women; particularly in America, not all Muslim women will wear it, but this should not exclude them from participating within the community or even serving as leaders.[123] The impossibility of any concrete action regarding the *ḥijāb* in America thus renders the issue moot.

Other positions are far starker in their implications. Regarding modern science, for instance, Yusuf, while accepting its general validity, warns against the dangers of science conducted without a true purpose and argues for the necessity of moral grounding in scientific research. His position here is derivative of his broader rejection of secularization, and it is functionally the same critique that he offers for other, potentially problematic, aspects of modern society, such as the economic or educational systems: that scientific research conducted without moral purpose has no real meaning and serves no real benefit.

He argues, however, that science without such meaning is also dangerous. For Yusuf, religion and morality serve as limits; they force people to question why they are doing something and whether it is worth doing, thereby providing higher meaning and purpose.[124] People lacking such limits do "unnatural" things, in the sense that they act in ways contrary to their nature. Unlike animals, which always act in their nature and understand their limits, people can act "demonically," in an inhuman fashion.[125] Science without moral grounding is particularly perilous because as currently constructed it encourages "hubris" on the part of scientists, fostering innovations that take humanity away from its nature.[126] Yusuf offers the example of a group of scientists studying ocean plant life who, following a mistaken hypothesis, ruined the ecosystem of an area of the ocean in an experiment. Upon finding the results, the scientists' initial, "natural" reaction was to be disgusted, but Yusuf states that they soon became elated at what they had found, even if it was disastrous, which he considers a clear sign of an inhuman motivation in their work.[127] Yusuf also identifies things like eugenics, foods created to be addictive rather than nutritious, and nihilism and atheism as similarly unnatural things caused and fostered by science lacking moral grounding.[128] Moreover, the pursuit of science for base reasons, as with economics or consumerism, merely perpetuates the meaninglessness of modern society. Technologies created with only profit in mind serve to isolate people and weaken human relationships, just as food produced to make money rather than nurture undermines people's bodies and spirits.[129]

At the same time, Yusuf embraces certain forms of science. Astronomy was one of the major sciences practiced within the Islamic scholarly tradition, and, perhaps fittingly, it is the only natural science subject taught at Zaytuna.[130] But Yusuf also relies on it for important ritual purposes. In a video showing him and some students attempting to locate the new moon at the end of Ramadan, he repeatedly cites measurements for the location of the moon prepared by astronomers. Calling astronomy "a very precise and exact science," he argues for relying on these measurement aids in determining the correct end of the fast, to be supplemented by physically sighting the moon. He also criticizes Muslims who rely only on eyesight, stating that they are more likely to be mistaken.[131] He has furthered described the ritual and historical importance of astronomical calculations and the physical sighting of the moon in his book *Caesarean Moon Births*.[132]

Yusuf distinguishes in his criticism between problematic *conceptions* of science and science as an intellectual endeavor. Yusuf undoubtedly considers knowledge of the natural world important, and he praises Muslims' past contributions to science and the place of scientific inquiry in Islamic tradition.[133] He also decries what he sees as people's separation from nature in modern society as something that has been lost, something essential for humanity.[134] This is most frequently expressed in terms of "the heavens" (i.e., the stars). Yusuf often uses knowledge of the stars and their function in navigation as a metaphor for moral guidance, which he links with the loss of tradition. He states that people used to use the stars to know where they were going, but without that knowledge people are lost, overly reliant on technology.[135] Yusuf in fact argues that electric lights are to blame for humans' separation from the heavens, and he suggests that cities should institute short intervals of darkness to allow people to again see the stars.[136]

It is clear that, for Yusuf, the critique itself is the point. Yusuf's goal is reminding people of the limitations of science, affirming that it is not the be-all and end-all of life, but that there are things more important, more fundamental than what can be measured or experimentally verified, and of its dangers when left unchecked and divorced from morality or purpose. Rather than offering specific injunctions to avoid certain subjects or types of scientific research, which would draw him into controversies over the precise boundaries of "Islamic" science, Yusuf maintains a distinction between science and religion—between the measurable and the immeasurable, he says—that allows him to limit the scope of the latter. Instead of getting bogged down in science/religion debates (or debates on essentially scientific topics), Yusuf is primarily concerned with promoting moral awareness and spiritual mindfulness, which is foundational for his Islamic authority. Additionally, by focusing on his critiques Yusuf can avoid alienating those Muslims who are positively disposed to science (or engineering or technology), who make up a significant portion of the American Muslim community. While his failure to address specific questions and issues may irk some Muslims—as many Internet comment boards attest—it is likely that weighing in on those issues would drive away many others.

By focusing on the shortcomings in the way that science is utilized and currently understood, Yusuf can articulate a response that is grounded in Islamic morality and is part of his constant call for mindfulness and purpose in people's everyday lives. If, as al-Attas argues, the crisis of knowledge stems from Muslims' unawareness of the moral dangers of secularization and its corrupting effects, then the mere act of critiquing secular science serves to ameliorate the crisis. And, indeed, this seems to be the impact for Zaytuna's students. As Faatimah Knight, the college's first valedictorian, stated upon her graduation:

> I came here at 18; I had habits to break, patterns to unlearn, beliefs to reconsider. I leave here at 22, and I still have habits to break, patterns to unlearn, and beliefs to reconsider. The difference is now I know what many of those habits, patterns, and beliefs are, whereas before I may have been so ignorant of them that I could not even begin to get to the real work of rectifying them. The difference is now I have some answers.[137]

While the crisis of knowledge exists for Muslims, as Yusuf's vocal opposition to purposelessness and moral blindness makes clear, these problems do not affect Muslims uniquely, but are rather endemic to modern societies. Yusuf's critique may be based in Islam and in the Islamic tradition, but it has relevance for America, which benefits by the knowledge that Zaytuna imparts to its students: "The greatest, truest, and only permanent good bestowed upon humanity is that of true knowledge. From such knowledge, all other goods flow, even faith."[138]

Notes

1. Information on Yusuf's early life and conversion is found in the video interview Hamza Yusuf, "Why I Came To Islam" [Video], *YouTube*, February 24, 2007, accessed August 10, 2016, https://www.youtube.com/watch?v=HAPdXDlLdXk; also Zareena Grewal, *Islam is a Foreign Country: American Muslims and the Global Crisis of Authority* (New York: New York University Press, 2013),159–68.
2. Yusuf's time in Mauritania in described in his post "Another Mother of the Believers," which has been reposted on numerous websites; cf. Hamza Yusuf, "Another Mother of the Believers," April 16, 2009, accessed August 1, 2016, http://www.mujahideenryder.net/2009/04/16/another-mother-of-the-believers-by-shaykh-hamza-yusuf/.
3. Geneive Abdo, *Mecca and Main Street: Muslim Life in America after 9/11* (Oxford: Oxford University Press, 2006), 17–18; cf. Ahmed Elewa and Laury Silvers, "'I Am One of the People': A Survey and Analysis of Legal Arguments on Woman-Led Prayer in Islam," *Journal of Law and Religion* 26 (2010), 141–71, esp. 160.
4. Nadia Inji Khan, "'Guide Us to the Straight Way': A Look at the Makers of 'Religiously Literate' Young Muslim Americans," in *Educating Young Muslims of America*, eds Yvonne Haddad, Farid Senzai, and Jane Smith (New York: Oxford University Press, 2009), 123–54, esp. 134–40; also Scott Alan Kugle, *Rebel between Spirit and Law: Ahmad Zarruq, Sainthood, and Authority in Islam* (Bloomington: Indiana University Press, 2006), 16.
5. Ibid.
6. Abdo, *Mecca*, 12–13. Yusuf asked Bin Bayyah for advice before accepting the invitation to the White House: Hamza Yusuf, "America's Tragedy: An Islamic Perspective," lecture, Zaytuna Academy, Hayward, CA, September 30, 2001, formerly available at http://www.zaytuna.org/tragedy.html.
7. Grewal, *Islam is a Foreign Country*, 164–6.
8. Jack O'Sullivan, "If You Hate the West, Emigrate to a Muslim Country," *The Guardian*, October 8, 2001, accessed August 10, 2016, https://www.theguardian.com/world/2001/oct/08/religion.uk.
9. Mozammel Haque, "Introducing Global Center for Renewal and Guidance," *The Official Website of His Eminence Shaykh Abdallah Bin Bayyah*, accessed July 30, 2016, http://binbayyah.net/english/2012/06/19/introducing-global-center-for-renewal-and-guidance/.
10. Yusuf, "Why I Came to Islam."
11. Sadek Hamid, "The Rise of the 'Traditional Islam' Network(s): Neo-Sufism and British Muslim Youth," in *Sufism in Britain*, eds Ron Geaves and Theodore Gabriel (London: Bloomsbury, 2013), 177–96.
12. Hamza Yusuf, "The Central Purpose of the Human Being," (undated lecture) [Audio], *YouTube*, published April 20, 2013, accessed August 10, 2016, https://www.youtube.com/watch?v=rsWbTgtZv1E; cf. Kugle, *Rebel Between Spirit and Law*, 9–10.

13. Yusuf's approach to home-schooling is connected with those of secular education reformers John Taylor Ghatto and Dorothy Sayers, with whom he has co-authored multiple works.
14. Kugle, *Rebel between Spirit and Law*, 9; Grewal, *Islam is a Foreign Country*, 167.
15. Bill Moyers, "Transcript: Bill Moyers Talks with Imam Zaid Shakir," *Bill Moyers Journal*, June 22, 2007, accessed August 10, 2016, http://www.pbs.org/moyers/journal/06222007/transcript2.html.
16. Zaid Shakir, "About Imam Zaid Shakir," *New Islamic Directions*, accessed August 10, 2016, http://www.newislamicdirections.com/nid/about/.
17. Line Khatib, *Islamic Revivalism in Syria: The Rise and Fall of Ba'thist Separatism* (Abingdon: Routledge, 2011), 90–1. A number of Zaytuna College's current faculty have studied at Abu Nur.
18. Shakir, "About."
19. See United for Change Facebook page, accessed August 10, 2016, https://www.facebook.com/unitedforchange/.
20. Abdo, *Mecca*, 34.
21. Hamza Yusuf, "Translator's Introduction," in *Purification of the Heart: Signs, Symptoms and Cures of the Spiritual Diseases of the Heart* (n.p.: Sandala, 2012), 6–10.
22. Zaid Shakir, "American Muslims and a Meaningful Human Rights Discourse in the Aftermath of September 11," *Cross Currents* 52 (2003), accessed August 10, 2016, http://www.crosscurrents.org/Shakirwinter2003.htm.
23. Moyers, "Transcript."
24. Zaid Shakir, *Twitter*, August 22, 2014, accessed August 10, 2016, https://twitter.com/imamzaidshakir/status/502873595992084480.
25. Mucahit Bilici, *Finding Mecca in America: How Islam is Becoming an American Religion* (Chicago: University of Chicago Press, 2013), 117–18.
26. Cf. Grewal, *Islam is Foreign Country*, 312; Scott Korb, *Light without Fire: The Making of America's First Muslim College* (Boston: Beacon Press, 2013), 16.
27. Winter's position was met with considerable controversy among American Muslims; Grewal, *Islam is Foreign Country*, 310.
28. Sherman Jackson, *Islam and the Blackamerican: Looking toward the Third Resurrection* (Oxford: Oxford University Press, 2005).
29. Zaytuna College, "Reclaiming Our Faith: Lecture 7 by Sherman Jackson," [Video], *YouTube*, July 1, 2013, accessed August 10, 2016, https://youtu.be/KIRtp9KZzUc.
30. Moyers, "Transcript."
31. For instance, Grewal notes that, despite marked theological disagreements with the Salafi-leaning American Muslim leader Yasir Qadhi (who has condemned Zaytuna as unorthodox), Zaytuna faculty members accept the Islamic validity of his views: Grewal, *Islam is a Foreign Country*, 387 n. 77; also Laurie Goodstein, "US Muslim Clerics Seek a Modern Middle Ground," *The New York Times*, June 18, 2006, accessed August 10, 2016, http://www.nytimes.com/2006/06/18/us/18imams.html.
32. Cf. Abdo, *Mecca*, p. 17.
33. Hamza Yusuf, "Success in This World and the Next," [Video], *YouTube*, December 28, 2011, accessed August 10, 2016, http://youtu.be/ldvz6LZ6BdU.
34. Cf. Korb, *Light without Fire*, 25–6.
35. Rollo Romig, "Where Islam Meets America," *The New Yorker*, May 20, 2013, accessed August 10, 2016, http://www.newyorker.com/books/page-turner/where-islam-meets-america.
36. Moyers, "Transcript."

37. Cf. Zaytuna College, *Zaytuna College Catalog 2014–2015*, accessed August 10, 2016, http://zaytunacollege.org/downloads/2014_Catalog.pdf, 7–10.
38. Moyers, "Transcript."
39. Ibid.; cf. Goodstein, "US Muslim Clerics."
40. Hamza Yusuf, "America: Commerce & Benevolence," [Video], *YouTube*, July 3, 2014, accessed August 10, 2016, http://youtu.be/lo31MMcW43s.
41. O'Sullivan, "If You Hate the West."
42. Korb, *Light without Fire, passim*; Moyers, "Transcript."
43. Korb, *Light without Fire*, 31, 21.
44. Zaytuna College, *Catalog 2014–2015*, 1; see also Romig, "Where Islam Meets America."
45. E.g. Korb, *Light without Fire*, 54; Grewal, *Islam is a Foreign Country*, 308, 312; Abdo, *Mecca*, 25. Mahdi Tourage argues insightfully that Yusuf's whiteness elicits particular skepticism among immigrant Muslims, and accordingly Yusuf's (and other white converts') Islamic leadership is contingent upon upholding certain "Islamic" norms of behavior and comportment. Tourage, following Marcia Hermansen, labels this "performing Islam"; see Mahdi Tourage, "Performing Belief and Reviving Islam: Prominent (White Male) Converts in Muslim Revival Conventions," *Performing Islam* 1 (2012), 207–26.
46. Cf. Korb, *Light Without Fire*, 25–6; Hamza Yusuf, "Success in This World and the Next" (undated lecture) [Audio] *YouTube*, December 28, 2011, accessed August 10, 2016, http://youtu.be/ldvz6LZ6BdU; Moyers, "Transcript"; on the appeal of this approach, see Abdo, *Mecca*, 27.
47. Yusuf, "Success in This World."
48. Korb, *Light Without Fire*, 52, 54–5; Grewal, *Islam is a Foreign Country*, 312.
49. Hamza Yusuf and Tariq Ramadan, "Rethinking Islamic Reform" (University of Oxford debate, May 26, 2010), [Video], *YouTube*, September 29, 2011, accessed August 10, 2016, https://www.youtube.com/watch?v=qY17d4ZhY8M.
50. Korb also notes that Shakir held extracurricular classes for students to memorize legal texts not part of the main course of study; Korb, *Light without Fire*, 40.
51. See the discussion on Zaytuna's conservatism in Romig, "Where Islam Meets America." See also the section on "Campus Policies and Etiquette (*Adab*)" in the College *Catalog*; Zaytuna College, *Catalog 2014–2015*, 48–9.
52. Elewa and Silvers, "I Am One of the People," 141–71.
53. Zaytuna, *College Catalog 2014–2015*, 7.
54. Muhammad Naguib Al-Attas, *Prolegomena to the Metaphysics of Islam: An Exposition of the Fundamental Elements of the Worldview of Islam* (Kuala Lumpur: International Institute of Islamic Thought and Civilization, 1995), 29.
55. Ibid., 29.
56. Hamza Yusuf, "Transcript: Vision of Islam," lecture, April 2005?, accessed August 10, 2016, http://shaykhhamza.com/transcript/Vision-of-Islam.
57. Hamza Yusuf, "When the Social Contract Is Breached on One Side, It's Breached on Both Sides," *Sandala*, February 7, 2011, accessed August 10, 2016, https://sandala.org/blog/-when-the-social-contract-is-breached-on-one-side-its-breached-on-both-sides.
58. Yusuf, "When the Social Contract is Breached."
59. Hamza Yusuf, "Islamic State and Shariah Law are Fantasies," [Video], *YouTube*, August 14, 2013, accessed August 10, 2016, https://www.youtube.com/watch?v=dUe5OsGbhM0.

60. Hamza Yusuf, "Prohibitions of the Tongue, Session 2," [Video], *YouTube*, November 24, 2013, accessed August 10, 2016, https://www.youtube.com/watch?v=XVNFnaJxeRc; Hamza Yusuf, "Higher Education for a Higher Purpose," [Video], *YouTube*, September 18, 2014, accessed August 10, 2016, https://www.youtube.com/watch?v=8NCM97NOp7g.
61. Yusuf has used this analogy in multiple recorded speeches, e.g., Hamza Yusuf, "Healing Self, Healing Society," [Video], *YouTube*, May 18, 2014, accessed August 10, 2016, http://youtu.be/M-ddKKNttFQ; Hamza Yusuf, "Global Tawbah," [Video], *YouTube*, September 19, 2014, accessed August 10, 2016, https://www.youtube.com/watch?v=jwGeWE9zPV0.
62. Hamza Yusuf, "On Education, Philosophy and Science in our World," lecture, Toronto, 2013, [Audio], *YouTube*, March 7, 2014, accessed August 10, 2016, http://youtu.be/OYcNgANdX1Y; also Yusuf, "Healing Self."
63. Yusuf, "Translator's Introduction."
64. Hamza Yusuf, *Purification of the Heart: Signs, Symptoms and Cures of the Spiritual Diseases of the Heart: Translation and Commentary of Imam al-Mawlud's* Matharat al-Qulub (n.p.: Starlatch Books, 2004); Imam Ghazali and Hamza Yusuf, *The Alchemy of Happiness* [Audio CD] (Alhambra Productions, 2006); Hamza Yusuf, "The Critical Importance of Al-Ghazali in our Times," [Video], *YouTube*, January 3, 2012, accessed August 11, 2016, https://www.youtube.com/watch?v=lJezFjbn-6M.
65. Moyers, "Transcript."
66. Ibid.
67. Hamza Yusuf, "Prohibitions of the Tongue, Session 1," [Video], *YouTube*, November 24, 2013, accessed August 11, 2016, https://www.youtube.com/watch?v=buT8oWI-S9U.
68. Korb, *Light without Fire*, 34.
69. Zaytuna College, *Catalog 2014–2015*, 9.
70. Muhammad Naguib Al-Attas, *Islam and Secularism* (Kuala Lumpur: Muslim Youth Movement of Malaysia, 1978), 16–17; this definition is not Cox's originally, but comes from Cornelius A. van Peursen, see Harvey Gallagher Cox, *The Secular City: Secularization and Urbanization in Theological Perspective* (Princeton: Princeton University Press, 2013), 2.
71. Zaytuna College, "Our Mission," accessed November 7, 2014, http://www.zaytunacollege.org/about/our_mission/.
72. Ibid.
73. Yusuf, "On Education, Philosophy"; Yusuf, "Prohibitions, Session 2"; Hamza Yusuf, "Thoughts on the Science Delusion," (Zaytuna Monthly Videocast) [Video], *YouTube*, December 23, 2009, accessed August 11, 2016, http://youtu.be/HUfd_z-4ZPY.
74. Ira M. Lapidus, "Knowledge, Virtue, and Action: The Classical Muslim Conception of *Adab* and the Nature of Religious Fulfillment," in *Moral Conduct and Authority: The Place of Adab in South Asian Islam*, ed. Barbara Daly Metcalf (Berkeley, C.A.: University of California Press, 1984), 38–61, esp. 40.
75. Al-Attas, *Islam and Secularism*, 15.
76. Hamza Yusuf, "Interview on IKIMfm, September 4, 2014," [Video], *YouTube*, September 18, 2014, accessed August 11, 2016, https://www.youtube.com/watch?v=_MHPc5wIE48.
77. Hamza Yusuf, "The Crisis of Knowledge," [Video], *YouTube*, September 5, 2014, accessed August 11, 2016, https://www.youtube.com/watch?v=NIc-4CdIF9U.

78. Al-Attas, *Islam and Secularism*, 106.
79. E.g., Hamza Yusuf Hanson, "A Time for Introspection," accessed February 24, 2015, http://www.masud.co.uk/ISLAM/misc/shhamza_sep11.htm.
80. Hamza Yusuf Hanson, "A Time for Introspection," accessed February 24, 2015, http://www.masud.co.uk/ISLAM/misc/shhamza_sep11.htm.
81. For use of the term "Neo-Traditionalism," see Gavin Picken, "Review of *A Textbook of Ḥadīth Studies: Authenticity, Compilation, Classification and Critisism of Ḥadīth* by Mohammad Hashim Kamali," *Journal of Qur'anic Studies* 8 (2006), 131–8; Alexandre Caeiro, "Fiqh Al-Aqalliyyat," *Oxford Bibliographies Online*, Islamic Studies, July 27, 2011, accessed February 26, 2015, DOI: 10.1093/obo/9780195390155-0027.
82. Zaytuna College, "Faculty," accessed August 11, 2016, http://www.zaytunacollege.org/academics/faculty/. Ali is frequently a teacher in Zaytuna's "Living Links" broadcast, a series of free classes that are live streamed online and then reposted on *YouTube*: Abdullah bin Hamid Ali, "Watch Live Weekly: The Roots of Interpretative Disagreements, Session 1," September 11, 2014, accessed August 11, 2016, https://www.youtube.com/watch?v=nfT0HWQbgh8&feature=youtube_gdata_player.
83. Abdullah bin Hamid Ali, "'Neo-Traditionalism' vs 'Traditionalism'," *Lampost Education Initiative*, January 22, 2012, accessed August 11, 2016, http://www.lamppostproductions.com/neo-traditionalism-vs-traditionalism-shaykh-abdullah-bin-hamid-ali/.
84. Ibid.
85. Ibid.
86. Ibid.
87. Abdullah bin Hamid Ali, "Preserving the Freedom for Faith: Reevalutaing the Politics of Compulsion," *Lamppost Productions*, September 12, 2014, accessed August 11, 2016, http://www.lamppostproductions.com/files/articles/PRESERVING%20THE%20FREEDOM%20FOR%20FAITH.pdf, 5.
88. Ibid., 5.
89. Yusuf and Ramadan, "Rethinking."
90. Ibid., 28:30.
91. Ibid., 33:10.
92. Ibid., 31:45.
93. Ibid., 31:30.
94. Abdallah Bin Bayyah, "Fiqh of Reality: When Fiqh Meets Fact, How Do We Act?" RISTalks [Video], *YouTube*, January 9, 2015, accessed August 11, 2016, https://www.youtube.com/watch?v=rgBwGmfXi5E.
95. Ibid., 57:19.
96. Abdullah Bin Bayyah, "Muslims Living in Non-Muslim Lands," talk at the Santa Clara Convention Center, Santa Clara, CA on July 31, 1999, accessed February 12, 2015, http://www.themodernreligion.com/world/muslims-living.html.
97. Hamza Yusuf, "Interview: In Collaboration with Hamza Yusuf," September 19, 2014, accessed December 5, 2014. https://www.youtube.com/watch?v= _MHPc5wIE48&feature=youtube_gdata_player.
98. Zaytuna College, *Catalog 2014–2105*, 7.
99. Ibid., 7–9.
100. Tim Lacy, *The Dream of a Democratic Culture: Mortimer J. Adler and the Great Books Idea* (Basingstoke: Palgrave Macmillan, 2013), 1.

101. Ibid.; Robert Maynard Hutchins, "The Great Conversation," *Encyclopedia Britannica Blog*, December 11, 2008, accessed August 11, 2016, http://blogs.britannica.com/wp-content/pdf/The_Great_Conversation.pdf.
102. Romig, "Where Islam Meets America"; Columbia College, "Mark Van Doren," accessed July 30, 2016, https://www.college.columbia.edu/core/oasis/profiles/van_doren.php.
103. Zaytuna College, *Catalog 2014–2015*, 2; Hutchins, "Great Conversation."
104. Zaytuna College, *Catalog 2014–2015*, 8.
105. Ibid., 10–12.
106. Hamza Yusuf, "Follow a Madhab or Follow a Wahabi / Salafi? 2013/2014," [Video], *YouTube*, October 10, 2013, accessed August 11, 2016, http://youtube/S-01WsNKNAE.
107. Zaytuna College, *Catalog 2014–2015*, 17.
108. Yusuf, "Another Mother of the Believers."
109. Some examples of Yusuf's commentaries are Hamza Yusuf, *The Burda of Al-Busiri: The Poem of the Cloak (Arabic and English Edition)* [Audio CD] (Sandala, 2002); idem, *Purification of the Heart*; idem, *The Creed of Imam al-Tahawi* (Louisville: Fons Vitae, 2009); Ghazali and Yusuf, *Alchemy*; Hamza Yusuf, *The Vision of Islam* [Audio CD] (Alhambra Productions, 2002).
110. Hamza Yusuf, "Islam Has a Progressive Tradition Too," *The Guardian*, June 19, 2002, accessed August 11, 2016, http://www.theguardian.com/world/2002/jun/19/religion.september111.
111. Hamza Yusuf, "Transcript: What Happened to Poetry?" lecture, Fremont, CA, 2009, accessed August 11, 2016, http://sheikhhamza.com/transcript/what-happened-to-poetry.
112. Yusuf, "Higher Education."
113. Yusuf, "What Happened to Poetry?".
114. Ibid.
115. E.g., Yusuf, *Burda*; Yusuf, *Purification of the Heart*; Ghazali and Yusuf, *Alchemy*.
116. "Favorites," *Sandala*, accessed July 30, 2016, https://sandala.org/favorites/.
117. Hamza Yusuf, "Reading 'Ozymandias' with Shaykh Hamza Yusuf," [Video], *YouTube*, October 12, 2013, accessed August 11, 2016, https://www.youtube.com/watch?v=Bz8oSl5A36s.
118. "Favorites," *Sandala*.
119. Yusuf states that in it, "Dostoyevsky deals with every major theme of the current crisis in the West": ibid. Yusuf also praises it in the lecture "What Happened to Poetry" for its depiction of the struggles in modern society with morality.
120. Zaytuna College, *Catalog 2014–2015*, inside cover.
121. Elewa and Silvers, "I Am One of the People."
122. Hamza Yusuf, "Women, Shari'ah And Islam," [Video], *YouTube*, March 25, 2011, accessed August 11, 2016, https://www.youtube.com/watch?v=4EpINIa0bd0.
123. Hamza Yusuf, "Men and Women (In Islam)," [Audio], *YouTube*, August 21, 2012, accessed August 11, 2016, https://www.youtube.com/watch?v=H8PrFABsVcQ; Hamza Yusuf, "How Do We Respond? Part 3," December 12, 2010, accessed August 11, 2016, https://sandala.org/blog/how-do-we-respond-part-3.
124. See Yusuf's statement that the actor Dave Chappelle refused to wear women's clothing in a movie because "he's a Muslim, and he's got limits, right, of where he's gonna go": Hamza Yusuf, "Dave Chappelle on How Hollywood Emasculates

Young Black Men, Part 1," [Video], *YouTube*, January 05, 2013, accessed August 11, 2016, http://youtu.be/3qd37nBI5B8.
125. Yusuf, "Thoughts on the Science Delusion."
126. Yusuf, "On Education, Philosophy"; Hamza Yusuf. "The Antichrist (Dajjal) and the New World Order," [Video], *YouTube*, November 07, 2011, accessed August 11, 2016, http://youtu.be/HVVtns1_O0w.
127. Hamza Yusuf, "Secularism: The Greatest Challenge Facing Islam," [Video], *YouTube*, September 07, 2011, accessed August 11, 2016, http://youtu.be/0AX8ck7jjtU.
128. Ibid.; Hamza Yusuf, "You Have Been Manipulated Like 'Mice in a Maze,'" [Video], *YouTube*, March 9, 2013, accessed August 11, 2016, http://youtu.be/_DYusqIXpzo.; Yusuf, "On Education, Philosophy."
129. Hamza Yusuf, "Higher Education for a Higher Purpose"; idem, "On Photography," [Audio], *YouTube*, December 30, 2011, accessed August 11, 2016, http://youtu.be/tTgEukrY_tQ; idem, "Secularism: The Greatest Challenge"; idem, "Healing Self, Healing Society"; idem, "You Have Been Manipulated."
130. Zaytuna College, *Catalog 2014–2105*, 7, 11.
131. Hamza Yusuf, "Moon Sighting," [Video], *YouTube*, October 23, 2006, accessed August 11, 2016, http://youtu.be/gkk9RroPOGw.
132. Hamza Yusuf, *Caesarean Moon Births: Calculation, Moon Sighting, and the Prophetic Way* (Berkeley: Zaytuna Institute, 2010). (The title is somewhat misleading. The work strictly addresses issues of determining the beginning of lunar months.)
133. He gave a speech in Sharjah, U.A.E. in April 2013 entitled "Contributions of Muslims in Science and Technology." A recording of this speech has unfortunately not been made available, but on the event see "Renowned Islamic Scholar Hamza Yusuf Speaks at AUS," *American University of Sharjah Website*, accessed August 11, 2016, https://www.aus.edu/news/article/498/renowned_islamic_scholar_hamza_yusuf_speaks_at_aus.
134. Yusuf, "Healing Self, Healing Society."
135. Ibid.; Hamza Yusuf, "The Critical Importance of Al-Ghazali"; Yusuf, "Jewels and Pearls of The Qur'an," [Video], *YouTube*, December 25, 2011, accessed August 11, 2016, https://www.youtube.com/watch?v=mNAEI2_YfyI.
136. Yusuf, "Healing Self, Healing Society."
137. Zaytuna College, *Catalog 2014–2015*, 3.
138. Ibid., 6.

CHAPTER

2

THE NEO-TRADITIONALISM OF TIM WINTER

Christopher Pooya Razavian

Timothy John Winter, or Shaykh Abdal Hakim Murad, is a university lecturer, a religious leader, and an influential speaker on Muslim affairs. Tim Winter has developed a neo-traditionalist understanding of Islam that values diversity and spirituality. His neo-traditionalism is grounded in his understanding of a balanced rationality and the pluralism of Islamic tradition. This understanding of Islam is also seen as a natural progression of British values. Thus, while Islam's origins may be foreign, its values are not. Winter also sees Wahhabism as being a threat to this understanding of Islam. A major focus of Winter's works is on describing the difference between this neo-traditionalist approach and the modern materialistic secular imaginary. His neo-traditionalist approach combines a traditional *madhhab* approach to Islamic law with spirituality in a way that has a deep respect for diversity.

Winter's multiple academic duties include being the Shaykh Zayed lecturer in Islamic Studies at the Faculty of Divinity at the University of Cambridge, the Director of Studies at Wolfson College, and the Dean of the Cambridge Muslim College.[1] He is an alumnus of the University of Cambridge where he studied Arabic as an undergraduate in 1983. He subsequently moved to Cairo to study at al-Azhar for three years, and then moved to Jeddah to study for another three years. In 1989, after returning to England, he attended the University of London to learn Turkish and Persian.

Although Winter is a lecturer at the University of Cambridge he is more of a public intellectual than a traditional academic. His works are mostly reflections—some academic, some more general—about various issues about Islam and Muslim life in the modern world. Winter has written seven books; however, most of these books are printed editions of essays available online and not necessarily academic in nature. For example, his *Understanding the Four Madhhabs: The Facts about Ijtihad and Taqlid* is a printed version of his essay

"Understanding the Four Madhhabs: The Problem with Anti-Madhhabism." His book *Bombing without Moonlight: The Origins of Suicidal Terrorism* is a reprint of an essay by the same name.[2]

A part of Winter's project is to make Islam accessible to non-Muslim audiences. For example, he has co-authored an introductory book about Islam titled *Understanding Islam and the Muslims: The Muslim Family, Islam and World Peace* published in 2002.[3] This book is written in a question-and-answer format and covers the basic fundamentals of Islam. It covers introductory questions related to Muslim beliefs and how one becomes a Muslim, as well as several social issues, such as the importance of family to Muslim life.

In an interview on BBC with Joan Bakewell, Winter describes the events that led to his conversion to Islam as a teenager.[4] He states that his conversion was in part due to the religious climate in England during the 1970s that no longer saw Anglicanism as being the default option. He himself had difficulty understanding the concept of the trinity within Christian thought, and this was exacerbated by John Hick's publication of *The Myth of God Incarnate.* John Hick (d. 2012) was an English philosopher of religion who had put forward a progressive understanding of theology. In *The Myth of God Incarnate*, as the title suggests, he critiques the conception of Jesus as God incarnate.[5] In a radio interview with Joan Bakewell, Winter states that this book:

> sort of pushed me in the direction of knowing that I really wanted to believe in God, that was the only explanation that could possibly suit my mind . . . but I could never with fullness of heart accept the classic doctrines of the Christianity with which I had been raised, so I started to look for alternatives.[6]

Initially, Winter had no intention of studying the religion of Islam in any great depth. He had enrolled in evening classes in Arabic with the "intention being not to learn about God, but to do Economics at Cambridge with Arabic, so that I could go and make a killing in the Gulf."[7] It was through this Arabic course that he was introduced to Islam. The theology of Islam "ticked all the boxes that my inherent Christianity had left vacant."[8] Islam had answered the theological questions that plagued Winter. It answered not only the monotheism that Winter was moving toward, but it also allowed Winter to still consider Jesus as part of his religious vision.

Neo-traditionalism

Winter can be described as a neo-traditionalist. Abdullah bin Hamid Ali, an American self-styled neo-traditionalist also associated with Zaytuna College (see Chapter 1), describes neo-traditionalism as having the following characteristics: a return to the classical schools of law, contextualization of mainstream Sunni doctrine, the practice of text-based Islamic spirituality, and an understanding that the past cannot be recreated today.[9] Tim Winter aptly fits this profile. He calls for a return to the classical schools of law, teaches and translates works in mainstream Islamic doctrine, values Sufism, and all this while trying to bring these classical teachings in coherence with modernity.

Winter is a strong defender of the classical schools of law. He believes that the classical schools of law, *madhhabs*, have developed an internal cohesion and a method that helps to minimise mistakes in deriving Islamic law. This defence of the *madhhab* is also a critique of the anti-*madhhab* approach of Salafism. Winter criticizes the Salafis for threatening the cohesion that has been established by the *madhhabs*, creating conflict, and ultimately threatening the existence of Islam itself.

Winter is quite clear about the necessity of following a tradition when it comes to understanding Islamic texts. In his article "What is Scriptural Reasoning?" Winter lays out the way that Muslims can approach "Scriptural Reasoning." Scriptural Reasoning is a modern interfaith movement where adherents of different religions come together to discuss common themes through the various holy texts.[10] Winter is quick to note that Muslims have "formal restraints on the reflections they are likely to offer."[11] These restraints come in the form of traditional authorization:

> Properly speaking, a Muslim may only interpret scripture after authorisation (*ijāzah*) from traditional masters, who have themselves been authorised as part of an unbroken succession (*isnād*) stretching back to the Prophet himself.[12]

One should not assume that Winter is calling for a single understanding of Islamic text. As will be shown below, Winter in fact believes that the difficulties of understanding Islamic text leads to various interpretations. What he is arguing for, however, is that Muslims are not as free as their religious counterparts to understand the text as they see fit. They are bound to a certain tradition. This necessity of being within the tradition is also reflected in Winter's writings on Islamic law.

Winter begins his article "Understanding the Four Madhhabs: The Problem with Anti-Madhhabism" by stating that "the ummah's greatest achievement over the past millennium has undoubtedly been its internal intellectual cohesion," and writes that "Sunni Muslims have maintained an almost unfailing attitude of religious respect and brotherhood among themselves." He praises Sunnism for this "unusual outcome" and for bucking the trend of violence and factionalism, and it is for this very reason that Sunni cohesion "demands careful analysis."[13]

Winter admits that there are "painful exceptions" to this trend, but limits these exceptions to the "earliest phase of our history." This early period of Islam is the period immediately after the Prophet until the establishment of the four schools of law. He writes that there was "disunity and fitnas" that "divided the early Muslims despite their superior piety," but there was "solidity and cohesiveness of Sunnism after the final codification of the *sharīʿah* in the four Schools of the great Imams."[14] The "disunity and fitnas" of the early period consist of the revolt against ʿUthmān, and the wars during the caliphate of ʿAlī ibn Abī Ṭālib. The schisms that formed after these conflicts led Sunni Islam to occupy the "middle ground between the two extremes of egalitarian Kharijism and hierarchical Shi'ism."[15] For Sunni thought, authority was "vested in the Quran and Sunnah." Yet, the number of sources that Muslim scholars had to reference were too great and their apparent contradictions too complex to interpret. This led to the development of certain rudimentary hermeneutics, such as *naskh* (abrogation), but it was not until al-Shāfiʿī's systematization of *uṣūl al-fiqh* that any consistent methodology was formed.[16]

Al-Sh*āfiʿī*'s approach to law was soon incorporated by the other schools of law. Thereafter, Muslims scholars, Winter notes, recognized the brilliance of the four great *imāms*, and the various schools of law began to take shape. Winter argues that it was at this time that "the attitude of toleration and good opinion between the Schools became universally accepted."[17] Thus, while "it was necessary for the Muslim to follow a recognised madhhab in order to avert the lethal danger of misinterpreting the sources, he must never fall into the trap of considering his own school categorically superior to the others." The *madhhab* methodology was necessary to correctly interpret religion, but should not itself become a source of conflict.

This inter-Muslim conflict in his view, however, is being flamed by the Salafis and their utter disregard for classical schools of law. This is due to Salafi claims that individuals can derive Islamic law for themselves. Winter states that this belief that "ordinary Muslims, even if they know Arabic, are qualified to derive rulings of the Shariah for themselves, is an example of this egotism running wild." He states that "Western-influenced global culture" urges individuals to challenge authority and to adhere to their own rationality and this makes it difficult to recognize that one simply does not have the hermeneutical tools to decipher Islamic law. Ultimately, the "danger of less-qualified individuals misunderstanding the sources and hence damaging the Shariah is a very real one."

He gives examples of the "Pharisaic atmosphere" created by the Salafis. He writes that it is common to see young Arabs hoarding collections of *ḥadīth*, trying to decipher Islamic law, and then forcing their own understanding on others. These young Arabs are "prowling the mosques" in order to critique Muslims for actions and beliefs that they believe to be deviant. This in turn has discouraged many from attending the mosque in general. Moreover, "No-one now recalls the view of the early *ʿulamā*', which was that Muslims should tolerate divergent interpretations of the Sunnah as long as these interpretations have been held by reputable scholars."[18] Winter also implies that the Salafis are, in essence, doing the work of the enemies of Islam. He writes that the reason Salafis are well funded is because they are detrimental to Islam.

> This is not to suggest in any way that those who attack the great madhhabs are the conscious tools of Islam's enemies. But it may go some way to explaining why they will continue to be well-publicised and well-funded, while the orthodox alternative is starved of resources.[19]

Another cornerstone of Winter's neo-traditionalism is the conception of a balanced reason. It is a middle way between pure rationality and pure religious experience expressed in Sufism. In a paper titled "Reason as Balance: The Evolution of *'aql*" Winter argues that very few Muslim thinkers have tried to find a balance between these two paths. He follows Sachiko Murata and William Chittick in their description about the two dimensions of Islamic thought: the *tanzīh* (God as Transcendence) and the *tashbīh* (God as Immanence). Chittick and Murata, husband and wife, are renowned authors on Islamic philosophy and Sufism; they have co-authored *The Vision of Islam*, a book that has found traction among neo-traditionalist thinkers. Hamza Yusuf has highly praised this book, and as discussed in the previous chapter, has even dedicated a series of lectures to its study.[20] Winter himself references this book in relation to the concept of balanced rationality. Winter summarises the two approaches of the *tanzīh* and the *tashbīh* as thus:

> Sachiko Murata and William Chittick have reflected extensively on this inner Islamic metabolism, identifying kalām with the principle of drawing inferences about God as Transcendence (*tanzīh*); and Sufism with the principle of experiencing God as Immanence (*tashbīh*); the dyadic categorisation of divine names as Names of Rigour and Names of Beauty is one outcome. Their conclusion is that these two inexorable consequences of the postulate of monotheism run like twin constants through Islamic religious history. Each is allocated its own realm, form of discourse, and even, on occasion, ritual life and structured authority.[21]

This quote catches the essence of Winter's conception of balanced reason. It is a commitment to both approaches of Islamic understanding. The rational discussion of the philosophers and theologians is to be balanced by the spiritual approaches of the mystics. In the same paper, Winter compares the variety of ways that Muslim thinkers have approached this issue, and ultimately presents Abū Ḥamid Muḥammad ibn Muḥammad al-Ghazālī (d. 1111)—the famous mystic, theologian, jurist, and philosopher—as the model thinker that synthesized both approaches.

Winter cites thinkers such as the modernist Egyptian reformer Rashid Rida (d. 1935) as an example of a scholar that went too far towards the rational camp.[22] Winter argues that these modernist polemics were "reactive against a European belief in 'Oriental unreason'."[23] On the other end of the spectrum are thinkers such as the celebrated poet and mystic Jalāl ad-Dīn Muhammad Rūmī (d. 1273). Winter quotes a few verses from Rūmī's poetry that highlight the degree to which Rūmī valued love and spiritual experience over reason and rationality. He summarizes Rūmī's opinion as such: "Reason, the steed of the formal theologians, is a noble part of God's creation, but is desperately slow and limited."[24] Winter finds it surprising that very few scholars try to bring about a synthesis between these two viewpoints:

> It is striking that only in a few texts do we observe an attempt to provide a grand synthesis of the two approaches, which we might, to borrow European terminology, describe as the logical and the passional [*sic*]. Ghazālī (d.1111) is the most obvious, and successful, example.[25]

Winter goes on to cite other thinkers that also take up this task, namely the famous Sufi Ibn 'Arabī (d. 638/1240), the Ottoman *Shakyh al-Islām* Ibn Kamāl (d. 940/1534), the influential Indian thinker Shāh Walī Allāh al-Dihlawī (d. 1176/1762), and the Turkish religious leader Said Nursi (d. 1960). It is however, Ghazālī that takes centre stage. This is not surprising given Winter's numerous speeches about Ghazālī and his translations of a few sections of Ghazālī's multivolume book on Islamic ethics the *Iḥyā' al-'Ulūm*.[26]

The final aspect of Winter's neo-traditionalism is the role he gives to spirituality. Winter writes about the necessity of spirituality in relation to increasing radicalization. He writes that Islam is in need of a spiritual revival. He criticizes current Islamic movements for forgetting spirituality and pushing a line of activism that pushes towards burnout. He labels this "salafi burnout", and blames "neo-Kharijite" Wahhabism as being a major source of the problem. The solution is for Muslims to "improve the state of our hearts, and fill them with the Islamic virtues of affection, respect, tolerance and reconciliation."[27]

In a talk given in Vrije Universiteit Amsterdam titled "Is Orthodox Islam Possible Without Sufism?" Winter discusses the centrality that Sufism should play within Sunni thought.[28] He argues that the classical Azhari scholarly opinion is that it is not possible to be an orthodox Muslim without incorporating Sufism. He makes this argument by quoting the famous didactic poem *Jawharah al-Tawḥīd*, by the Ash'arī theologian Ibrāhīm al-Laqqānī (d. 1041/1632). The *Jawharah al-Tawḥīd* is considered as a standard work of Ash'arī theology, and it is widely read in many traditional Islamic educational institutions, including al-Alzhar. Hassan al-Banna memorised this text,[29] and many influential Azhari scholars, such as Ibrahim al-Bajuri (d. 1860), have written extensive commentaries on the text.[30] The section that Winter quotes roughly constitutes two verses from the poem indicating the need to follow the *imāms* of Islamic law and also the spiritual *imāms*. Al-Laqqānī names Abū al-Qasim, which is in reference to the famous Persian mystic Abū al-Qasim ibn Muḥammad ibn al-Junayd (d. 298/910), as one such example.

Winter uses this poem to mention that the standard traditionalist reply to the question at hand is that no, it is not possible to have orthodox religious belief without Sufism. He adds that Sufism has always been a part of traditional Islamic understanding, and that for thousands of years there were no real debates about this. Moreover, he argues that "Sufism" as a category was only invented 200 years ago. Sufism was never an "ism", he argues it was rather a verb "*taṣawwuf*." It was something that one did rather than something one joins. He asked the audience to not use orientalist categories when Muslims are trying to define themselves but to rather use indigenous vocabulary. Thus, it would be more relevant to ask if a Muslim performs *taṣawwuf* rather than if one is a Sufi. The essence of *taṣawwuf* is to have an inward detachment from the world and an eye to find humans who might be in service:[31] "The indigenous definition is simply transcending yourself and applying that inner dimension of the sunnah."[32]

Tied in to his discussions of Sufism and rationality is his understanding of pluralism. In the same speech titled "Is Orthodox Islam Possible Without Sufism?" Winter spends more time explaining the concept of orthodoxy than he does explaining Sufism. He emphasizes the point that there has always been pluralism within Islamic thought. There is no orthodoxy in Islam, one correct teaching, rather Islam is a conversation. A conversation that has been ongoing between scholars and laypersons for thousands of years:

> It is a much more diverse tradition. And this has always been a sign of Islamic authenticity that it is of the *jamā'a*, in other words it is of conversation. An ongoing accumulated wisdom based on discussions and arguments and polemic and fraternal remarks discussed in commentaries and amongst Muslims in their meetings for hundreds of years. And that is what it is to be a part of the *ahl al-sunnah wa-al-jamā'a*.[33]

Thus, there is a type of pluralism that is innate to Islamic thinking. The difficulty in understanding the text itself leads to various scholarly positions. To be authentically Islamic is not to be dogmatic about an understanding of the text, but to acknowledge that there are multiple understandings of the Islamic text. He also states that it has been the establishment of plural-vocal religious cultures that has made Muslim civilisations great in the past: "It's always been a sign of the strength of the *ummah* that this necessary diversity within this large grab bag category of orthodox Islam has underpinned the moment of greatness in our civilisation and the florescence of a wide range of different perspectives."[34]

Opposing this Islamic pluralism, however, is our more modern attempt to find a single voice for Islamic understanding. Winter attributes this to modernity and the rapidly changing context. He believes that in times like these, people tend to feel threatened and seek refuge within singular understandings of religion. In comparison, when the *ummah* feels strong then it welcomes a pluralism of different voices:

> In times of turbulence and rapid change people tend to move away from an understanding that the umma is defined in terms of multiple voices and towards a fearful anxiety about a possibility of an internal Islamic pluralism.[35]

Gender, Science, and British Muslim Identity

This understanding of neo-traditionalism has an impact on how Winter approaches real life issues. The website that hosts most of his essays (masud.co.uk) has marked that the two major themes of Winter's works are British Muslim identity and gender. However, a major sub-theme that develops under gender issues is science. The reason is that Winter uses biology to support his claims of "difference feminism". Winter has tackled the issue of gender in a few of his writings. He argues that early forms of feminism that called for complete equality have failed, and this failure has given rise to a new strand of feminism that recognizes the differences between males and females leading to rise of "difference feminism" as opposed to earlier efforts at "equality feminism".

One of Winter's more popular essays on this subject is "Boys Will Be Boys," which Hamza Yusuf has also referenced in one of his own talks on gender.[36] Winter argues that many debates about gender from Muslim intellectuals are limited to the classical issues of *fiqh*. While he does not deny that there is great importance to understanding the *fiqh* background to these issues, he argues that this approach has been too apologetic. What he wishes to do is "construct a language of gender which offers not a defence or mitigation of current Muslim attitudes and establishments, but a credible strategy for resolving dilemmas which the Western thinkers and commentators around us are now meticulously examining."[37]

Thus, Winter is trying to move past a dichotomy where Muslims are trying to defend their positions on gender difference to a Western audience, and is trying to reframe the issue in dialogue with the new gender paradigm being debated in the Western academic circles. This is precisely why Winter begins his article with Germaine Greer's *The Whole Woman* as her work personifies the "ways in which the social and also scientific context of Western gender discourse has shifted over this period."[38]

Greer authored an influential book in 1970 titled *The Female Eunuch*. She argued that the typical suburban nuclear family rendered females as eunuchs. Yet, in a book written in 1999, *The Whole Women*, Greer became critical of what earlier feminism had achieved leading to a shift from "equality feminism" to "difference feminism". Winter describes "equality feminism" as "committed to the breakdown of gender disparities as social constructs amenable to changes in education and media generalisation." On the other hand "difference feminism" is "rooted in the growing conviction that nature is at least as important as nurture in shaping the behavioural traits of men and women."[39]

Winter states that Greer's position is that sexual liberation has harmed women. The sexuality that has been liberated is male sexuality, and promiscuity harms women more than men. There has been an increase in infidelity, and a rise in divorce and single parenthood. Moreover, pornography has led to an increased "dehumanisation and objectification of women."[40] The fashion industry is seen as "a major contributor to the contemporary enslavement of women."[41] Women now lead unhappier lives than before with increased levels of depression. Thus women have not been liberated, but have exchanged one type of dependence, on the husband, for another, on the pharmaceutical industry.

In order to add weight to difference feminism, Winter appeals to science. He cites how women are physically weaker than men, that men are biologically more aggressive and competitive so they can be more successful reproductively, that the nature of their intellect is different, and that men seek novelty. Ultimately, Winter concludes that the *sharīʿah* "upholds the dignity and the worth of women more reliably than secularity ever can."[42] Materialism, here equated with secularism and capitalism, measures human worth in terms of wealth and sex, and this will "inexorably glorify the male."[43] He adds that: "Materialistic civilisations will, in the longer term, favour and revere male traits."[44] Yet, "[a]s Muslims, we refuse such a favouritism."[45] Islam is about absolute justice. Thus while the *sharīʿah* might "favour the male in functional, material terms" Muslims are "able to insist on the worth of women in a way that is not possible outside a religious context."

He develops this approach to gender by drawing on the understanding of the ninety-nine names of Allah, and the polarity in the name of majesty (*jalāl*) and the name of beauty (*jamāl*). Although Winter does not go into depth about the meanings of these names of Allah, he references an early written article on the subject, "Islam, Irigaray, and the Retrieval of Gender," where he delves into the significance of the names of majesty (*jalāl*) and the names of beauty (*jamāl*).Winter's appeal to the image of God in order to understand problems of gender follows a line of thinking put forward by the feminist theologian Rosemary Reuther. Reuther, in her book *Sexism and God-Talk*, argues that the way that we understand the image of God affects how we understand gender relations.[46] From this premise, Winter build his argument that the image of God in the Islamic thought can bring about a balance between the genders. In order to argue this Winter uses the concept of *jalāl* and *jamāl* as developed by the feminist Sufism of Sachiko Murata.

Sachiko Murata is a Professor of Religion and Asian Studies at Stony Brook University, where she conducts research into the interrelationship of Islam and Far Eastern thought. In 1971, she was the first woman and the first non-Muslim to study at the Faculty of Theology at the University of Tehran.[47] Murata has authored a book about Islam and gender, *The Tao of Islam*, and it can be described as a work of feminist Sufism. Her goal in this book is to push the reader to look beyond Islamic law and to understand gender in terms of Islamic spirituality. She argues that the balance between genders will become apparent if gender is viewed from this perspective. However, she is not stating that this is how Muslims are living in Muslim-majority countries. She is in fact critical of the treatment of women in many Muslim countries, and clearly states that what she has written in this book is unfortunately not put in the practice.[48]

The way that Murata shows the balance between the genders in Islamic thought is through the concepts of the divine names of God (*al-asmāʾ*

al-ḥusnā), Considered to be 99 in number, these names of God[49] have been invoked by some Sufi scholars to develop a distinction between the names of majesty (*jalāl*) and the names of beauty (*jamāl*). The names of majesty are seen as pre-eminently masculine, whereas the names of beauty were seen as feminine.[50] The names of majesty include names such as the Mighty, the Great, the Majestic, and the names of beauty include names such the Near, the Compassionate, the Forgiving. Murata labels the names of majesty as "yang names" and the names of beauty as "yin names".[51] These two names together create the "Tao of Islam", the yin and the yang. Murata argues that the legalistic approach to Islam puts greater emphasis on the "yang names" where as a spiritual approach emphasizes the "yin names". She is not trying to give greater weight to one over the other but tries to show the two must come to balance.

According to this categorization there are many aspects of God that are considered feminine. And it is here that Winter makes use of Murata's work. Winter mentions how *raḥmah*, mercy, is seen as a feminine quality but is identified with creation: "Creation itself is the nafas al-Rahman, the Breath of the All-Compassionate."[52] This is contrast to Christian theology that sees God as the father. Islamic theology is, therefore, beyond gender.

Thus, while Winter agrees that there are differences in the two genders they are still equal. That equality, however, extends beyond material attributes and towards the metaphysical. Thus Islamic theology provides a gender-neutral context that helps one to value traditionally feminine attributes, attributes that are not valued in today's materialistic consumerist culture.

Winter then uses this approach to rethink the meaning of some of the injunctions in Islamic law. He does not rethink the law itself, but what this law means. For example, he discusses the possibility of having female *imāms*. Rather than discussing legal aspects and the legal theory behind the permissibility or impermissibility of having female *imāms*, Winter focuses on the role that *imāms* play in Muslim life. Rather than changing the law he deemphasizes the importance of the *imām*. He writes that the role of the *imām* is merely a marker of time, and that it is possible to be a valuable Muslim leader without being an *imām*. It is for this reason that many women in the Muslim world have not tried to become *imāms*.[53]

He also discusses issues of gender segregation. Again, he does not focus on the legal theory behind gender segregation. Rather, he focuses on the benefits that a segregated, dedicated space can have for women themselves. He quotes feminists such as Luce Irigaray, who similarly argue for such women's spaces within the Western world.[54] Winter therefore believes that normative Islamic society is both patriarchal and matriarchal. It would be inappropriate to assume that Winter is simply being apologetic for traditional Islamic norms. His use of feminist theories has the potential to be more revolutionary then he himself has so far admitted; he is critical of the dominant Islamic legalistic approach towards gender norms. He writes that ignoring the spiritual aspects of religious law leads to a diminished respect for women:

> This is why the contemporary Muslim interpretation of *shari'a* in ways which diminish *haqiqa* is so often accompanied by a diminished respect for women. The sexes are only regarded with equivalent esteem when *batin* and *zahir* are spoken of with equal frequency by believers.[55]

The primary intent of these essays is not to reform Islamic law, but to make Islamic norms of gender difference understandable to a contemporary Western audience. His goal is to take a practice that is seen as alien, and show how it can have solidarity with contemporary Western thinkers. In doing so, however, there is an undertone of critique of current Muslim practices as is evident by the statement above. This undertone is even picked up by other neo-traditionalists such as Hamza Yusuf. In one of his lectures, Yusuf criticizes the myth that men are better than women, and he refers to Winter's paper "Boys will be Boys" as a critique of this myth.[56] For Yusuf, this essay is not simply trying to justify difference feminism, but it also tackles the myth of gender preference.

Thus, in the process of trying to define difference feminism, Winter develops an understanding of gender that critiques contemporary Muslim practices Winter's appeal to spirituality enables him to move past the debate on gender in terms of Islamic law. In fact, he views the debate about gender as being solely framed by Islamic law and uses Sufism and Islamic spirituality as a means of bringing balance to the debate on gender. It should be noted however, that Winter never references any of the other Islamic feminists working in the field. It would be interesting to see what Islamic feminists think about Winter's approach to gender, although Winter's opinions on gender do not seem to have gained any attention outside of the neo-traditionalists discussed in this volume.

A major subtopic within Winter's discussion on difference feminism is the relationship between science and religion. As with many other neo-traditionalists, Winter tries to find a common ground between Islamic values and science. In the same essay, "Boys will be Boys," Winter strives to "show that an opposition to the Shari'ah is an opposition to science."[57] This search for common ground is aided by the fact that he lives in the West which he argues puts him "more in touch with contemporary trends in science and social theory"[58] compared to thinkers in Muslim-majority countries. The issues that he raises are the physical weakness of women, patterns of behaviour due to evolutionary biology, and difference in psychology.

The first issue that Winter raises is the physical weakness of women. Winter argues that the call for equality amongst the sexes has shown the limitations of such a strategy. One case in point is the United Kingdom's use of female recruits in the military. In 1998, "gender-free" selection procedures where adopted to ensure that men and women had identical tasks. Women were therefore required to perform more strenuous physical activities, which in turn led to more physical harm. Winter cites Ian Gemmell's study that showed that while stress fractures were at 1.5 per cent for males it was between 4.6 per cent and 11.1 per cent for females.[59] The same study also stated that because of their different physical builds, there was 33–39 per cent more stress on the female skeleton. Winter concludes that the result is that "although social changes have eroded the traditional moral reasons for barring women from active combat roles, the medical evidence alone compels the British army to bar women from the infantry and the Royal Armoured Corps."[60]

The second issue that Winter raises is about evolutionary biology. According to Winter, evolutionary biology argues that "biological success amounts to one factor alone: the maximal propagation of an organism's genetic material."[61] Since males and females have different reproductive strategies, they will also have different behaviours. One such example is "parental investment," a term popularised by the foremost evolutionary biologist Robert Trivers.[62] Females have nine months of pregnancy plus a period of weaning, whereas males are free of such commitments. Thus, sex becomes a limited resource, one in which males gain reproductive success through having multiple partners, and this explains the basis for competition and aggression amongst males. There is also a biological explanation for the strong nurturing instincts of women, due to estrogen and oxytocin, because women have "a far greater investment to lose if they neglect their children."[63]

For males, reproductive success was determined by aggression and competitiveness. These are traits that we still see in males today. Winter cites studies that show that the drive for competitiveness is why males choose fields such as math and science. At Harvard the male/female ratio for in the science department is seven to one: "the conclusion is not that women are less intelligent than men—the new biology clearly rules that out—but that they prefer to exercise it in specific fields."[64] Males also have a biological advantage to taking university examinations. The male endocrine system was designed to focus on a single task, like hunting, which gives males the edge in exams. Thus universities are looking for replacements to the examination system.[65]

There are a series of psychological traits that Winter also appeals to. He argues that the nature of male and female intelligence is different. Girls play games that are collaborative with deeper levels of discourse, whereas boys play games that are more rule based. 65 per cent of boy's games are rule based compared to 35 per cent of games played by girls.[66] Thus boys are more rule-oriented. Men are also more risk takers, due to reasons of biological survival: in order to attract and keep mates the men had to take risks. This is why, today, more men than women participate in high-risk sports. Women are better suited for chores at the home because male biology seeks out novelty with a dislike for repetitive tasks.

Winter also relies on the works of psychologists such as Carol Gilligan, who have argued that there are psychological differences between the genders. Many of these works were originally seen to be emancipatory; they were written so women could be understood as they are and not be made to conform to male standards. For example, Gilligan argues that the "objective" position taken by psychologist during the 1970s "was based on an inherent neutrality which concealed power and falsified knowledge."[67] Gilligan argues that men and women have different moral voices and approach moral problems from different angles. Winter uses Gilligan's work to argue the reason women define themselves in terms of relationships is due to the fact that in the pre-modern world women were primarily involved in care.[68] Winter argues that the new science of difference feminism and the *sharīʿah* vindicate each other: "Equality is no more envisaged by nature than it is by the law of God; indeed, the law of God, for us, is commensurate with natural law."[69] Both the *sharīʿah* and the science of difference feminism state that the concept of equality as sameness is not an effective approach to gender. They are also in agreement that it is better to approach the issue in terms of opportunity and respect: "We insist, therefore, that our revealed law, confirmed so magnificently in its assumptions by the new science, upholds the dignity and the worth of women more reliably than secularity ever can."[70]

Although Winter makes use of biology and evolutionary biology he is against the idea that humans evolved from pre-historic apes, even though he agrees with the concept of microevolution. Thus, animals can evolve to gain certain traits but they cannot evolve from one type of species into another. Winter touches on this topic in passing, while he is discussing the biological differences between men and women.

Winter states that the theory of evolution has come under attack from philosophers and physicists alike: "Darwinism and neo-Darwinism are of course under attack now, particularly by philosophers and physicists, rather more seriously than at any other time over the past hundred years." However, he does not offer any references to support this view. The only critical engagement with the theory of evolution that he does site is an article written by Shaykh Nuh Keller: "And as Shaykh Nuh Keller has shown, a thoroughgoing commitment to the theory of evolution is incompatible with the *Qurʾānic* account of the origins of humanity."[71] Following Keller, Winter accepts micro-evolution or the "perpetuation and reinforcement over time of genetically successful strategies for survival . . ."[72]

The article that Winter is referencing is Keller's *Islam and Evolution*. Keller's article is not a denial of science or the scientific method, but instead reaches its conclusions by analysing the claims for evolution particularly through a philosophy of science. He references a variety of different Western scholars such as Charles Darwin, Charles Peirce, and Jürgen Habermas. Keller's conclusion is that the claim "that man has evolved from a non-human species . . . is unbelief (kufr);"[73] this is diametrically opposed to the position of Yasir Qadhi, an American Salafi reformer (see Chapter 5) who believes that the theory of evolution is an established fact.

Nonetheless, Winter's theory of difference feminism is well grounded in scientific research. He cites many of the top feminists, psychologists, and biologists that have worked on this topic. This does not mean that the scientists will necessarily agree with Winter's interpretation of their research. This does, however, highlight how Winter believes science and Islamic thought overlap, and that he is comfortable in coming to a dialogue with science. In a way, it shows how he is applying his theory of balanced rationality.

Creating British Islam

One of the other major topics that Winter discusses is British Muslim identity. The website that hosts many of Winter's essays (masud.co.uk) lists numerous essays under this category. As a British Muslim convert, it is a subject that is quite close to Winter. He writes that the issue of British Muslim identity will determine the future of Islam in the U.K.: "My own belief is that the future prosperity of the Anglo-Muslim movement will be determined largely by our ability to answer this question of identity."[74]

Winter's understanding of the British Muslim identity is rather unique. He believes that Islam is the natural progression of Britishness. He sets up his argument on the premises that Islam is a universal religion, and that moral and religious temper of the British best match Islam. Islam "is the most suitable faith for the British."[75]

Winter's first claim is that "Islam, as a universal religion, in fact as the only legitimately universal religion, also makes room for the particularities of the peoples who come into it." He illustrates this point by looking at the history of Islam. He draws attention to the fact that Muslims were able to "accommodate those aspects of local, pre-Islamic tradition which did not clash absolutely with the truths of revelation."[76] A striking example is the history of Islam in China. Winter writes how many of the leading mandarins of the Ming dynasty were Muslim, and that Chinese mosques look like traditional garden-temples without idols and with Qurʾānic calligraphy.

Winter also describes how converts have an initial period where they view everything that pious Muslims do as angelic and everything outside of that as demonic. He labels this as "convertitis." While it is difficult to deal with those who have been afflicted with "convertitis" the effects of it soon wear off. The majority of converts that came to Islam for spiritual and intellectual reasons continue on their journey, but those who sought Islam for identities remain in search of sects and factions. British Muslims must keep a positive view towards diversity alive:

> Islam is, and will continue to be, even amid the miserable globalisation of modern culture, a faith that celebrates diversity. Our thinking about our own position as British Muslims should focus on that fact, and quietly but firmly ignore the protests both of the totalitarian fringe, and of the importers of other regional cultures, such as that of Pakistan, which they regard as the only legitimate Islamic ideal.[77]

On the other side, Winter does not see Europe as having a history of diversity: "Only in Europe was there a consistent policy of enforcing religious uniformity."

The reason for this religious uniformity stems from Church theology where everyone was tainted by the original sin, and was seen as an instrument of the devil unless one believed in Christ's redemptive suffering. With such a set of beliefs "it was only natural that Europe constantly strove for religious uniformity."[78]

Winter supports his claim that Islam is closer to the British moral and religious temper by citing the works of great British thinkers such as Henry Stubbe, Thomas Carlyle, and George Bernard Shaw. It was due to England's protestant past that England became the "the first country in Europe where medieval images of Islam could be challenged." He cites Stubbe as the "first European Christian to write favourably of Islam."[79] Stubbe was an English physician and scholar who trained in Oxford and Westminster and held radical religious and political views. He was eventually accused of heresy and died in prison. Winter states that Stubbe "constantly shows Islam to be a purer and more rational form of religion than Christianity,"[80] a stance that is also corroborated by other scholars, such as James Jacob, who have studied Stubbe's writings on Islam.[81]

Thomas Carlyle was considered as one of the most influential social commenters in the nineteenth century. In 1840 he presented a lecture on *The Hero as Prophet* which was a positive appreciation of the Prophet of Islam, and he used the example of the prophet of Islam as a warrior saint against Christian notions of pacifism. George Bernard Shaw, the famous twentieth-century playwright and winner of the Nobel Prize for literature, was also impressed by this image of the prophet. Shaw had been thinking about writing a play about the prophet, but feared protests from the Turkish ambassador.[82] It is, nonetheless, Stubbe's writings about Islam to which Winter gives the most weight. As Winter argues, Stubbe saw Islam as a pragmatic and practical religion. This is why Stubbe was attracted to Islam's view towards sex and polygamy, the practicality of Islamic practices, as well as the notion of jihad. Christianity in contrast, Stubbe believed, had a negative attitude towards sex, was cumbered with troublesome ceremonies, filled with abstruse notions, and its idea of pacifism was impractical.[83]

According to Winter, Islam as a universal religion with its respect for diversity coupled with Britain's moral temper, its appreciation of pragmatic and practical moral norms, means that Islam "is the most suitable faith for the British. Its values are our values."[84] This overlap between Islam and British values is summarized by Winter as such:

> Its moderate, undemonstrative style of piety, still waters running deep; its insistence on modesty and a certain reserve, and its insistence on common sense and on pragmatism, combine to furnish the most natural and easy religious option for our people.[85]

On the other hand, "Christianity, formerly a Greek mystery religion advocating a moral code against the natural law, is in fact foreign to our national temperament."[86] The origin of Islam is no more foreign to the British than Christianity; yet its values are more British than those of Christianity.

The Cambridge Muslim College

Tied in to Winter's endeavours to cultivate British Muslim identity is his work at the Cambridge Muslim College. The Cambridge Muslim College (CMC) is dedicated to teaching graduates from British Islamic seminaries, namely the *dār al-ʿulūms*, in order to augment their religious learning with a liberal arts training. The goal is to have these students better understand the realities of contemporary British society so that they can better serve their communities. Moreover, they have started to offer a four-year programme in Islamic Studies starting this year. The goal of this programme is to offer religious education to Muslims living in Britain.

The CMC was established in 2002 by three trustees of the Muslim Academic Trust. These trustees consisted of Yusuf Islam (the famous British convert singer-songwriter Cat Stevens), Shaykh Tijani Gahbiche, and Tim Winter. The CMC has made a slow but steady progression towards their goals. One of its stated goals is to be "a recognised centre of excellence offering a B.A. and M.A. in Islamic Studies, taught by a team of Islamic scholars in conjunction and collaboration with the expertise available at the University of Cambridge."[87]

The CMC's curriculum for their four-year programme is based on the curriculum of the Al Fatih Islamic Institute (*Maʿhad al-Fatiḥ*) in Damascus.[88] Al Fatih was established by the late Syrian scholar Shaykh Muhammad Salih Farfour (d. 1986). It was an outgrowth of Farfour's popular teaching circles that were held in the Umayyad Mosque.[89] The undergraduate department was established in 1971 and consisted of three specializations: Islamic Jurisprudence and its Foundations, Arabic Language and Literature, Sciences of *ḥadīth* and Sciences of the Qurʾān.[90] Al Fatih had established itself as being a stepping-stone towards al-Azhar. Three years of the B.A. programme was to be held at al Fatih but the fourth year was to be held at al-Azhar itself. Thus the al Fatih curriculum was based on al-Azhar's curriculum but with slight modifications: its website describes the curriculum as being "almost the same as al-Azhar University with minor modification to cope with the social and structural differences of modern age [sic]."[91] Initially graduates attained an "official international university degree signed by the head of al-Azhar University," but starting from the 2005 academic year graduates obtained their degrees from the Syrian Minister of High Studies.[92]

While Al Fatih had three departments and allowed for three separate specializations, the CMC has streamlined their curriculum into one general path. The aim of CMC's four-year programme is to teach the fundamentals of the Islamic tradition as a coherent intellectual and spiritual body of knowledge, and to examine the ways that contemporary life might "challenge, reinforce or reshape the Islamic tradition." [93] It is hoped that these graduates will be able to better apply their knowledge and understanding of Islam to contemporary society.[94]

The first year of the programme is to be held at the Qasid Arabic Institute, and this year is dedicated solely to Arabic. The Qasid Arabic Institute, based in Jordan, is one of the leading centres for study of the Arabic language, and it works in conjunction with various universities such as Harvard and Oxford.[95] The subsequent three years cover a variety of topics such as Qur'ān and *ḥadīth* studies, history, theology, and Islamic literature. A more detailed outline curriculum can be found in Table 2.1.

It is still unclear as to how this degree is accredited. The CMC website states that enrolment in the course is dependent upon "completion of an external validation agreement with a major U.K. university."[96] There are no details about this university, and there are no specifics about the type of accreditation. Nonetheless, accreditation does take time and more details will probably be presented in the future. Absent from this curriculum are courses that are focused on British life and contemporary society. The reason for this is that the CMC also offers a Diploma in Contextual Islamic Studies and Leadership. This is their most active degree, and it currently defines CMC's identity. This degree was established over a year-long effort by two Cambridge Ph.D. students, Mujadad Zaman and James (Abdul Aziz) Brown. The curriculum of this degree was an outgrowth of the "non-traditional" segment of the B.A. curriculum. This "non-traditional" segment consisted of courses that would help students better understand contemporary society.[97] In an interview Tim Winter describes the goal of this degree as such:

> Here in the United Kingdom we're blessed with the existence of at least 80 major Islamic intellectual institutions. These are the *dār al-'ulūms*. Miniature Islamic universities that for years now have been turning out a great generation of young scholars. What we have at the Cambridge Muslim College is an opportunity for those graduates to remain fully faithful to what they've learned, to their scholars, to their teachers, to their professors, to their institutions and tradition, while augmenting that by exposing them in a sensitive but profound way to the realities of the modern British society in which they are going to be working.[98]

The curriculum for the Diploma in Contextual Islamic Studies and Leadership has, as the title suggests, a mix of courses that introduce various topics within the liberal arts as well as courses designed to develop leadership skills. The first term consists of courses in British Islam Today, Introduction to the Social Sciences, the U.K. State, World History, World Religions, and Islamic Counselling. The second term consists of courses in Effective Community Leadership, Modern British Political History, Islam and Religious Pluralism, and introductory

Table 2.1 Curriculum of CMC

Year 1	**Description**
Intensive Arabic	Memorisation Requirement: *Juz'* 30
Year 2	**Description**
RF1 – The Revealed Foundations (I): Introduction to the *Qur'ān* and *ḥadīth*	General introduction to *Qur'ānic* and *Ḥadīth* studies. Includes studies on *maṭn* and *isnād* along with *tajwīd*
ID1 – Introduction to Islamic Doctrine: kalam, falsafa and Sufism	General history of *kalām, falsafah* and Sufism. Covers topics such as creation, free will, and the uncreated *Qur'ān*
IH1 – Introduction to Islamic History	Covers the life of the Prophet, general Islamic history to the present and Islam in the Indian Subcontinent
IL1 – Introduction to Islamic Law	Covers jurisprudence (*uṣūl al-fiqh*) along with rulings related to worship, personal status law, marriage and divorce
Year 3	**Description**
RF2 – The Revealed Foundations (II): Further Studies in the *Qur'ān* and *ḥadīth*	Covers a selection of *Qur'ānic* and *ḥadīth* commentators
ID2 – Intermediate Studies in Islamic Doctrine	A study of al-Bayjūrī's commentary on the *Jawharah al-Tawḥīd*
IL2 – Intermediate Studies in Islamic Law	Covers contemporary issues in marriage, divorce and inheritance law as well as *ijtihād* and *iftā'*.
WL1 – Literatures of the Islamic World	A study of various types of Islamic literature including Arabic prose from the medieval period, Sufi poetry, and British Muslim literature
Memorisation Requirement: *Juz'* 28 & *Jawharah al-Tawḥīd*	

Source: Cambridge Muslim College website

courses in Astronomy, Science and Western Intellectual History. The third term covers Islam and Gender, Modern British Intellectual History, Modern Muslim History, Modern Religious Thinkers, Religious Ethics in the Modern World, and Sacred Art and Architecture.

What differentiates this course from a traditional liberal arts course is that it is designed for the graduates of Islamic seminaries. Thus, the courses will usually present material in comparison to Islamic thinkers and concepts that students are already familiar with. For example, the course on Modern Religious Thinkers introduces various Christian religious thinkers and examines "the notion of a public theologian and how it differs from the Islamic classical roles of a scholar."[99] The course on Western Intellectual History presents the main trends of "Western" thought with reference to "the points of convergence and divergence with the intellectual history of Islamic civilisations."[100]

CMC's vision for the M.A. programme, on the other hand, is a two-year part-time research based qualification.[101] The goal of the programme is to train students to "gain research skills necessary to enable them to apply for a Ph.D. in a major university; but the M.A. is also envisaged as a valuable terminal degree in its own right."[102] There is no official statement about when this M.A. programme will begin.

The CMC helps to provide a type of education that it believes can help the graduates from British Islamic seminaries apply their knowledge more effectively to the contemporary British context. It is an extension of the type of curriculum reform movements that have held sway in al-Azhar and various other Islamic institutions of learning. The difference is that the CMC has a specific focus on the British context, where as other Islamic institutions focus on Muslim-majority countries. It remains to be seen what type of effect this approach is having on the students.

Notes

1. "Dr Timothy Winter [Profile]," *University of Cambridge, Faculty of Divinity Website*, accessed July 30, 2015, http://www.divinity.cam.ac.uk/directory/timothy-winter.
2. C.f. Abdal Hakim Murad, *Bombing Without Moonlight: The Origins of Suicidal Terrorism*, (Bristol: Amal Press, 2008).
3. John Alden Williams and Timothy Winter, *Understanding Islam and the Muslims* (Louisville: Fons Vitae, 2002).
4. Joan Bakewell, "Tim Winter," *Belief, Series 4, BBC Radio 3*, December 24, 2009, formerly available at http://www.bbc.co.uk/programmes/b00g42xy. Although this interview was originally conducted by the BBC, it is currently not available on their website. Individual fans of Tim Winter have uploaded the interview online on YouTube: Timothy Winter, "Why I Converted to Islam, Part 1/2" [Audio], *YouTube*, January 27, 2015, accessed November 2, 2016, https://www.youtube.com/watch?v=GGfc6Ob1UAY.

5. John Hick, ed., *The Myth of God Incarnate* (London: SCM Press, 1977).
6. Bakewell, "Tim Winter".
7. Ibid.
8. Ibid.
9. Abdullah bin Hamid Ali, "'Neo-Traditionalism' vs 'Traditionalism'," *Lamppost Education Initiative Website (Home/Answers)*, January 22, 2012, accessed June 30, 2016, http://www.lamppostproductions.com/neo-traditionalism-vs-traditionalism-shaykh-abdullah-bin-hamid-ali/.
10. "What is Scriptural Reasoning?," *Scriptural Reasoning Online*, accessed May 21, 2016, http://www.scripturalreasoning.org/what-is-scriptural-reasoning.
11. Tim Winter, "Qur'ānic Reasoning as an Academic Practice," *Modern Theology* 22 (2006): 449–63 at 454.
12. Ibid., 454.
13. Timothy Winter, "Understanding the Four Madhhabs: The Problem of Anti-Madhhabism," *masud.co.uk (Shaikh Abdal Hakim Murad–Fiqh)*, July 6, 2014, accessed July 31, 2015, http://masud.co.uk/understanding-the-four-madhhabs-the-problem-with-anti-madhhabism/.
14. Ibid.
15. Ibid.
16. Abū 'Abdullāh Muhammad ibn Idrīs al-Shāfi'ī (d. 820/204) is one of the four great Imams in Islamic legal theory. His works led to the development of the Shafi'i school of law.
17. Winter, "Understanding the Four Madhhabs."
18. Ibid.
19. Ibid.
20. Hamza Yusuf, *Vision of Islam* [Audio CD] (Alhambra Publications, 2004).
21. Tim Winter, "Reason as Balance: The Evolution of *'aql*," *CMC Papers* 3 (Cambridge Muslim College, n.d.), accessed April 16, 2016, http://cambridgemuslimcollege.org/download-papers/CMCPapers3-ReasonAsBalance.pdf.
22. Ibid., 1.
23. Ibid., 2.
24. Ibid., 6.
25. Ibid., 7.
26. See, for example, Abu Hamid Muhammad Ghazali, *Al-Ghazali on Disciplining the Soul and on Breaking the Two Desires: Books XXII and XXIII of the Revival of the Religious Sciences*, trans. Timothy J. Winter (Cambridge: Islamic Texts Society, 1995); Abu Hamid Muhammad Ghazali, *Al-Ghazali on the Remembrance of Death and the Afterlife: Book XL of the Revival of the Religious Sciences*, trans. Timothy J. Winter (Cambridge: Islamic Texts Society, 1989); Timothy Winter, "The Life and Works of al-Ghazali (Part 1/2)" [Video], *Matters of Faith, YouTube*, October 15, 2010, accessed November 3, 2016, https://www.youtube.com/watch?v=HMWEggenO3c; Shaikh Abdulhakim Murad Winter, "Master Classes on Imam Al Ghazali – 1" [Video], *Al Ghazali Week 2013, Alqueria de Rosales Andalusia, YouTube*, October 28, 2014, accessed November 3, 2016, https://www.youtube.com/watch?v=8_tQs717ngs.
27. Timothy Winter, "Islamic Spirituality: The Forgotten Revolution," *masud.co.uk (Shaikh Abdal Hakim Murad–Sufism)*, July 6, 2014, accessed August 3, 2015, http://masud.co.uk/islamic-spirituality-the-forgotten-revolution/.

28. Shaykh Abdal Hakim Murad (Dr. Timothy Winter), "Is Orthodox Islam Possible Without Sufism?" [Video], *Sufi World, YouTube*, December 27, 2015, accessed November 3, 2016, https://www.youtube.com/watch?v=uQWNeGyRu0k.
29. Daniel Lav, *Radical Islam and the Revival of Medieval Theology* (Cambridge: Cambridge University Press, 2012), 51.
30. Aaron Spevack, *The Archetypal Sunnī Scholar: Law, Theology, and Mysticism in the Synthesis of Al-Bājūrī* (Albany: State University of New York Press, 2014), 25–6.
31. Winter, "Is Orthodox Islam Possible Without Sufism?".
32. Ibid.
33. Ibid.
34. Ibid.
35. Ibid.
36. Hamza Yusuf, "Men and Women (In Islam)" [Audio], *TheHamzaYusufChannel, YouTube*, August 21, 2012, accessed November 3, 2016, https://www.youtube.com/watch?v=H8PrFABsVcQ.
37. Timothy Winter, "Boys will be Boys: Gender Identity Issues," *masud.co.uk (Shaikh Abdal Hakim Murad–Gender Issues)*, July 6, 2014, accessed January 29, 2015, http://masud.co.uk/boys-will-be-boys-gender-identity-issues/.
38. Ibid.
39. Ibid.
40. Ibid.
41. Ibid.
42. Ibid.
43. Ibid.
44. Ibid.
45. Ibid.
46. Rosemary Radford Ruether, *Sexism and God-Talk: Toward a Feminist Theology* (Boston: Beacon Press, 1993).
47. "Professor Sachiko Murata [Profile]," *Stony Brook University, Department of Asian & Asian American Studies Website*, accessed May 17, 2016, http://www.stonybrook.edu/commcms/asianamerican/facultystaff/SachikoMurata.html.
48. Sachiko Murata, *The Tao of Islam: A Sourcebook on Gender Relationships in Islamic Thought* (Albany: State University of New York Press, 1992), 1.
49. L. Gardet, "al-Asmā' al-Ḥusnā," *EI*².
50. Murata, *Tao of Islam*, 9.
51. Ibid.
52. Timothy Winter, "Islam, Irigaray, and the Retrieval of Gender," *masud.co.uk*, April 1999, accessed June 30, 2016, http://masud.co.uk/ISLAM/ahm/gender.htm.
53. Winter, "Islam, Irigaray, and the Retrieval of Gender."
54. Luce Irigaray, *An Ethics of Sexual Difference* (Cornell, N.Y.: Cornell University Press, 1993).
55. Winter, "Boys will be Boys."
56. Yusuf, "Men And Women (In Islam)."
57. Winter, "Boys will be Boys."
58. Ibid.
59. Ian Gemmell, "Injuries Among Female Army Recruits: A Conflict of Legislation," *Journal of the Royal Society of Medicine* 95 (2002), 23–7.
60. Winter, "Boys will be Boys."

61. Ibid.
62. Robert Trivers, "Parental Investment and Sexual Selection," in *Sexual Selection and the Descent of Man, 1871–1971*, ed. Bernard Grant Campbell (London: Heinemann Educational, 1972), 52–95.
63. Winter, "Boys will be boys."
64. Ibid. Here Winter is referencing Kingsley Browne's summary of Camilla Benbow and David Lubinski's research. See Kingsley Browne, *Divided Labours: An Evolutionary View of Women at Work*. (London: Weidenfeld & Nicolson, 1998).
65. Ibid.
66. Winter attributes this research to Janet Lever although he does not offer citations. See Janet Lever, "Sex Differences in the Games Children Play," *Social Problems* 23 (1976), 478–87.
67. Carol Gilligan, *In a Different Voice: Psychological Theory and Women's Development* (Cambridge, M.A.: Harvard University Press, 1993), xviii.
68. Winter, "Boys will be Boys."
69. Ibid.
70. Ibid.
71. Ibid.
72. Ibid.
73. Nuh Ha Mim Keller, "Evolution and Islam," masud.co.uk July 14, 1995, accessed June 30, 2016, http://www.masud.co.uk/ISLAM/nuh/evolve.htm.
74. Timothy Winter, "British and Muslim?" *masud.co.uk (Shaikh Abdal Hakim Murad–British Muslim Heritage)*, July 2, 2014, accessed May 19, 2016, http://masud.co.uk/ISLAM/ahm/british.htm.
75. Ibid.
76. Ibid.
77. Ibid.
78. Ibid.
79. Ibid.
80. Winter, "British and Muslim?"
81. James R. Jacob, *Henry Stubbe: Radical Protestantism and the Early Enlightenment*. (Cambridge: Cambridge University Press, 1983), 71.
82. Hesketh Pearson, *Bernard Shaw: His Life and Personality* (London: Collins, 1942), 375.
83. Winter, "British and Muslim?"
84. Ibid.
85. Ibid.
86. Ibid.
87. "History," *Cambridge Muslim College Website*, accessed May 19, 2016, http://www.cambridgemuslimcollege.org/about/history/.
88. Ibid.
89. "Welcome to Al Fatih Islamic Institute," *Al Fatih Islamic Institute Website*, accessed May 19, 2016, http://www.alfatihonline.com/en/.
90. Ibid.
91. "The Institute Departments," *Al Fatih Islamic Institute Website*, accessed May 19, 2016, http://www.alfatihonline.com/en/departments.htm.
92. Ibid.
93. "Objective," *Cambridge Muslim College Website*, accessed May 20, 2016, http://www.cambridgemuslimcollege.org/programmes/four-yp/objective/.

94. Ibid.
95. *Qasid Arabic Institute Website*, accessed May 20, 2016, http://www.qasid.com/.
96. "Four-Year Programme," *Cambridge Muslim College Website*, accessed May 20, 2016, http://www.cambridgemuslimcollege.org/programmes/four-yp/.
97. "History," *CMC Website*.
98. "Cambridge Muslim College" [Video] *MishkatMedia*, *YouTube*, accessed May 19, 2016, https://www.youtube.com/watch?v=is8QeocY5AU&feature=youtu.be.
99. "Course Modules," *Cambridge Muslim College Website*, accessed May 19, 2016, http://www.cambridgemuslimcollege.org/programmes/diploma/modules/.
100. Ibid.
101. "History," *CMC Website*.
102. Ibid.

PART II

♦ ♦ ♦

NEO-LEGALISTS

The second part captures another very popular approach among Muslim scholars in the West to reconciling Islam and modernity: shifting their focus to *maqāṣid al-sharīʿah* (principles of *sharīʿah*) rather than to the specifics of particular Islamic legal rulings. In so doing, they emphasize moves towards reconciling the tension between the Western liberal tradition and Islamic law by focusing on the underlying ethical and moral principles shared by both. Chapter 3 focuses on the Institute of Islamic Intellectual Thought (IIIT) operating out of Washington D.C., which has long been an important platform for bringing together many scholars (including Tariq Ramadan) working on operationalizing the concept of *maqāṣid al-sharīʿah*. Chapter 4 looks at the work of Tariq Ramadan and the methodological tools that are being developed under his guidance at the Centre for Islamic Legislation and Ethics (CILE) to answer contemporary questions.

CHAPTER
3

FROM "ISLAMIZATION OF KNOWLEDGE" TO "AMERICAN ISLAM": THE INTERNATIONAL INSTITUTE OF ISLAMIC THOUGHT (IIIT)

Nathan Spannaus

The International Institute of Islamic Thought (IIIT) is an organization built around research and scholarship on Islam suited for the contemporary period. Often called a think tank, IIIT's main activities are publishing, hosting conferences and workshops, and supporting research. It also runs a small educational division called The Fairfax Institute (TFI). These activities lead to IIIT's unique character. Headquartered in suburban Washington, D.C. but with autonomous branch offices around the world, IIIT is quite diffuse as an organization, with a number of figures only loosely associated with it, and its focus is simultaneously local and global. In addition, it does not engage in advocacy or political outreach, making any ideological inclinations difficult to pin down.

IIIT's primary aims are intellectual and religious. It describes itself as "dedicated to the revival and reform of Islamic thought and its methodology in order to enable the Ummah to deal effectively with present challenges, and contribute to the progress of human civilization in ways that will give it a meaning and a direction derived from divine guidance."[1] IIIT presents itself at the forefront of a global movement of Islamic intellectual reform, necessary for adapting Islamic thought to contemporary circumstances. Throughout its history, dating back to its very founding, it has been connected with some of the major contemporary trends in Islamic thought, and the changes in its intellectual orientation over time have mirrored broader shifts globally.

Today, IIIT is at once concerned with "preserving the authenticity of Islamic values in the twenty-first century" and reconciling faith and reason, science and religion, and "establishing peace, prosperity and freedom for all humanity."[2] It intends to accomplish these goals through academic and scholarly endeavors.

Its diffuse character is important in this regard. Without having an explicit orientation beyond promoting the reform of Islamic thought, IIIT is able to maintain a degree of distance from intra-Muslim disputes. This is furthered by IIIT's extensive connections with mainstream academia, which allows for a degree of scholarly objectivity in its activities.

Focusing primarily on the headquarters in Herndon, Virginia, IIIT is engaged in an ambitious project to integrate itself into American academia—current executive director Abubakar Al-Shingieti states that its "goal is to become the primary institution for the scholarly study of Islam"[3]—while leading an effort to reform Islamic thought from within. At the same time, IIIT stands as a prominent institutional representation of Islam in America, a fact its leaders are very conscious of. Its existence as an organization for a controversial religious minority colors IIIT's activities as well as its intellectual orientation, and it plays a significant role in its history.

Founding and History

IIIT was founded in 1981 in Washington, D.C., moving to its current home in nearby Herndon soon after. It was founded by a partnership of Ismail Raji al-Faruqi (1921–86) and AbdulHamid AbuSulayman (1936–), along with Taha Jabir Al-Alwani (1935–2016).[4] These three are the major figures in IIIT's history.

Al-Faruqi was the driving impetus for founding IIIT. A political figure in his native Palestine, he immigrated to the United States in 1948, where he subsequently attained advanced degrees in philosophy and religion from Indiana University and Harvard. Al-Faruqi then spent the years 1954–8 pursuing Islamic Studies at al-Azhar in Cairo. After holding teaching positions in religious studies at McGill University (with Wilfred Cantwell Smith), the Institute of Islamic Research in Karachi (under the leadership of Fazlur Rahman) and Syracuse University, he settled permanently in Philadelphia as professor of religion at Temple University in 1968.[5]

Al-Faruqi was very active both in promoting the study of Islam in American academia and in supporting Muslims' civic participation and organizations. He had helped found the Muslim Students Association (MSA) while a graduate student, and he was instrumental in the 1971 establishment of the Association of Muslim Social Sciences (AMSS), an organization for bringing together Muslim graduates and scholars of Islam and coordinating their academic and religious activities. The AMSS was co-founded with the Saudi AbuSulayman, then an engineering student at the University of Pennsylvania, who provided financial support for the organization.[6]

The AMSS was part of a wave of Islamic-oriented academic organizations arising in the United States following the influx of Muslim immigrants in the 1960s, all of which sought to promote an explicitly Islamic approach to their respective fields. The AMSS was oriented around a project called the

"Islamization of knowledge", an effort by a segment of Muslim academics to support scholarship and research by Muslims and to resist what they saw as pervasive Eurocentrism and epistemological bias in the conventional social sciences. (See below.)

In 1977, the AMSS convened a conference with a number of scholars from the Muslim world in Lugano, Switzerland to address the lack of scientific knowledge among Muslims and widespread shortcomings in their education. Participants included the prominent intellectuals Seyyed Hossein Nasr and Yusuf al-Qaradawi, and al-Faruqi and al-Alwani, an Azhar-educated *faqīh* from Iraq who was at the time teaching in the *sharīʿah* faculty of Muhammad ibn Saud University in Riyadh. A second conference on Muslim education was held in Mecca that year with many of the same attendees. The conferences focused on how best to carry out the Islamization of knowledge as a type of epistemic and educational reform, and one of the main conclusions reached at Lugano was the need to establish an institution devoted to analyzing Muslims' decline and determine the way to remedy the situation: "The participants unanimously agreed that the contemporary crisis of the Ummah was intellectual—a crisis of thought—and that the remedy was to be sought within that framework . . . [T]he Muslim thought process and methodology needed to be given priority in the effort to achieve reform and that a specialized body needed to be established to conduct research into these areas."[7] This led directly to the founding of IIIT four years later.[8]

These origins have played a large role in shaping IIIT's intellectual orientation. The belief that modern sciences as currently constituted are not compatible with an Islamic way of thinking, emphasized very strongly by Al-Faruqi, served as its initial impetus, and IIIT set out to develop scholarship and research that would adapt Western academic disciplines to Islam (in other words, to Islamize them). This was built on the position that Islam is a total, comprehensive way of thinking that is not reflected in modern scholarship, even—or especially—scholarship produced by Muslims, because the fundamental premises of modern scholarship are foreign to Islam. Therefore, these fields must be reformulated based on Islam—to have a "*tawḥīd*ic" orientation.[9] The alternative was a hopelessly divided mindset for Muslims: "the main locus and core of the *Ummah*'s malaise is the prevalent education system" Al-Faruqi writes, in which the consciousness of Muslim youth is "moulded into a caricature of the West". Educational opportunities for Muslims are split between traditional religious schooling, which has little contemporary applicability, and modern sciences that do not align with Islamic sensibilities.[10]

By the 1970s, notions of the "Islamic" and the importance of reasserting Islamic identity had grown in political and cultural force. This has been labeled the global Islamic revival, linked with the post-colonial environment that followed the independence of Muslim countries in Africa, the Middle East, and South and Southeast Asia in the 1950s and 1960s.[11] Numerous new Islamic organizations and politico-religious projects emerged in this period, including both the Islamization of knowledge and IIIT. The latter was linked with the Muslim Student Association of North America, founded in 1963, with several of its leaders extensively involved in the organization. The MSA in turn was connected with the Muslim Brotherhood, and there is a degree of ideological influence from the Brotherhood on the early activities of IIIT.[12] That the Brotherhood had such influence with IIIT is not surprising; their goal of forming an Islamic model for society and governance parallels the Islamization of knowledge as a drive for an Islamic epistemology.[13] Al-Faruqi speaks approvingly of Hasan al-Banna (founder of the Muslim Brotherhood) and his efforts against secularism.[14] Indeed, the conceptual linkage between the Islamist political project and the Islamization of knowledge becomes clear in Arabic, where the term for "Islamization", *islāmīyah*, is closely connected with the common Arabic label for Islamists, *islāmīyīn*. The Islamization of knowledge project was connected with the influence of Brotherhood members in Saudi academia as part of the *Ṣaḥwah* (the "Islamic awakening"), a movement that combined a purist religious orientation with Islamist approaches to society. Muhammad Qutb (1919–2014), the Egyptian Islamist ideologue who became a prominent professor in Saudi Arabia, for instance, wrote a book on the Islamization of the social sciences, and Islamization was pushed by Islamists in fields like economics and psychology as well.[15]

Yusuf al-Qaradawi, the Egyptian intellectual and *muftī* and Brotherhood member, was one of the prominent participants at the early Islamization of knowledge conferences, but the project attracted figures of diverse interests and religious orientations. Seyyid Hossein Nasr, the Iranian academic and longtime professor of Islamic Studies at George Washington University, was another participant, but his background in Islamic mystical philosophy was altogether distinct from any Islamist leanings. Nasr was instead connected with the twentieth-century Perennialist school, led by Frithjof Schuon (1907–98), a Swiss religious thinker who espoused the belief in the unity of all religions.[16] Similarly, the influential Malaysian intellectual Naquib al-Attas, who claims to have coined the term Islamization of knowledge, like Nasr grounds his understanding in Islamic metaphysics as a means of unifying different forms of epistemologies with creation and existence, but, as evidence of the breadth of the movement, the project also includes the British-Asian cultural theorist Ziauddin Sardar, who uses Islamic moral concepts to critique Western imperialistic and ethnocentric paradigms.[17]

The International Institute of Islamic Thought began with a goal of closing the separation between Islam and modern academics, by developing a *tawḥīd*ic methodology for the social sciences in particular, through the support for academic research, conferences and publishing. This was made explicit in the "Institutional Agenda" which lays out IIIT's mission:

- To create awareness in the Ummah of the crisis of ideas. This involves enlightening the Ummah about the place and methodology of the crisis of Islamic thought in the perspective of its cultural and civilizational existence.

- To foster a deeper understanding of the nature of the crisis of ideas in contemporary Islamic thought, its causes, and its solutions.
- To define the critical relationship between the failure of Islamic thought and its methodology; the current absence of the Ummah as a civilization; and its failure to succeed as a free, progressive, and prosperous nation.
- To work toward reviving the ideologies of the Ummah, reinvigorating and gradually redeveloping its methodology, and elucidating its viewpoints and its intimate relationship with original Islamic goals.
- To work for adopting and incorporating comprehensive Islamic methodology in the fields of social sciences and the humanities, as well as to foster and fund scientific studies in actual individual and social life conditions.
- To implement the requisite steps to allow the developing contemporary Islamic culture and methodology to avail themselves of the fountains of Islamic principles and legacy, as well as of modern sciences and knowledge, by making them accessible and digestible to Muslim students.
- To provide help in researching studying, and working on the methodology and its presentation, with a view toward elucidating Islamic concepts and intellectual outlook and toward laying the foundation for the evolution of Islamic social sciences and humanities.
- To prepare the requisite intellectual cadres to broaden the field of Islamization of knowledge through providing stipends for studies, providing academic supervision, and establishing academic programs of Islamic studies in all fields of contemporary social sciences and humanities.[18]

There was the distant goal of establishing a full-fledged university based on this new methodology, but more concrete were the efforts toward producing and distributing textbooks that existing Islamic schools could use to teach modern subjects. Work with the AMSS continued, and *The American Journal of Islamic Social Sciences* (*AJISS*), a peer-reviewed academic journal, was founded by IIIT in 1984 for the purpose of disseminating Muslim scholars' work.[19]

The International Institute of Islamic Thought endeavors underwent a major setback in 1986 with the murder (sometimes labeled "assassination") of Al-Faruqi by Yusuf Ali, an acquaintance affiliated with the Nation of Islam.[20] In the aftermath, AbuSulayman (president of IIIT from 1981 to 1984) took over leadership of the AMSS and the journal *AJISS*, while Al-Alwani assumed the presidency of IIIT. In response to Al-Faruqi's murder, Al-Alwani set about establishing branch offices around the world, in fear that the Islamization of knowledge movement could be wiped out with the deaths of its leaders.[21]

IIIT underwent further change in 1987, after the failure of its conference, co-sponsored and hosted by the University of Khartoum, on the "Methodology of Islamic Thought and Islamization of the Behavioral Sciences." Describing the feeling following the conference, IIIT member (now-president) Jamal Al Barzinji writes:

> It became evident to us that the Muslim *Ummah*, represented by its scholars and intellectuals is not yet ready to make an original contribution to human thought, more specifically in the Behavioral Sciences, based on the *Tawḥīdic* paradigm . . . Further, it became clear that Muslim specialists in the Western disciplines of Social and Behavioral Sciences are not able to present an in-depth evaluation and criticism of their own specialization.[22]

In response, IIIT decided that its goal of adapting academic disciplines to a *tawḥīd*ic perspective was insufficient for addressing the problems of Muslims' education and intellectual vibrancy. Instead, it was determined that a broader, more comprehensive reformulation of Muslim thought was necessary. The development of an entire new way of thinking, a full *tawḥīd*ic episteme, became IIIT's main goal, as described in the new 1989 edition of *Islamization of Knowledge: General Principles and Work Plan*, revised by AbuSulayman from the 1981 original.[23]

IIIT pursued this goal through new publications and smaller workshops of Muslim scholars under Al-Alwani's leadership. AbuSulayman left to become rector of the International Islamic University of Malaysia (IIUM) in 1988, where he sought many of the same intellectual reforms. IIUM has had a very close relationship with IIIT—its founding was also inspired by the 1977 conference in Mecca—and relocating IIIT's headquarters to Kuala Lumpur was seriously considered in 1994.[24]

In 1996, Al-Alwani and his British-Egyptian wife, Professor Mona Abul-Fadl (d. 2008), helped found the School of Islamic and Social Sciences (later the Graduate School of Islamic and Social Sciences [GSISS]) with the goal of furthering the Islamization of knowledge in a formal academic setting and instructing students in this epistemic approach.[25] According to Stenberg, it was oriented toward "reinstitut[ing] the true nature (cultural, intellectual and civilizational) of the *ummah* through the Islamization of the humanities and social sciences . . . If these goals are fulfilled, a rectified methodology of Islamic thought can contribute to the progress of human civilization in general and guide it toward Islamic values and norms."[26]

GSISS offered master's degrees in Islamic Studies and Imam Studies (see below). Though there was considerable overlap between the faculty of GSISS and IIIT members, the two were institutionally and administratively separate.[27] IIIT in this period began to focus less on theoretical issues of the Islamization of knowledge (leaving that largely to GSISS), and more on practical, quotidian matters facing the Muslim community. Family and financial issues became a major point of emphasis, and the majority of the workshops and lectures organized by IIIT at this time addressed these topics.

This is still the case today. After the founding of GSISS, IIIT in Herndon devoted most of its attention to developing a model for Muslim life in America, moving away from the earlier concentration on the Islamization of knowledge. Al-Alwani has in fact criticized the earlier Islamization of knowledge paradigm as too narrowly focused.[28] The bulk of the publishing was carried out by the London branch, which began to serve in some respects as a second headquarters.[29]

The particular focus on the American context became more important after September 11th. Following the attacks, both IIIT and GSISS fell under considerable government scrutiny, with their offices and affiliates' homes raided by the FBI.[30] Subsequently, IIIT has emphasized its American setting to a greater degree than before, having previously presented itself as a primarily international body. A short self-produced video from 2014, for instance, features a segment on the importance of American society, complete with a set of patriotic images, including the Statue of Liberty and Mount Rushmore.[31]

As a part of this effort to focus on a specifically American vision of Islam, IIIT established the Fairfax Institute as an in-house educational institution. In contrast to GSISS, TFI is aimed at instructing members of the local Muslim community in practical knowledge for Muslim life in America. According to Christopher Furlow and Muslih, in the wake of the government investigation GSISS changed its name to Cordoba University and continued its educational mission, and TFI is an entirely separate institution officially under the umbrella of IIIT.[32] (Cordoba University's operations appear to have ceased; its two listed websites are currently non-existent.)

Moving away from Islamization of knowledge, IIIT today is focused upon crafting a "methodology" for Islam in America, an aspect which is strongly emphasized. IIIT's website lists five objectives, four of which are explicitly oriented toward this goal:

1. [To] serve as a think tank in the field of Islamic education, culture and knowledge.
2. *Formulate a comprehensive Islamic vision and methodology* that will help Muslim scholars in their critical analysis of contemporary knowledge.
3. *Develop an appropriate methodology* for understanding the Qur'an and Sunnah of the Prophet.
4. *Develop an appropriate methodology* for dealing with Islamic legacy and contemporary knowledge, in order to draw on the experiences of both past and present, to build a better future for the Ummah and humanity at large.
5. *Develop an appropriate methodology* for understanding and dealing with the present situation of both the Ummah and the world in general, and the field of education in particular, in view of contemporary challenges and opportunities.[33]

The development of this methodology is intended specifically "to bridge the intellectual divide between the Islamic tradition and Western civilization." Through this, "IIIT endeavors to promote moderation, inter-faith dialog and good citizenship."[34] In addition to the classes offered at TFI, IIIT remains active as a think tank, supporting Muslim scholars' research, connecting with academic institutions, organizing conferences and workshops, and disseminating Islamic learning through classes, lectures and publishing.

It is their publishing activities that are most important to understanding IIIT's standing and significance among Muslims. Unlike the conferences and lectures, which are only seen by small numbers of people even when recorded (most videos posted online receive a few hundred views), IIIT's publications are the primary vehicle for spreading its message and associated research. In addition to the articles in *AJISS* and its sister Arabic-language journal, *Islāmīyat al-Ma'rifah*, IIIT has published hundreds of books in English and Arabic, a significant number of which have been translated into some 20 other languages.[35]

Publishing also plays a large role in IIIT's connections with other organizations and individual scholars. IIIT has formed partnerships with institutions around the world to organize conferences and co-publish books.[36] In addition, IIIT will often form publishing agreements with affiliated scholars (or use a publishing agreement to affiliate a scholar to them). For instance, recipients of IIIT's research grants are obliged to publish the results of their research through IIIT, either in book form or in one of the journals.[37]

Intellectual Orientation

Despite the basic function of IIIT having changed little since its founding, its intellectual orientation has undergone considerable shifts over its 30-year history. There is a single trajectory to this development, however, and it is possible to trace the evolution of IIIT's outlook. This history can be divided into two phases: the first, beginning with its establishment by Al-Faruqi, AbuSulayman and Al-Alwani, revolved around the Islamization of knowledge project. As the project changed and the approach to Islamization of knowledge evolved, a new focus on the practical began to emerge in the mid-1990s (as noted above). During this phase the Islamization of knowledge gradually diminished in importance and was largely abandoned in favor of finding new ways to apply Islamic knowledge in daily life. This second phase is focused on "methodology", specifically the methodology for Islam in American/Western society, and the ways in which it can be brought to bear on practical matters.

Despite this shift, a major aim from IIIT's founding can still be seen in its orientation: the notion that Islam can, or must, remain dynamic and vibrant in Muslims' thought process. At the point of its establishment its founders bemoaned:

> . . . the current estrangement between the Ummah and its legacy—a rift that has turned Islam's great achievements into merely historical ones—mere fossils of a bygone age, recalled, if at all, to muster nostalgic feelings or an intellectual sense of pride. The legacy of Islam, to many, no longer presents the basis for dynamic creativity.[38]

This, it was argued, was the source of Muslims' intellectual shortcomings, and IIIT was started to revive not only knowledge of the past glories of Islamic scholarship, but also—and I would say much more importantly—to restore dynamic creativity to Islamic thought, to make it benefit Muslims in their current circumstances, as it had in the past. This is still the goal of IIIT, and its importance to the founders is clear in the original "Institutional Agenda", quoted above.

Beyond the main goals and orientation, however, it's difficult to attribute specific views to IIIT. Its diffuse nature as an organization certainly plays a role; while a handful of figures are directly affiliated, either as board members or administrators, many associated individuals have a far more tenuous connection. Published authors, invited speakers or visiting scholars do not necessarily conform to any particular intellectual model. For instance, IIIT awards grants to researchers whose work focuses on the *maqāṣid al-sharīʿah*, minority *fiqh*, educational reform or social sciences with Islamic epistemologies, but otherwise, scholars appear free to pursue these subjects however they choose.[39] IIIT seems to allow considerable space for disagreement within these overall goals; Imad al Din Khalil, in his *Islamization of Knowledge: A Methodology*, for example, classifies the natural sciences as morally neutral, and therefore beyond the scope of the Islamization project, something Al-Faruqi would reject.[40]

Nevertheless, IIIT is very strongly oriented around its goals, and it is not so diffuse as to be incoherent. The best indication of its intellectual stance is through its published works, largely the writings of its central figures and major books by outside authors. The room for debate fostered by IIIT in its conferences and classrooms is far less visible in its publications. Moreover, many of IIIT's publications are derivative works, further enhancing their coherence: a significant proportion of its books are translations, re-editions, abridgments or collections of earlier publications. In addition, many works are relatively repetitive, restating—though often expanding upon—arguments made before (particularly in the case of the early figures affiliated with IIIT). For instance, al-Alwani's short book *Ijtihad* was published in 1993, based on two articles he had written in 1991 for *AJISS*. Those articles were then included verbatim in his *Issues in Contemporary Islamic Thought*, published by IIIT in 2005, which was translated into Turkish in 2006.

Alongside the two major goals of Islamization of knowledge and methodology, there are a smaller number of IIIT publications devoted to specifically religious themes (guides to the Qur'ān and *ḥadīth*, the Islamic calendar, comparative religion) and to historical aspects of Islamic civilization. In total, these two kinds of books collectively make up probably less than 10 per cent of all of IIIT's titles. The former are unremarkable, but the latter are interesting for the light they shed on IIIT's view of the Islamic past. Many authors decry the lack of knowledge that contemporary Muslims have of their intellectual and cultural heritage, which they attribute to the broad failures of Muslim education and thought.[41] These works seemed to be aimed at correcting this through focusing on aspects of Islamic history; but apart from an isolated academic study,[42] these works belie an apologetic approach, arguing for the global importance of Islamic history in the face of Eurocentrism. This is most apparent in *Studies in Islamic Civilization: the Muslim Contribution to the Renaissance*, a monograph that recites the well-established narrative of Muslims preserving Greek knowledge and transmitting it, along with Persian and Indian science and technology, back to Europe in the Dark Ages.[43] Though the apologetic slant is not surprising in a book on this topic, it also shows up in other works where its presence and function is less obvious. For instance, Jasser Auda, in his major work on *maqāṣid al-sharīʿah*, includes as an aside the contention that Islamic philosophy "paved the way for renaissance [*sic*] and modernist philosophy" in Europe.[44]

This apologetic stance begins to make more sense in light of IIIT's initial purpose, the Islamization of knowledge, which seeks to maintain the validity and applicability of Islamically-derived knowledge in the face of modern Western epistemes' predominance. As such, the assertion that those Western epistemes were themselves reliant upon previous forms of Islamic knowledge serves to justify their would-be Islamization.[45]

Islamization of Knowledge

The notion underlying the Islamization of knowledge is unity. This is the foundation for the *tawḥīd*ic episteme, Al-Faruqi writes, which brings the unification of all types of knowledge in order to understand "the telic nature of creation" and to serve the Ummah. The Islamization of knowledge thus represents a unity of epistemology and purpose, reflecting the fundamental unity of God. Knowledge is intended to comprehend the nature of all of God's creation to serve humanity. All disciplines and fields are therefore simply different expressions of the same singular field of knowledge. Unlike in modern sciences, where each field has its own paradigm and conventions, geology, psychology, political science and history are all part of the same discipline, based on the same premises, studying the same subject—creation. This is the *tawḥīd*ic episteme.[46]

The use of the term "episteme" is significant here. It's commonly used in modern philosophy and critical theory to signify whole systems of knowledge—e.g. the scientific episteme, the overarching paradigm for the natural sciences—and its use for the Islamization of knowledge speaks to the project's ambitions, to forge an epistemic frame that rivals, if not surpasses, modern Western thought. As Al-Alwani writes in 1991, "What is needed is the erection of an Islamic methodology which can replace its Western counterpart. This is no easy undertaking, for it involves establishing a unique framework of knowledge."[47]

Al-Faruqi was at the forefront of the formulation of the *tawḥīd*ic episteme. Interestingly, he produced two English translations of works on *tawḥīd* by Muḥammad ibn ʿAbd al-Wahhāb around the time IIIT was founded, and there are some similarities between the Wahhabi conception of *tawḥīd* and al-Faruqi's *tawḥīd*ic episteme.[48] For ibn 'Abd al-Wahhāb, *tawḥīd* entailed not simply monotheism, but absolute unity of worship, belief, purpose and action. For a Muslim to act in an immoral way, to commit misdeeds, was not merely a moral failing, but a reflection of a failing in their belief in God, a sign that their adherence, their worship was not oriented solely to God (if it had been, they would not have committed the misdeed), therefore they are guilty of a type of polytheism (what ibn 'Abd al-Wahhāb calls "lesser *shirk*").[49]

Al-Faruqi does not go so far as to declare modern sciences polytheism, but the difference between ibn 'Abd al-Wahhāb's unity of belief and action and the unity of knowledge and purpose that underlies the *tawḥīd*ic episteme is one of degree.[50] One of the major objections that Al-Faruqi puts forward to modern sciences is their lack of moral grounding; their basis in materialist positivism places the emphasis on what *can* be done, rather than what *should* be done. They are not oriented toward any moral aim, and in fact can work at cross-purposes to each other. The *tawḥīd*ic episteme, by contrast, orients the production of knowledge and its application toward a single moral purpose.

Within IIIT's approach to the Islamization of knowledge, the principle of unity underpins everything. There are not multiple, separate fields, but rather the same episteme focused on different topics. As a result, interdisciplinary distinctions lose their significance. This is not a problem, as everything is part of creation, which is itself based on *tawḥīd*. The *tawḥīd*ic episteme, as the type of knowledge suited to understanding *tawḥīd*, is thus the best way to approach any subject. By extension, the Qur'ān, as the perfect source of knowledge about *tawḥīd*, is useful in understanding myriad subjects, including finance, sociology, nutrition, computer science and geology.[51] Although the Qur'ān's contribution to these subjects is described as a form of "guidance" [*hidāyah*] rather than scientific, strictly speaking, it is noted that any scientific fact will not/cannot contradict the Qur'ān.[52]

Again paralleling ibn 'Abd al-Wahhāb, al-Faruqi believed that this paradigm of unity underpinned—or should underpin—all aspects of Muslims' lives and Islamic society. He saw a totality encompassing the entire Ummah's knowledge, purpose and actions.[53] He viewed Islamic behavior as necessary for an Islamic society, and he believed that secularism disrupts the natural unity between religion and politics. He blamed secularism for Muslims' decline, and he also believed that Muslims in America should actively engage Americans in order to spread Islam.[54]

These concerns were largely secondary, however, to the Islamization of knowledge project, which focused on "thought, ideology and a normative and ideational human pattern—and how such a pattern, its constituents, its roots in reason, psyche, and conscience may be built."[55] In order to develop the *tawḥīd*ic episteme, the advancements and contributions of the modern sciences would have to be understood, mastered, and then adapted into an Islamic framework. This was the goal of the Western Thought Project, an effort begun by Al-Faruqi shortly before his death to compile the most important scholarship in the major disciplines (primarily the social sciences and philosophy) so that an advanced, Islamized version of each field could be shaped as part of the eventual formation of the *tawḥīd*ic episteme.[56]

Islamized social science research had been one of the goals behind the founding of *AJISS*, and it was determined that common discourse with Western sciences was an obvious necessity for any intellectual project.[57] After Al-Faruqi's death, this was taken up by Mona Abul-Fadl, who strove through the late 1980s and 1990s to craft a cultural hermeneutic for the *tawḥīd*ic episteme. An expert in critical and political theory, Abul-Fadl focused on discourse for the *tawḥīd*ic episteme as a critique of modern epistemology.[58] She writes in her monograph *East Meets West*:

> It has been the practice for the dominant paradigm to set the terms of rational discourse and for the "Other" to defer in reverence—if it wanted to be admitted to the circle of respectability. In this case, the tables are turned and the dominant paradigm, which is secularist, is viewed critically through the lens of a re-emerging *tawḥīdi* paradigm.[59]

The goal, as before, was the formulation of truly Islamized disciplines, wherein Islam served as a comprehensive intellectual system on a par with the Western systems of liberalism and socialism. It was at this time that Akbar Ahmed published his work on Islamic anthropology, as an attempt to Islamize humanities theory.[60]

For Abul-Fadl, however, the purpose of the *tawḥīd*ic episteme was not merely to relativize Western epistemology, to resist its claims to universalism by rendering it culturally specific. Rather, she saw the true goal of the Islamization of knowledge project as superseding the Western paradigm with the *tawḥīd*ic episteme, which is itself truly universal and not subject to shifts in culture.[61]

This approach to Islamization was not unanimously shared within IIIT, however. Most notably, Al-Alwani took a broader, more ecumenical approach to the Islamization of knowledge project. He considered the focus on the specifically Islamic as opposition to the Western to be too narrow. He argued instead for an identification of *tawḥīd* with monotheism, thus allowing for the inclusion of Christian and Jewish approaches within the Islamization perspective.[62] Abul-Fadl, for her part, believed that Western approaches that benefit humanity—as a Qur'ānic principle—could be incorporated into the *tawḥīd*ic episteme, but this was obviously a matter of subordinating the former to the latter—i.e., the contributions of Western sciences are valid only insofar as they conform to Qur'ānic principles.[63]

Al-Alwani's approach is evinced in a 1997 article linking *ijtihād* and economics, in which he argues that mainstream economics is incorrect in assuming that economic theories are morally neutral, and that Muslims must utilize the advancements of economics to craft an Islamized approach to economic policy that is underpinned by Islamic values and morality. (Such an approach, he notes, cannot simply omit interest.) But in making these arguments, al-Alwani cites Frithjof Schuon as the source for his claims about the necessity of a spiritual and moral foundation for economics. Thus, although the presentation of Al-Alwani's argument is indeed couched in Islamic terminology—*ijtihād* is the interpretive method by which he believes economics should be brought in line with Islamic principles—the very moral premises for the argument are broadly religious, rather than specifically Islamic.[64] Interestingly, Schuon, as noted above, was a major influence on Seyyed Hossein Nasr, who taught courses in the late 1990s at GSISS and was actively engaged in debates over the Islamization of knowledge.[65]

In addition to showing the contours of al-Alwani's position on the *tawḥīd*ic episteme, this article also shows many of the shortcomings of the Islamization of knowledge project. Al-Alwani's claim that conventional economic theory ignores moral concerns is stated in some detail, as is his contention that *ijtihād* is needed as a way of interpreting both the Qur'ānic message and economic theory in order to create a new, Islamized approach to economics. In fact, he writes that adopting Marxist economics is simply another form of *taqlīd*.[66] In the end, al-Alwani states that capital markets that are not based on interest are Islamically acceptable, and he lists a handful of common business practices that he says are Islamically invalid.[67]

These statements, however, are given as disjointed pronouncements (not dissimilar from *fatwā*s) that lack any specific explanation of his reasoning and, more importantly, any discussion of specifically *economic* principles or theories that could be considered Islamic. In essence, what al-Alwani provides in this article is a detailed justification for why, from an Islamic point of view, an approach to economics based on a moral framework is necessary (and currently non-existent).[68] The framework itself, however, is missing; what the article offers instead is a critique of mainstream economics from a religious standpoint, followed by a description of common economic practices that are illegitimate from that perspective. Yet the underlying economics are unchanged.

This in a nutshell is the main problem with the Islamization of knowledge project. The development of a new epistemological paradigm that would not only incorporate all knowledge disciplines, but also rival (if not supplant) the existing paradigm(s) is an immense undertaking. To their credit, al-Faruqi, AbuSulayman, al-Alwani and Abul-Fadl articulated specific goals and formulated a serious critique of modern sciences. Unfortunately, such a project proved far too ambitious, and, despite the goals put forward, the end product was much too vague or scattered to serve as fully formed epistemology of any kind.[69]

Nevertheless, out of the research that contributed to the Islamization of knowledge emerged new understandings of the relationship between Islamic morality and ethics and Western modes of thinking and organization. As we see in al-Alwani's article, the lack of an overarching *tawḥīd*ic framework does not preclude issuing practical advice for Muslims that is based in some manner on Islamic principles. Given the failure of the Islamization of knowledge project, these contributions proved much more viable, and they gradually became the main focus of IIIT and its associated research.

A Methodology for Contemporary Islam

The move toward the practical began in the late 1990s, and it was definitively completed following the disruptions of the post-September 11th period. The shift was significant; if Al-Faruqi dominated IIIT in its earlier era, Al-Alwani laid out the approach for the later. Unlike Al-Faruqi's totalizing approach to the *tawḥīd*ic episteme, Al-Alwani views the Islamization of knowledge more in terms of a synthesis, wherein multiple paradigms of thought—relevant Western sciences, the universal message of Islam, and historical paradigms from the Islamic past—are brought together to serve the ends of sound research and study. This, Al-Alwani argues, represents the *tawḥīd*ic episteme, as all of these different paradigms can be used to further the goals of humanity as determined by God.[70]

As shown in the discussion of economics above, al-Alwani's later approach is decidedly pragmatic. His view of the Islamization of knowledge is concerned primarily with finding ways for morally grounded behavior to flourish in an environment where questions of morality and purpose are largely ignored. Islamization of knowledge is thus necessarily a kind of *ijtihād*, used for determining the methodology for being Muslim in contemporary times. As the Islamization of knowledge project strove for new ways of thinking, it ran counter to *taqlīd*, as al-Alwani—and others at IIIT—frequently characterized the adoption of older forms of Islamic thought or Western types of knowledge.

If earlier efforts toward the Islamization of knowledge were aimed at how Muslims should think and learn as part of modern society, al-Alwani's emphasis on *ijtihād* was aimed at how Muslims should act as part of modern society. As with epistemology, this required novel approaches. Comparing today with Muhammad's time, al-Alwani writes, "Obviously that reality differed considerably from that in which we live at the present. It is this realization that leads us to construct a methodology based on how the Prophet applied the teachings of revelation to real situations, rather than one based in imitation springing from deference or *taqlīd*."[71]

The practical goal then was a methodology for determining moral action for Muslims adapted to the circumstances in which they currently find themselves. Replacing the Islamization of knowledge project, the development of this methodology became IIITs primary focal point (as noted in their present mission statement, quoted above). For al-Alwani, the first part—determining moral action—was of course the essence of *fiqh* throughout history. But it was the second part—adapted to current circumstances—that was most important, and also what al-Alwani saw as a severe shortcoming in existing Islamic institutions, highlighting the "failure of many contemporary *fuqahā'* to provide workable solutions to contemporary problems, due to their incomplete understanding of the issues or their inability to fully realize the significance of their premises and predicates."[72] Muslims have a dire need for a workable model of the Islamic that was suited to modernity, Western Muslims in particular. A *faqīh*, then, has to be aware not only of *fiqh*, but also needs knowledge of how modern society operates. Therefore, al-Alwani states that the modern *faqīh* is a "social scientist" who must work in concert with all others types of social scientists to serve the *Ummah*'s current needs.[73] Here some influence of Islamization of knowledge remains.

But this methodology was still a type of *ijtihād*—interpretation, in other words—and it needed a hermeneutical strategy through which the sources of revelation could be understood. The strategy that al-Alwani seized on is the *maqāṣid al-sharīʿah*, a long-established but relatively marginal aspect of Islamic legal theory. The *maqāṣid al-sharīʿah* are the principles or objectives of the *sharīʿah*, the fundamental aims toward which the divinely mandated law is oriented, such as human flourishing, protection of property and family, peace and justice. For al-Alwani, the *maqāṣid* are three: "*tawḥīd* (the absolute unity of God and acknowledgment that God is the Absolute), *tazkiyah* (purification from evil), and *ʿumrān* (building of civilization to accomplish the good)."[74] These broad principles are the standard by which any type of Islamic action must be validated. That which violates any of these three objectives is illegitimate, and that which upholds and furthers them should be pursued.

Al-Alwani considers the *maqāṣid* the key to developing the necessary methodology for contemporary Islamic morality. Their flexibility and lack of connection with conventional pre-modern *fiqh* are important attributes. Speaking of the utility of older legal rulings, he notes that "Old solutions in new guises are still old solutions and will never bring about the sort of reform that is needed, or serve the higher purposes of Islam's universal message." Instead, Muslims must find a relationship with the Islamic legal tradition that is based on rational aims (i.e., confirming the *maqāṣid*) as opposed to outright rejection, total acceptance, or arbitrary borrowing.[75]

While using the past legal tradition as an inspiration, al-Alwani argues for a wholly new approach for Muslims living in the West, part of *fiqh al-aqallīyāt* (*fiqh* of minorities). This approach rethinks *fiqh* on a fundamental scale, based on the *maqāṣid*. *Muftī*s and *faqīh*s should broadly interpret them to provide flexibility, making the *sharīʿah* suitable and functional for Muslims in non-Muslim societies. Along these lines, al-Alwani argues that legal scholars should consult with other specialists in order fully to understand the circumstances and significance of the issues at work: "For example, a question regarding economics could be dealt with jointly by an economist, a legal expert, and a religious jurist, each dealing with the subject from his/her specialist angle."[76]

The end result of this approach to *fiqh* is similar to al-Alwani's work on finance and economics. Unlike the Islamization of knowledge, the aim is not a new, Islamized way of understanding these endeavors, but rather practical guidance for engaging in them in a morally Islamic way. Thus, the goal for finance is not solely monetary gain, but monetary gain (which in itself conforms to the principle of *'umrān*) that is used for moral purposes and not attained through immoral—even if legal—means.

The *maqāṣid* represent a major aspect of IIIT's drive for a methodology for understanding contemporary Islam. Since the early 2000s, IIIT has convened a number of conferences and workshops focusing on the *maqāṣid* and has launched a book series devoted to the subject (to say nothing of additional, related titles). These works include translations of older *fiqh* texts on the *maqāṣid*, as well as newer studies analyzing them and applying them in the contemporary context. In terms of the latter, there is Muhammad Umer Chapra's *The Islamic Vision of Development in the Light of Maqāṣid al-Sharī'ah*, which applies the theory of the *maqāṣid* to the subject of economic activity. In contrast to Al-Alwani, Muhammad Chapra puts forward a number of *maqāṣid*, arranged into a hierarchy, with the most fundamental, human wellbeing, at the top. Secondary is faith, to which posterity, intellect and wealth are subordinated.[77] As such, wealth and its accumulation must serve faith and, by extension, human wellbeing in order to conform to the *sharī'ah*. Wealth is not an end in itself, but rather:

> a trust form [*sic*] God and needs to be developed and used honestly and conscientiously for removing poverty, fulfilling the needs of all, making life as comfortable as possible for everyone, and promoting equitable distribution of income and wealth. Its acquisition as well as use need to be primarily for the purpose of realizing the *maqāṣid*.[78]

A more theoretical view of the *maqāṣid* has been put forward by Jasser Auda, previously a researcher associated with IIIT London and the Qatar Foundation. Auda's understanding of the *maqāṣid* is much more structured than al-Alwani's, and it takes its contours from pre-modern *fiqh* discussions. Auda separates the *maqāṣid* into necessities and needs, with the former subordinate to the latter (somewhat similar to Chapra). For example, protection of lineage is a necessity, while marriage is a need. Islamic morality upholds both as good, but marriage is less important in that it is a means of protecting lineage. Thus, as long as lineage is protected, there can be some flexibility in terms of marriage. This is where the adaptability of the *maqāṣid* theory is expressed; necessities are far more fundamental (and broad) than needs—some scholars label them ends and means, to reflect this hierarchy—and as such, necessities are universal and unchanging. Needs, however, can vary, rendering them historically and culturally contingent. Needs must change with the times, and this is legitimate as long as they continue to uphold the necessities.[79]

Unlike al-Alwani, who views the *maqāṣid* as a broad moral framework, Auda relates them to very technical aspects of legal theory (*uṣūl al-fiqh*). He advocates applying the *maqāṣid* theory as a way of dealing with conflicting scriptural evidence in legal reasoning, which is a major issue in the history of Islamic law. Instead of weighing varying pieces of evidence according to different textual, hermeneutical or derivative criteria, as is the case in classical *fiqh*, Auda also argues for viewing the evidence through the lens of the different types of *maqāṣid*. Such an approach, he contends, is more comprehensive, allowing for a wider range of scriptural evidence to be incorporated into legal reasoning.[80]

Auda's "*maqāṣidi* approach" to *fiqh* is unusual. Most applications of *maqāṣid* theory are overwhelmingly pragmatic in nature. In its flexibility and adaptability to different situations, the theory of the *maqāṣid* is used to formulate Islamic ways to be modern and to justify the capability of Islam and Islamic morality with capitalist modernity. Currently, it forms the basis for a number of approaches to Islamic finance, banking, business and development.[81] Not coincidentally, it has become prominent in the last two decades in financial centers, particularly Doha, where Auda, Tariq Ramadan and Yusuf al-Qaradawi all have adopted *maqāṣid* theory to different degrees.[82] It similarly receives considerable attention in Malaysia, and Mohammed Hashim Kamali, a retired scholar at IIUM, has published a guide to *maqāṣid* with IIIT.[83]

Educational Activities

The shift away from the ambitious theoretical work of the Islamization of knowledge to the search for a more practical methodology of Muslim life was mirrored by the evolution of IIIT's ventures in education. GSISS was founded in 1996 with the express purpose of putting the principles of the Islamization of knowledge project into action in a formal academic setting. As noted, it began by offering master's degrees in Islamic Studies and Imam Studies, with the intention of adding further Islamized subject matter.[84] Ultimately, the goal was the development of a mainstream educational institution that was integrated into American academia, teaching common humanities and social sciences subjects from an Islamic perspective.[85] This was long a dream of al-Faruqi, who was himself involved in the founding of the American Islamic College in Chicago in 1983, serving as its first president.[86] The Imam Studies programme was not originally planned, but was suggested by the American Muslim Council and Fiqh Council of North America, who were attempting to address the lack of qualified Muslim chaplains for the U.S. military. GSISS became an official training center for military clergy, and the Imam Studies programme attracted a significant proportion of the students and the majority of attention. GSISS quickly became known—to al-Alwani's dismay—as primarily an Islamic seminary (even according to some of its own students). Other organizations came forward looking for trained *imāms* and chaplains, making the programme one of the most important sources of Muslim clergy in the country.[87]

The Fairfax Institute was founded as part of IIIT's reorientation in the post-September 11th period, more in line with the goal of crafting ways for

Muslims to understand how to live in American/Western society. It works very closely with IIIT, and many of its teachers are associated scholars. IIIT also provides the academic approach, which aligns with the kinds of research and publications it supports. According to IIIT, the main purpose of TFI is community outreach, and it offers a combination of public lectures, formal academic programmes and night classes. In addition to Arabic and calligraphy, it offers courses on subjects such as Islamic banking and finance and Islamic management. The courses focus on practical aspects, reflecting IIIT's shift away from the theoretical to people's day-to-day concerns.[88] Likewise, TFI provides training in religious subjects for teachers in Islamic schools and certificate programmes for *imāms* and Muslim chaplains.

The connection with the U.S. military was revoked following the federal investigation, but TFI currently has an educational relationship with Hartford Seminary in Connecticut, the only accredited Muslim chaplaincy programme in the country, and in 2013 IIIT gave a $1 million donation for the creation of an endowed chair there in Islamic chaplaincy.[89] While TFI remains quite different from a full-fledged college (as well as from GSISS), connections with local, mainstream universities have been made, including a credit transfer programme with nearby Shenandoah University. The Fairfax Institute also has links with foreign universities, namely the University of Science and Technology in Yemen and Huron University College in Canada.[90]

Global Networks and Connections

Many of the relationships between IIIT and academic institutions are in fact personal, rather than institutional. Because its activities are so diffuse, many people are connected with IIIT—giving lectures there, participating in workshops, contributing publications—while maintaining a primary affiliation and engaging with other organizations elsewhere. In some instances, this leads to formal relationships, as in the case of Hartford Seminary, or looser connections. An example of the latter is with Tariq Ramadan's Center for Islamic Legislation and Ethics (CILE), a think tank headquartered in Qatar (see Chapter 4). It has no official relationship with IIIT, but Ramadan himself has been an active participant in IIIT-sponsored activities, going so far as to endorse IIIT in its 2014 self-produced introductory video.[91] And Auda, formerly deputy director of CILE, is, as noted, associated with IIIT in London.

Al-Alwani had similar connections. Living in Egypt from the late-2000s until his death in 2016, he served on different *fiqh* bodies around the world, including the International Fiqh Council in Jeddah (through which he was affiliated with the Organization of Islamic Conferences) and the European Council for Fatwa and Research in Dublin. Yusuf al-Qaradawi is a central participant in both of these organizations, and he and al-Alwani worked closely together on projects related to *fiqh al-aqallīyāt*. Similarly, al-Alwani was a member of the Fiqh Council of North America, which is part of the

Islamic Society of North America (ISNA). Despite his participation in these *fiqh* bodies, al-Alwani did not consider himself a *muftī*, and he did not issue *fatwās*. Rather, he passed the questions he received along to *muftīs* (including, at times, al-Qaradawi) and would comment on the responses they gave. Al-Alwani was also associated with Iranian organizations in the 1980s, as a member of the World Forum for the Proximity of Islamic Schools of Thought (headquartered in Tehran) and published articles in the Iranian journal *Majallat Qaḍāyā Islāmīyah*.[92]

The current executive director of IIIT, the Sudanese Abubaker al Shingieti, has similarly worked with a number of different Islamic organizations. A former official in the Sudanese government, al Shingieti has been a member of the Society for Islamic Thought and Culture in Khartoum, and he is prominently involved (as many IIIT affiliates have been) in the group American Muslims for Constructive Engagement (AMCE), and he is the vice-president of the International Center for Religion and Diplomacy.[93]

In addition to these personal connections, IIIT does have long-standing relationships with a number of Islamic institutions in America, primarily the group of organizations founded in the late 1970s and early 1980s for American Muslims that grew out of the Muslim Student Association, in which al-Faruqi had been a central figure. These include IIIT and AMSS, as well as ISNA. ISNA became the umbrella organization for Muslim groups, with the AMSS and MSA coming under its administration. IIIT, ISNA and ISNA's financial wing, the North American Islamic Trust (NAIT) have long had a continually close (but bureaucratically separate) relationship.[94]

As noted, this group of Islamic organizations has distant ties to the Muslim Brotherhood, with many of their early founders being members, before coming to the United States. While the Muslim Brotherhood's influence was limited in scope, IIIT's potential link with them, as well as Hamas, has attracted intense government scrutiny. Much of this attention came as a result of the investigation into the Holy Land Foundation, a Texas-based Islamic charity accused of funneling money to Hamas. During this investigation, the government discovered a 1991 memo written by a high-ranking member of the Egyptian Muslim Brotherhood that names IIIT among the Brotherhood's potential "friends" in North America. Though never charged with any wrongdoing—it was labeled an "unindicted co-conspirator" in the 2007–2008 Holy Land Foundation trial—controversy surrounding IIIT remains, and it is a constant subject of speculation about potential ties to terrorist organizations.[95]

A number of sources contend that IIIT is—or has been—funded by either the Muslim Brotherhood or the Saudi government, but there seems to be little evidence for this. In fact, much of IIIT's funding appears to be piecemeal, with support coming from various sources on a temporary basis. For instance, GSISS was founded thanks to a one-time $5 million donation from the Kuwaiti government.[96] Many projects are coordinated with other organizations, allowing for outside funding. IIIT has co-sponsored conferences with institutions like al-Azhar University and IIUM, which receive financial support from their respective governments. Similarly, in 2008 AMCE began a small publishing project with IIIT that was funded by a grant from the Saudi-based Kingdom Foundation.[97]

According to IIIT, it is supported by a "*waqf*", though it does not say where its endowment comes from.[98] IIIT has worked with the World Congress of Muslim Philanthropists, but it does not actively seek donations.[99] In its early years, IIIT's operations were funded by the members themselves; according to Furlow, its first headquarters were a house in Herndon purchased by two members, Hisham al-Talib and Jamal al Barzinji.[100]

Position in the American Context

One result of the scrutiny aimed at IIIT has been a greater focus on its activities as part of the American setting. In the first decade of IIIT's existence, it was primarily an international organization, with an emphasis on the global scope of the Islamization of knowledge project. Any consideration for the American environment specifically was secondary. For instance, in 1986 al-Faruqi wrote a guide to "Islamic English", in which he develops an English vocabulary for Islamic terminology to avoid misrepresentations. While such a work has obvious importance for American Muslims, al-Faruqi explicitly presents it as directed toward a global audience.[101] He authored a German version shortly after.[102] Certain activities, such as IIIT's close relationship with ISNA or the chaplaincy programme, were particularly focused on (North) American Muslims, but these caused some difficulty for IIIT's global self-presentation. In fact, the description of the chaplaincy programme in GSISS English-language materials was far more prominent than in Arabic-language versions, where it was downplayed.[103]

The major emphasis on IIIT's location in America was used to further its international aims. It presented itself and the Islamization of knowledge project within America as free from interference or control by any Islamic government, and outside the political and religious tensions of the Islamic world.[104] The American environment held some importance, to be sure, but it was decidedly secondary to IIIT's international scope.

This focus changed after September 11th and the subsequent investigations into its operations. The investigations into IIIT were built around its possible overseas connections, and in the aftermath its place as an *American* Islamic institution became a much greater part of its self-presentation. As noted, TFI, which was established in this period, is aimed explicitly at serving the American Muslim community, and IIIT now frequently emphasizes the American importance of its reform goals. (It should be noted that the generically American name "Fairfax Institute"—particularly in comparison with the "The Graduate School of Islamic and Social Sciences"—was chosen after September 11th.) The earlier shift in focus away from the Islamization of knowledge project toward a methodology for Islamic life in the West was furthered by the new focus on the American environment.

Nevertheless IIIT's history remains tied with broader trends in global Islamic thought. Its foundation and enthusiastic embrace of the Islamization of knowledge project were part of the push in the initial post-colonial period for the reassertion of Islamic identity and intellectual vitality. Similarly, its research into new *fiqh* frameworks beginning in the 1990s overlapped with related efforts around the world, particularly with the *maqāṣid al-sharīʿah* and *fiqh al-aqallīyāt*, which as documented in these two volumes, are perhaps the most widely embraced types of Islamic legal reform globally. *Fiqh al-aqallīyāt* especially remains a major priority for IIIT, allowing it to balance its focus on the practical concerns of American Muslims with the theoretical research of its pre-2001 orientation.

Notes

1. IIIT, "About IIIT," accessed May 10, 2016, http://www.iiit.org/about.html.
2. IIITMedia, "About IIIT" [Video], *YouTube*, February 7, 2014, accessed May 10, 2016, https://www.youtube.com/watch?v=LGu1orUNc-w.
3. Ibid. That he refers to it as "scholarly study *of* Islam" is telling for IIIT's approach.
4. Juliane Hammer, "International Institute of Islamic Thought," in *EM-AH*, vol. 1, 269; Christopher Furlow, "Islam, Science and Modernity: From Northern Virginia to Kuala Lumpur" (Ph.D. dissertation, University of Florida, 2005), 56–9; Leif Stenberg, *The Islamization of Science: Four Muslim Positions Developing an Islamic Modernity* (Lund: Lund University, 1996), 155–65; Muslih, "The International Institute of Islamic Thought (IIIT)-USA: A Project of Islamic Revivalism" (Ph.D. dissertation, Leiden University, 2006), 11–26. Muslih's study, though based on fieldwork at IIIT, contains some problematic and unfounded assumptions about IIIT as a conduit for Wahhabism; e.g., 14–15.
5. International Institute of Islamic Thought–London, "Ismāʿīl Rājī Al Fārūqī: An Expose of the Legacy of the *Mujtahid* in the Modern Age" (seminar program), 2010, accessed May 10, 2016, http://www.iiituk.com/docs/pdf/Ismail%20Faruqi%20Seminar%202010%20Programme.pdf; William Brown, "al-Faruqi, Ismail," in *EM-AH*, vol. 1, 189–90; Stenberg, *Islamization of Science*, 153–4; John Esposito, "Ismail R. al-Faruqi: Muslim Scholar-Activist," in *The Muslims of America*, ed. Yvonne Yazbeck Haddad (Oxford: Oxford University Press, 1991), 65–79.
6. Juliane Hammer, "Association of Muslim Social Scientists of North America," in *EM-AH*, vol. 1, 67–8.
7. *Islamization of Knowledge: General Principles and Work Plan*, 2nd ed., ed. AbdulHamid AbuSulayman (Herndon: International Institute of Islamic Thought, 1989 [1981]), xiii.
8. Hammer, "International Institute of Islamic Thought"; Stenberg, *Islamization of Science*, 157–8; Furlow, "Islam, Science and Modernity," 56.
9. Ismail Raji al-Faruqi, *Al Tawḥīd: Its Implications for Thought and Life* (Herndon: International Institute of Islamic Thought/Kuala Lumpur: International Islamic Federation of Student Organizations, 1992).

10. Ismail Raji al-Faruqi, "Islamization of Knowledge: Problems, Principles and Prospective," in *Islam: Source and Purpose of Knowledge* (Herndon: International Institute of Islamic Thought, 1988), 13–64 at 22.
11. See Maxime Rodinson, "Islam Resurgent?" republished in Janet Afary and Kevin Anderson, *Foucault and the Iranian Revolution: Gender and the Seductions of Islamism* (Chicago: University of Chicago Press, 2005), 223–8; Olivier Roy, *Globalised Islam: The Search for a New Ummah* (London: Hurst, 2004).
12. Peter Mandaville, "American Muslims and Global Islam," in *The Oxford Handbook of American Islam*, ed. Yvonne Yazbeck Haddad and Jane Smith (Oxford: Oxford University Press, 2014), 474–89, esp. 480–481; Esposito, "Ismail R. al-Faruqi," 73–5.
13. For a discussion of al-Faruqi's intellectual connections with the Brotherhood, see Mona Abaza, *Debates on Islam and Knowledge in Malaysia and Egypt: Shifting Worlds* (London: Routledge, 2002), 77–84.
14. Cf. Esposito, "Ismail R. al-Faruqi," 74; Stenberg, *Islamization of Science*, 163; see also Mandaville, "American Muslims," 480.
15. Muhammad Qutb, *Hawla al-taʾṣīl al-islāmī li-al-ʿulūm al-ijtimāʿīyah* (Cairo: Dār al-shurūq, 1418/1998); cf. Stephane Lacroix, *Awakening Islam: Religious Dissent in Contemporary Saudi Arabia* (Cambridge, M.A.: Harvard University Press, 2011), esp. 47; Lacroix places the main thrust of this influence in the 1970s; see also the relevant chapters on Saudi Arabia in Volume 1.
16. See Mark Sedgwick, *Against the Modern World: Traditionalism and the Secret Intellectual History of the Twentieth Century* (Oxford: Oxford University Press, 2004).
17. Stenberg, *Islamization of Science*; also Abaza, *Debates on Islam and Knowledge*, Al-Attas's work is also discussed in some detail in Chapter 1.
18. *Islamization of Knowledge*, ed. AbuSulayman, 57–8.
19. Furlow, "Islam, Science and Modernity,"; Stenberg, *Islamization of Science*, 160; Hammer, "Association of Muslim Social Scientists," 68. IIIT also prepared a series of textbooks for American Muslim schoolchildren, published in the mid-90s; cf. Susan Douglass. "Developments in Islamic Education in the United States," in *Oxford Handbook of American Islam*, ed. Yvonne Haddad and Jane Smith (Oxford: Oxford University Press, 2014), 246, 250 n. 34.
20. Brown, "al-Faruqi," 190.
21. Furlow, "Islam, Science and Modernity," 58–9.
22. Quoted in ibid., 60.
23. *Islamization of Knowledge*, ed. AbuSulayman; see also Taha Jabir Al-Alwani, *The Islamization of Knowledge: Yesterday and Today* (Herndon: International Institute of Islamic Thought, 1995).
24. Furlow, "Islam, Science and Modernity," 58–9; Stenberg, *Islamization of Science*, 158.
25. Furlow, "Islam, Science and Modernity," 63–4; cf. Karen Leonard, "Organizing Communities: Institutions, Networks, Groups," in *The Cambridge Companion to American Islam*, ed. Juliane Hammer and Omid Safi (Cambridge: Cambridge University Press, 2013), 170–89, esp. 179–80.
26. Stenberg, *Islamization of Science*, 157; cf. al-Faruqi, "Islamization."
27. Furlow, "Islam, Science and Modernity," 66–7.
28. Ibid., 67–8.
29. In international literature and pamphlets, IIIT will sometimes list both the U.S. and U.K. as its home countries.

30. John Mintz and Douglas Farah, "In Search of Friends among the Foes; U.S. Hopes to Work with Diverse Group," *Washington Post*, September 11, 2004,, accessed August 11, 2016, http://www.washingtonpost.com/wp-dyn/articles/A12823-2004Sep10.html; Muslih, "The International Institute of Islamic Thought," 39–44.
31. IIITMedia, "About IIIT."
32. Furlow, "Islam, Science and Modernity," 65, 87 n. 6; Muslih, "International Institute of Islamic Thought," 32–3. There is some confusion as to the relationship between GSISS, Cordoba University and the Fairfax Institute. Juliane Hammer states that GSISS was reorganized post-September 11th and renamed the Fairfax Institute, and she makes no mention of Cordoba University. Neither does Karen Leonard, in her article. Muslih for his part writes that GSISS became Cordoba University in 2005, and the Fairfax Institute was established in 2003. However, a work by Al-Alwani published by IIIT in 2003 identifies him as professor of Islamic law "at The Graduate School of Islamic Social Sciences at Cordoba University": Taha Jabir Al-Alwani, *Towards a Fiqh for Minorities: Some Basic Reflections* (London, International Institute of Islamic Thought, 2003), back cover; Hammer, "International Institute of Islamic Thought," 269.
33. International Institute of Islamic Thought, "About IIIT"; emphasis added.
34. Ibid.
35. International Institute of Islamic Thought, "Other Languages," accessed May 11, 2016, http://www.iiit.org/other-languages.html.
36. Stenberg, *Islamization of Science*, 157–60.
37. International Institute of Islamic Thought, "Research Grants," accessed May 11, 2016, http://www.iiit.org/research-grants.html.
38. *Islamization of Knowledge*, ed. AbuSulayman, xiv.
39. International Institute of Islamic Thought, "Research Grants."
40. Imad al Din Khalil, *Islamization of Knowledge: A Methodology*, 2nd ed. (Herndon: International Institute of Islamic Thought, 1995 [1991]), 5–6, 8.
41. E.g. *Islamization of Knowledge*, ed. AbuSulayman, xiv.
42. A re-edition of Bernard Weiss' major study of classical *fiqh*, co-published with University of Utah Press: Bernard Weiss, *The Search for God's Law: Islamic Jurisprudence in the Writings of Sayf al-Din al-Amidi*, 2nd ed. (Salt Lake City: University of Utah Press/Herndon: International Institute of Islamic Thought, 2010 [1992]).
43. Ahmed Essa and Othman Ali, *Studies in Islamic Civilization: The Muslim Contribution to the Renaissance* (Herndon: International Institute of Islamic Thought, 2010).
44. Jasser Auda, Maqāṣid al-Sharī 'ah *as Philosophy of Islamic Law: A Systems Approach* (London: International Institute of Islamic Thought, 2007), 27.
45. These kinds of apologetic claims appear in early IIIT publications as well; Stenberg, *Islamization of Science*, 191–3.
46. Al-Faruqi, "Islamization," 17.
47. Taha Jabir al-Alwani, "Taqlid and Ijtihad," *AJISS* 8 (1991), 129–42, esp. 131. The classic work on modern epistemes and their connection with Western power is Michel Foucault, *An Archaeology of Knowledge* (New York: Vintage, 1972).
48. *Sources of Islamic Thought: Three Epistles on Tawhid* (Indianapolis: American Trust Publications, 1980); *Sources of Islamic Thought: Kitab al Tawhid* (London: IIFSO, 1980); cf. Esposito, "Ismail R. al-Faruqi," 74.

49. On ibn ʿAbd al-Wahhāb, see also Chapter 5 in Volume 1.
50. A Wahhabi influence regarding certain religious practices is evident in Al-Faruqi, *Tawḥīd*.
51. S. M. Hasanuz Zaman, *Economic Guidelines in the Qur'an* (Dhaka: Bangladesh Institute of Islamic Thought, 1999); Ilyas Ba-Yunus, "Sociological Realism: An Islamic Paradigm," *AJISS* 8 (1991), 45–66; S. Imtiaz Ahmad, "Islamic Perspective on Knowledge Engineering," in *Islamization of Attitudes and Practices in Science and Technology*, ed. M. A. K. Lodhi (Herndon: International Institute of Islamic Thought, 1988), 75–88; Muhammad Ishaq Zahid, "Use of Islamic Beliefs in Mathematics and Computer Science Education," in *Islamization of Attitudes*, ed. Lodhi, 89–102; Z. R. El-Naggar, *Sources of Scientific Knowledge: The Geological Concepts of Mountains in the Qur'an* (Herndon: International Institute of Islamic Thought, 1991).
52. Ahmad, "Islamic Perspective on Knowledge Engineering," 75; cf. Stenberg, *Islamization of Science*, 213–14.
53. Al-Faruqi, *Tawḥīd*, esp. 77–8.
54. Stenberg, *Islamization of Science*, 202–203, 206; Brown, "al-Faruqi, Ismail," 190.
55. *Islamization of Knowledge*, ed. AbuSulayman, 84.
56. Furlow, "Islam, Science and Modernity," esp. 60-61.
57. Mona Abul-Fadl, *Where East Meets West: Appropriating the Islamic Encounter for a Spiritual-Cultural Revival*, 2nd ed. (Herndon: International Institute of Islamic Thought, 2010 [1992]).
58. Mona Abul-Fadl, "Beyond Cultural Parodies and Parodizing Cultures: Shaping a Discourse," *AJISS* 8 (1991), 15–44.
59. Abul-Fadl, *Where East Meets West*, 15–16; also Abul-Fadl, "Beyond Cultural Parodies," 16.
60. Akbar S. Ahmed, *Towards Islamic Anthropology: Definitions, Dogma, and Directions* (Herndon: International Institute of Islamic Thought, 1986).
61. Abul-Fadl, "Beyond Cultural Parodies," 16–24; Abul-Fadl, *Where East Meets West*, esp. 56–69.
62. Furlow, "Islam, Science and Modernity," 67.
63. Cf. Abul-Fadl, *Where East Meets West*, 25. On different understandings of the Islamization of knowledge, see Furlow, "Islam, Science and Modernity," 77–9.
64. Taha Jabir al-Alwani, "The Role of Islamic Ijtihad in the Regulation and Correction of Capital Markets," in *Issues in Contemporary Islamic Thought* (Herndon: International Institute of Islamic Thought, 2005), 129–58; repr. from *AJISS* 14 (1997).
65. Furlow, "Islam, Science and Modernity," 78.
66. Al-Alwani, "Role of Islamic Ijtihad," 144, 146.
67. Price-gauging, monopolies, maximizing current profit at the expense of future profit, etc.; ibid., 149–50.
68. The first part goes back to the earlier point about the repetitive character of IIIT's publications. Leaving aside the fact that this article itself has been republished, Al-Alwani's argument for including morality in mainstream economics is not in any way different from other works on the Islamization of knowledge, which take as a basic premise that modern sciences lack the moral grounding that the *tawḥīd*ic episteme would provide. Al-Alwani's article here merely adapts that claim to economics specifically.

69. It also was not without controversy. Seyyid Vali Reza Nasr criticized it for lacking both intellectual creativity and religious grounding: Seyyed Vali Reza Nasr, "Islamization of Knowledge: A Critical Overview," *Islamic Studies* 30 (1991), 387–400. Interestingly, this article was republished as a short monograph by IIIT Islamabad in 1992.
70. Al-Alwani, *Islamization.*
71. Ibid., 20.
72. Al-Alwani, "Taqlid," 141.
73. Ibid., 137.
74. Al-Alwani, "Role of Islamic Ijtihad," 134.
75. Al-Alwani, *Islamization*, 22–3.
76. al-Alwani, *Towards a Fiqh for Minorities*, 35.
77. See the chart of the various *maqāṣid*; Muhammad Umer Chapra, *The Islamic Vision of Development in the Light of Maqāṣid al-Sharīʿah* (Herndon: International Institute of Islamic Thought, 2008), 8.
78. Ibid., 36.
79. Auda, Maqāṣid al-Sharīʿah *as Philosophy.*
80. Jasser Auda, "A *Maqāṣidī* Approach to Contemporary Application of the *Sharīʿah*," *Intellectual Discourse* 19 (2011), 193–217.
81. E.g. Asyraf Wajdi Dusuki and Nurdianawati Irwani Abdullah, "*Maqasid al-Shariʿah, Maslaha*, and Corporate Social Responsibility," *AJISS* 24 (2007), 25–45; cf. Auda, Maqāṣid al-Sharīʿah *as Philosophy*, 25.
82. Cf. Adis Duderija, ed., *Maqāṣid al-Sharīʿa* [sic] *and Contemporary Reformist Muslim Thought: An Examination* (New York: Palgrave, 2014). See also the Chapter 4 on Tariq Ramadan in the present volume.
83. Mohammad Hashim Kamali, *Maqāṣid al-Sharīʿah Made Simple* (London: International Institute of Islamic Thought, 2008).
84. Furlow, "Islam, Science and Modernity," 68–70.
85. Stenberg, *Islamization of Science*, 206–7, 216.
86. Ibid., 154; Marcia Hermansen, "American Islamic College," in *EM-AH*, vol. 1, 51–2, esp. 51.
87. Furlow, "Islam, Science and Modernity," 70–4, 76.
88. Ibid., 65.
89. International Institute of Islamic Thought, "Seminary Marks Full Funding of Islamic Chaplaincy Faculty Chair," March 27, 2013, accessed May 13, 2016, http://www.iiit.org/news/seminary-marks-full-funding-of-islamic-chaplaincy-faculty-chair.
90. International Institute of Islamic Thought, "Scholarly Agreements with Institutions," accessed May 13, 2016, http://www.iiit.org/agreements.html.
91. IIITMedia, "About IIIT."
92. Said Fares Hassan, *Fiqh al-Aqalliyyāt: History, Development, and Progress* (New York: Palgrave, 2013), 88–90, 99.
93. International Institute of Islamic Thought, "Scholars' Biographies—2014," accessed May 10, 2016, http://www.iiit.org/2014---scholars-biographies.html; American Muslims for Constructive Engagement, "Leadership," accessed May 10, 2016, http://www.amceweb.net/2.html. AMCE's advisory council includes a number of figures associated with IIIT.
94. Furlow, "Islam, Science and Modernity," 53–4; Steve Johnson, "The Muslims of Indianapolis," in *Muslim Communities in North America*, ed. Yvonne Yazbeck

Haddad and Jane Smith (Albany: State University of New York Press, 1994), 259–78, esp. 270–2.

95. E.g. Kyle Shideler and David Daoud, "International Institute of Islamic Thought (IIIT): The Muslim Brotherhood's Think Tank," *Center for Security Policy Occasional Papers Series*, July 28, 2014, accessed May 13, 2016, http://www.centerforsecuritypolicy.org/2014/07/27/iiit-think-thank/.
96. Furlow, "Islam, Science and Modernity," 65–6.
97. International Institute of Islamic Thought, "AMCE Launches Book Digest Project," November 21, 2008, accessed May 13, 2016, http://www.iiit.org/news/amce-launches-book-digest-project-four-books-in-brief-released.
98. IIITMedia, "About IIIT."
99. World Congress of Muslim Philanthropists, "4th World Congress of Muslim Philanthropists: Defining the Roadmap for the Next Decade" (convention program), 2011, accessed May 13, 2016, http://thewcmp.org/oldsite/img/downloads/pdf/finalprgm0.pdf.
100. Furlow, "Islam, Science and Modernity," 58.
101. He even lists the United States behind the United Kingdom as English-speaking countries that would benefit from the work; Ismail Raji al-Faruqi, *Toward Islamic English* (Herndon: International Institute of Islamic Thought, 1986), 7; cf. Stenberg, *Islamization of Science*, 176–80.
102. Ismail Raji al-Faruqi, *Für Ein Islamisches Deutsch* (Herndon: International Institute of Islamic Thought, 1988).
103. Furlow, "Islam, Science and Modernity," 74.
104. Ibid., 74–5; Stenberg, *Islamization of Science,* 158 n. 45.

CHAPTER

4

TRANSFORMATIVE ISLAMIC REFORM: TARIQ RAMADAN AND THE CENTER FOR ISLAMIC LEGISLATION AND ETHICS (CILE)

Nathan Spannaus

Tariq Ramadan, currently a professor of contemporary Islamic Studies at the University of Oxford and head of the Qatar-based Center for Islamic Legislation and Ethics (CILE), is one of the most prominent Muslim intellectuals active today, and perhaps the foremost Muslim thinker in Europe. This prominence is due to some degree to his patrimony. He is the maternal grandson of Hassan al-Banna (1906–49), the Egyptian Islamist and founder of the Muslim Brotherhood, and son of Said Ramadan (1926–95), an activist prominent in mid-twentieth-century Islamist circles. This lineage has undoubtedly brought scrutiny and mistrust as well; Ramadan's public life has featured constant controversy, notably in European politics and media, and he was refused entry into the United States from 2004 to 2010.[1] He is also barred from a handful of Middle Eastern countries.

Ramadan was born in 1962 and raised in Geneva, where his family had settled following his father's expulsion by the Egyptian government a few years earlier. Educated in Switzerland, he studied French literature and philosophy at the University of Geneva before pursuing a doctorate in Islamic Studies there, which he completed in 1996. He also studied Islamic subjects with *'ulamā'* of al-Azhar in Cairo, including the former Grand Mufti of Egypt, Shaykh Ali Gomaa.[2] Following the completion of his Ph.D. he took on a teaching position at the University of Fribourg in Switzerland. He has worked in academia for his entire career, holding positions at various institutions throughout Europe.

It was also in the mid-1990s that Ramadan began writing, with his first book *Les musulmans dans la laïcité: responsabilités et droits des musulmans dans les sociétés occidentales* published by the Tawhid publishing house in

Lyon, France in 1994. Ramadan's partnership with Tawhid, an influential organization among French Muslims, proved beneficial, and he published a number of works with them over nearly the next fifteen years. He is an uncommonly prolific writer, which helped him grow in stature over this time, becoming a widely known public figure in France in particular. In the late 1990s his connections with British Muslim institutions began, and he spent a year associated with the Islamic Foundation of Leicester, who published his first English-language book in 1999.

September 11th brought new opportunities for international public engagement on Islamic issues, but also more government scrutiny. In 2003, a televised debate with then-French minister of the interior Nicolas Sarkozy caused a minor scandal when Ramadan, asked about the acceptability of stoning as a penalty for adultery, answered that there should be a "moratorium" on the practice, instead of an outright rejection of its validity.[3] In 2004 a professorial appointment to the University of Notre Dame was famously forestalled by the United States government rescinding his visa. Yet by that time Ramadan had published several books and innumerable articles, and had become a major figure in Western intellectual life generally. He first accepted a position at the University of Oxford in 2005, later becoming a permanent appointment in 2007.

Although his career up to this point has not followed a single trajectory, he has articulated and developed a sophisticated and nuanced programme of Islamic religious reform, one aimed simultaneously at Muslims in minority settings and in the Muslim world. Focusing on his major books on reform, the following is an analysis of the premises and developing contours of his project, and its implementation in recent years at CILE.

Being Muslim in Context

Ramadan is primarily concerned with the interrelated issues of context and reform. As he sees it, any viable legal or ethical framework must be suited to its environment to remain operative; if its circumstances change, it must change with them. Thus, shifts in context necessitate reform. The Islamic legal tradition's current predicament stems from its inability to adapt sufficiently or satisfactorily to the seismic transformations associated with modernity. It is for this reason that Ramadan calls for a radical rethinking of Islamic legal ethics, to fit the drastically altered context.[4]

Ramadan contrasts the current disconnect between Islamic legal thinking and its context with the situation during the earliest periods of Muslim history. He writes that the Muslim community in the past had been more at home in their context and historical setting, and therefore more open to flexibility and critical interpretation in their ethics. Muslims in the contemporary period are marginalized and at odds with their historical setting, thus more closed off and defensive.[5]

Ramadan has long argued that *fuqahā'* must have an understanding of their current setting and must take this into account in their legal interpretations and the religious guidance they offer, so that this guidance can be suited to that setting and the environment in which they will be enacted and the reality in which Muslims live. As early as 2002, he criticized the Dublin-based European Council on Fatwa and Research (ECFR)—and *muftīs* in Europe more generally—for its scholars' lack of familiarity with the prevailing habits, cultures and sensibilities of Europe, which he considered essential for an appropriately dynamic formulation of the *fatwā* as a viable form of legal guidance.[6]

Ramadan's interlinking of context and reform played a prominent role in his early work, which focused on questions regarding European Muslims' religious orientation and their place in the West. In his books *To Be a European Muslim* and *Western Muslims and the Future of Islam*, he addresses what he sees as necessary changes to Muslims' thinking in order to adapt to the European setting and to reduce their isolation, alienation and attendant defensive posture.[7] He identifies a lack of understanding of Islam and its essential aspects as one of the main problems, writing that European Muslims often present Islam as "a whole series of rules, interdictions or prohibitions, rulings which explain Islam within the framework of a specific relation of protection from an environment which is perceived as too permissive and even hostile." Muslims' religious identity is thus reduced to "a vague idea, an indistinct mix of different kinds of elements such as familial or local tradition imported from the country of origin, with its own peculiar rules and principles (and sometimes superstitions), without necessarily being linked to Islam, but often confused with it, or to a clear idea of what is the content of their identity."[8]

Instead, Ramadan argues for an increased focus on, and awareness of, the universal character of Islam and its viability in all times and places, that it "carries within itself a global understanding of creation, life, death, and humanity." Muslims in Europe must therefore understand and present the essential aspects of the religion in ways suited to and relevant for their European environment, which they can then approach positively rather than defensively.[9]

The goal here is the articulation of an Islamic religious identity that is at home in Europe or the West and that is to both Muslims and non-Muslims meaningfully "European" or "Western". This represents an important part of Ramadan's intellectual project, and the approach he uses to tackle the issue is quite illustrative of his thought. To begin with, he emphasizes that the message of Islam "is valid in every time and place," and thus there is nothing "Islamic" (in the normative sense of the word) preventing the crafting of a European Islam.[10]

He addresses the question of the so-called "abode of war" (*dār al-ḥarb*), a categorization of a territory as "non-Islamic", in contrast to the Islamic world (*dār al-Islām*). He writes that this notion lacks any scriptural basis, but rather was devised in response to historical circumstances faced by the early Muslim community and was utilized as a legal concept by later scholars. As such, it was created to serve a different time and different environment, a fact reinforced by the current difficulty in defining either the *dār al-ḥarb* or *dār al-Islām*, given the considerable global transformation of the past 200 years. With no sound religious or practical reason to maintain this binary view of the world, he calls for its abandonment and replacement by the notion of the *dār al-shahādah*, which he translates as the "land of witness" or "abode of testimony", in that Muslims in Europe can declare and practice their faith openly. But, due to globalization and Western hegemony, there is considerable overlap between the West and the "Islamic world", to the point that the entire planet could be considered the *dār al-shahādah*.[11]

This is not to say that the situation in Europe is the same as in Egypt or Pakistan, but rather that it is not fundamentally different—and, Ramadan would point out, the situation in Egypt is also distinct from the situation in Pakistan. Moreover, just as there is an Egyptian Islam and a Pakistani Islam, there can be a French Islam and a British Islam.

The formation of a European Islamic identity for Ramadan must focus on what is essential within the religion. He draws a significant distinction between the universal in Islam and the contingent, emphasizing the immutable nature of the former and the conditional and changeable nature of the latter. Quite simply, that which is changeable should almost necessarily be changed, on the grounds that the contingent norms reflect social and historical settings different from those found in Europe. As such, not only are they ill-suited to the contemporary environment, but they risk unduly shaping Muslims' perception of their European environment "through some previously conceived concepts formulated in another time for another context."[12] Contingent norms fall overwhelmingly in the arena of social practice (*mu'āmalāt*), meaning that they are both formulated and operative within a broader social context shaped by (ever-changing) historical circumstances. Even if based in the texts of scripture, their precise manifestation in practical action requires human "reasoning in time" and is therefore subject to change.[13]

It is those norms that have a clear and certain basis in the texts of scripture that form the essential and unchanging within Islam, limited primarily to the sphere of ritual (*'ibādāt*) and some matters of creed (*'aqīdah*). All other issues are potentially subject to change; adapting them to fit into the European context is thus key to forging a European Muslim identity. In this way, the maintenance of the essential aspects of the religion serves as a direct link with the universal and unchanging message of Islam, while the reform of *mu'āmalāt* (the process for which is discussed in detail below) offers the flexibility necessary to participate in European society. He writes that due regard for both can lead to a path for Muslims between "ghetto and dissolution," in which the immutable foundation of their religion is respected—thereby preserving their religious identity—but they also have the latitude to align their practices with their environment.[14]

The goal, as Ramadan sees it, is Muslims' integration into European or Western society as Muslims. No longer migrants or part of a "diaspora", he seeks a way for Muslims to consider themselves at home in Europe: "The aim is to protect the Muslim identity and religious practice, to recognize the Western constitutional structure, to become involved as a citizen at the social level, and to live with true loyalty to the country to which one belongs."[15] Such formal integration must be accompanied by a shift in attitude that opens Muslims up to outside influence, and he writes that:

> . . . it is a matter of integrating all the dimensions of life that are not in opposition to our terms of reference and to consider them completely our own (legally, socially, and culturally). We must clearly overcome the dualistic vision and reject our sense of being eternal foreigners, living in parallel on the margins or as reclusive minorities, in order to make way for the global vision of universal Islam that integrates and allows the Other to flourish confidently.[16]

Ramadan presents this attitude as part of Muslims' "faithfulness" to the "true universality of Islam," which calls for them to accept all that is good and does not contradict established, unchanging principles of the *sharīʿah*. He argues for a presumption of permissibility in social practice as basic within the *sharīʿah*, and thus abiding by Islamic morality entails an openness to that which is not expressly forbidden. And in Western societies where many *ḥarām* things are not outlawed, faithfulness requires only that those things are avoided by conscience, without extending their rejection to the society or government that allows them. Noting the legality of interest and alcohol in the West, Ramadan states that the *sharīʿah* commands Muslims' loyalty and allegiance to the country that they inhabit and that extends them peace and security and allows them to forego that which contradicts their beliefs. Faithfulness to the *sharīʿah* thus obliges respect for the legal system under which Muslims live.[17]

Faithfulness to the *sharīʿah* also obliges Muslims' moral and ethical engagement with their societies. If they are to be legitimately and meaningfully European or Western, then Muslims cannot simply remain a passive or marginal presence within their societies, but must work toward making the moral principles of Islam manifest. Ramadan argues that the imperatives of the *sharīʿah* should be not restricted or made private by Muslims' status as minorities, but rather that the comprehensiveness of the *sharīʿah* is not historically contingent (even if the precise form in which it is enacted is).[18] As such, and as full participants of society, Muslims have a right and a duty to strive to change and better their societies, to work toward justice and equity, while embodying Islamic moral imperatives in their daily lives, regardless of the setting.[19] He writes that:

> Nothing in Islam is opposed to individual engagement, social reform, to progress and well-being. On the contrary, one of the principles of *Uṣūl al-Fiqh* is to consider that all social reform and scientific progress that bring

> an improvement in the lives of men are permitted if they do not betray, in their articulation, the sense of the general orientations offered by the sources.[20]

Ramadan labels this effort "transformative reform" in *Radical Reform* (see below), but it underlies his aims in *Western Muslims*, which is intended to provide Muslims with a framework that is simultaneously based in Islamic tradition and allows them to participate fully in Western society as wholly religious and moral Muslims.

Acknowledging that the idea of an "Islamic" reform of Western society is certainly problematic, if not outright troubling, for non-Muslim audiences, Ramadan emphasizes the need for Muslims to reach out beyond themselves and to respect certain fundamental rights for people, irrespective of religion.[21] More significantly, he argues that any truly Islamic reform must reflect the universal character of Islamic morality, which is essential both for adapting to new circumstances and for finding commonalities with others as part of "a global commitment for the sake of justice and goodness."[22]

Ramadan's more recent work has focused on the universal nature of Islam and its moral priorities. *In the Footsteps of the Prophet: Lessons from the Life of Muhammad*, published in 2007, uses the biography of the Prophet to explore the values in Islam that Ramadan sees as timeless and essential, explicitly connecting them to the contemporary situation. To give a small example, he cites the young Muhammad's participation in an agreement to halt intertribal conflicts in Mecca, the so-called "pact of the virtuous" (*ḥilf al-fuḍūl*), and his later praise for the agreement as evidence for the importance of cooperation in the interest of peace and justice, as well as beneficial partnerships with non-Muslims. Switching focus from the event to its relevance to Muslims generally, Ramadan concludes that "Islam is a message of justice that entails resisting oppression and protecting the dignity of the oppressed and the poor, and Muslims must recognize the moral value of a law or contract stipulating this requirement, whoever its authors and whatever the society, Muslim or not." For Ramadan, the Prophet's working with non-Muslims toward a moral cause shows not only the importance of cooperation, but indeed the precedence of the moral cause as primary for Muslims; he goes on, "Far from building an allegiance to Islam in which recognition and loyalty are exclusive to the community of faith, the Prophet strove to develop the believer's conscience through adherence to principles transcending closed allegiances in the name of a *primary loyalty to universal principles themselves*."[23]

Ramadan's appeals to Muhammad's life are more aimed at a Muslim audience, of course, but he expands the scope of his religious inquiry in *The Quest for Meaning: Developing a Philosophy of Pluralism*.[24] Using Christian, Jewish, Buddhist and modern philosophical sources, this work focuses on universal aspects of religion as a basis for an ethos of pluralism, in a way relevant to his goal of using Islamic principles to enact broad reform of society, based on their universal applicability.[25]

Regardless of a principle's universal or comprehensive character, however, all norms and moral imperatives are manifested within a social and historical context, to which they therefore must be made suitable. This work requires reform and the engagement with the principle's source, to separate the principles from what is circumstantial and contextual in their implementation.

Promoting Reform

Alongside the concern for context within Ramadan's thought is his drive for reform, which, though following from context, is the most significant and prominent element of his intellectual project, and without question the basis for much of his prominence and notoriety. Ramadan's espousal of reform is unwavering. As he sees it, Muslims' failure to embrace true reform and understand the necessity of it has contributed to their current circumstances and difficulties in the contemporary world. He singles out the different ways of approaching scripture, in particular different conceptions of the role for human reasoning (equated with *ijtihād*) and its space to determine the precise significance of *Qur'ānic* and prophetic texts and their application in practice, as distinguishing the varying trends of thought among Muslims today.[26]

Laying out a typology of the major trends in *Western Muslims*, he uses the categories to criticize the shortcomings of the various approaches: "Scholastic Traditionalism" subjects the interpretation of scripture to the authority of the canonical legal schools, thereby precluding developments of doctrine beyond the boundaries of the *madhhab*s. "Salafi Literalism" excludes any innovation not present during the time of the first Muslim community as illegitimate, seeking instead explicit, literal validation for any belief or practice within the texts of scripture. "Political Literalist Salafism" combines the literalist view toward the text with political and social reformism overwhelmingly concerned with "the management of power" in Muslim hands apart from the West. "Liberal" or "Rationalist Reformism" relies on human reasoning and agency over and apart from the texts of revelation, which cease to be the main points of reference for understanding norms of behavior and conduct. Lastly, "Sufism", while indeed deeply grounded in scriptural texts, relies on moral prescriptions that are directed internally, away from the pragmatic and discordant function of society. Distinct from these trends lies Ramadan's own, "Salafi Reformism", which he presents as uniquely suited to maintain fidelity to the norms of Islam as contained in scripture while sufficiently flexible to incorporate reason into religious interpretations and therefore to adapt to different settings and circumstances. Emphasizing the centrality of reform to the trend, he lists several prominent examples of reformist figures: Jamal al-Din al-Afghani (1831–79), Muhammad 'Abduh (1849–1904), Rashid Rida (1865–1935), Said Nursi (1877–1960), Muhammad Iqbal (1877–1938), Ibn Badis (1889–1940), Hasan al-Banna, Allal al-Fasi (1910–74), Bennabi

(1905–73), Abu Ala Mawdudi (1903–79), Sayyid Qutb (1906–66) and Ali Shariati (1933–77).[27]

In these descriptions Ramadan makes clear the priorities that he considers important for both a functional and "Islamic" project of reform. Acknowledging that the West and their minority status represents a challenging and unsettling context for Muslims, as he does in *To Be a European Muslim*, Ramadan argues that reforms must be suited to this environment to be workable, but also remain committed to upholding Islamic moral norms in a meaningful, scripturally grounded way. Those trends which reject either the West or the current historical age—or both—or which turn their focus inward, are *ipso facto* ill-equipped to deal with contemporary circumstances, even if they rely on scripture to a significant degree. Sufism's aim of closeness with God is not primarily manifested in society, but rather, Ramadan writes, "is a call to the inner life."[28] Scholastic Traditionalism is similarly "uninterested in and even rejecting of any connection with the Western social milieu," but even those Traditionalists who are open to rethinking the religion through the mediation of their legal school insist "on rules for applying Islam, that rely on the opinions of scholars that usually were codified between the eighth and eleventh centuries."[29] Most critically, Salafi Literalism and Political Literalist Salafism, in their preoccupation with the "Islamic", are each premised upon visions for society that do not, and by definition cannot, exist in the West, and they accordingly reject any involvement in non-Muslim spaces.[30] By contrast, Liberal Reformism is undoubtedly suited to its context, as its basis is a "complete adaptation to a Western way of life," but in so adapting it abandons or subordinates adherence to the moral tenets of Islam and their comprehensive application, limiting the religion "to its spiritual dimension, lived on an individual and private basis."[31]

Ramadan evaluates these trends in terms of their use of "Text" [*sic*] and "reason", respectively. Adherence to scripture obviously guarantees a trend's Islamic character, which Liberal Reformism lacks, hence his criticism. He also explicitly excludes "sociological Muslims": Muslims by birth or by culture, but not by conviction.[32] But, as he sees it, the use of scripture is not in itself sufficient for a project of reform—nor, it should be noted, is it straightforward. Reason must be used for understanding the text, but also for determining its purpose. The text sets limits and determines priorities, while reason and the use of critical thinking is necessary for application within a particular social context. Salafi Reformism combines both sides effectively: "the Text still remains the source, but reason, applied according to the rules of deduction and inference (*qawāid al-istinbāṭ*), enjoys significant latitude for interpretation and elaboration through the exercise of *ijtihād*."[33]

The use of interpretive methods upon scripture in order to determine practical, moral action is of course the essence of *fiqh* and the articulation of Islamic law, as it has been practiced since the earliest periods of Islamic history. Bernard Weiss, a scholar of Islamic legal history, writes that "To the extent that the Law of God may be found at all in the mundane realm, it is only found in the formulations of jurists."[34] Scholastic Traditionalism, in Ramadan's typology, is premised on continuing the legal tradition and its pre-modern discourses, therefore sharing its effective elements with his Salafi Reformism. He argues, however, that Traditionalists' adherence to their *madhhab* precludes sufficient use of reason; rather, their continued reliance on legal norms laid out in medieval texts prevents amending those norms to fit contemporary circumstances.[35]

By maintaining the content of *fiqh* judgments articulated centuries earlier, Traditionalists eschew the basic spirit of reform that Ramadan considers so essential. This goes back to his first major publication in English, *To Be a European Muslim*, which he wrote in 1997–8, where he argued for the need for Muslims in Europe to adapt established notions of *fiqh* to fit the European setting. *Western Muslims* takes this drive toward reform further, putting forward specific ways in which Islamic legal thought can take into account aspects of Western society. Between the publication of *Western Muslims* in 2004 and *Radical Reform* four years later, however, Ramadan's position on the need for reform became even stronger, and in the latter he advocates a sweeping and seismic rethinking of Islamic law and its formulation (described in detail below).

Nevertheless, Ramadan's intellectual project is grounded in established (and quite conventional) *fiqh* discourses and methodologies, promoting the use of "the available juridical tools so as to facilitate a positive Muslim presence in the West."[36] His conception of this process aligns with the very traditional role of the *faqīh* (Islamic jurist)—to derive through a formal juristic hermeneutic of *uṣūl al-fiqh* (Islamic legal theory or jurisprudence) judgments or interpretations from the texts of scripture in the form of the *fatwā*. This process, as described by Ramadan, matches Weiss' observation quoted above. These judgments and interpretations, along with those of other scholars, stand as attempts to understand the divine will for humanity, encompassed in the *sharīʿah*, and the interpretive effort of scholars represents *ijtihād*, the work of articulating the content of *fiqh*, which serves as learned guidance for the community, forging a constant link between Muslims' quotidian existence and revelation. This is the role of the *ʿulamāʾ*, Ramadan writes in *To Be a European Muslim*:

> Faithfulness to such absolute principles [of the *sharīʿah*] is an important and permanent work of the *ʿulamāʾ* from whom it is expected that they formulate specific and precise rules and laws tuned to the historical and geographical context . . . just as the *fuqahāʾ* of the Muslim community have to provide their fellow Believers [*sic*] with appropriate answers fitting their environment, so they must also exert themselves in forming individual or community judgments so as to preserve the essential link between the absoluteness of the sources and the relativity of history and geography.[37]

Yet the interpretation of scripture and the dispensing of guidance to the community is not, Ramadan notes, in itself sufficient. Rather, jurists' textual engagement must necessarily be supplemented by knowledge and understanding of the community's context and circumstances, and the contemporary issues relevant within their current environment. The continuous articulation of *fiqh* that is the *'ulamā'*'s duty must necessarily be carried out in a way that is cognizant of their particular European setting:

> They must set about a two-fold work: a deep and precise interpretation of the Qur'an and the *Sunna* along with an appropriate analysis of the social, political and economic situation they are facing. They have to determine the *Fiqh* (Islamic Law) which is the product of rational human elaboration based on the unchangeable rulings of the *Sharī'ah* but with responses, adaptations and formulations which are in constant evolution."[38]

As Ramadan presents it, if European jurists issue *fatwā*s that are simultaneously grounded in scriptural norms and with due regard for Muslims' real, lived circumstances, the complexities of shaping a morally Islamic existence within a non-Muslim society can be assuaged.

Thus, in this earlier work reform is premised upon the very exercise of *ijtihād*. The problem is not so much in approach, but in attitude. Reliance on pre-existing *fiqh*—that is, judgments not made for a European setting—harms the community and hinders Muslims' progress towards becoming full members of European society, thereby necessitating new and continuously updated *fiqh* specific to their context. This is also a good example of the conjoining of context and reform in Ramadan's thought.

Beyond this call for new *fatwā*s, however, his project primarily uses concepts from the Islamic legal tradition, which are employed in largely conventional ways. Ramadan argues that *ijtihād* should be guided by *maṣlaḥah*/*istiṣlāḥ* (common good or public interest), a long-established legal principle that dates back to the work of Mālik ibn Anas (711–795), founder of the Mālikī school.[39] The common good should be a guiding concern for the *'ulamā'*, Ramadan writes, ordered according to the *maqāṣid al-sharī'ah*, the 'objectives of the *sharī'ah*' that underlie the norms contained in scripture. The *maqāṣid*, traditionally understood (as by Ramadan) as religion, life, progeny, property and intellect, represent the essential priorities upheld by the *sharī'ah*, with universal applicability within Islamic society. These necessities (*ḍarūrīyāt*), along with secondary needs (*ḥājāt*) and benefits (*taḥsīnāt*), collectively comprise *maṣlaḥah*, in the sense that promoting them is *ipso facto* beneficial for the common good.

Ramadan takes his understanding of the *maqāṣid* from the work of Abū Isḥāq al-Shāṭibī (ca. 1320–88), an Andalusian Mālikī jurist who formulated an approach to *fiqh* that closely connected it with changing social realities, based on a distinction between universal and particular norms, with the *maqāṣid* as the former.[40] Ramadan's reliance on Shāṭibī is not unusual, and the sources he employs in *To Be a European Muslim* come largely from the pre-modern Islamic legal tradition, attesting the conventional character of his *fiqh* reformism in his early writings.

It should be noted that, although he devotes much of *To Be a European Muslim* to issues of *uṣūl al-fiqh* and the importance of legal interpretation, Ramadan does not engage with substantive matters of legal theory, or even the content of *fiqh*. Instead he takes a wide, almost macro-perspective on the *fatwā* and its formulation: he argues for the need for new interpretations, and broad principles to orient those interpretations (for instance that *'ulamā'* should presume permissibility when evaluating an action's *sharī'ah* acceptability)[41], without delving into the details of exactly how interpretations should be carried out. This is not a negligible point. For example, he writes, when listing the qualifications for *ijtihād*, that a *mujtahid* must possess a "knowledge of Qur'ānic and *Ḥadīth* sciences in order to know how to understand and identify the evidences within the text (*adillah*) and, moreover, to infer and extract rulings."[42] Ramadan compiles his list of qualifications from (unnamed) pre-modern sources, and such a condition, although vague, is certainly conventional. That said, in a traditional text the meaning of how to "understand and identify the evidences" and "infer and extract rulings" would be clear: anyone with those abilities would already be well-versed in their school's methodologies and legal hermeneutic, since these were devised for the purpose of formalizing interpretation of the text and extracting rulings from it. However, Ramadan rejects the *madhhab* as a legal framework (as do large numbers of contemporary Muslims) while offering no substitute for the specifics of legal theory, leaving scholars—and would-be scholars—to their own devices, methodologically speaking.

Ramadan follows this same approach in *Western Muslims*. His two early works deal with many of the same issues and share significant points of overlap, as they both argue for Muslims living in the West to participate fully in their societies and for reform of Islamic legal thinking in a way that allows them to do so while remaining true to universal Islamic norms. As in *To Be a European Muslim*, in *Western Muslims* he advocates for renewed engagement in *ijtihād* to formulate new *fatwā*s suited to the Western context and guided by a concern for *maṣlaḥah*. He writes:

> . . . the "path to faithfulness" [the *sharī'ah*] *requires* the definition of the "common good" [*maṣlaḥah*] in a given society, the continuous exercise of "critical work on legal formulations," [*ijtihād*] and the exposition of "legal opinions" [*fatwās*] in step with the new realities of the world. Faithfulness in time is possible only if human reason, using the instruments put at its disposal, is active and creative in putting forward original proposals in tune with the time and place. In this sense, new answers connected with the Source [divine revelation] are *faithful* answers, just as there is no faithfulness without renewal.[43]

The exercise of *ijtihād* here represents the mechanism of reform, with the *fatwā* serving as the particular articulation of that reform, underpinned by faithfulness to the *sharīʿah* and concern for the common good combined with regard for Muslims' present, lived circumstances.

But *ijtihād*, Ramadan takes pains to note, is not just any kind of "critical legal formulation". Instead, he works to maintain a direct link between legal interpretation and the texts of scripture by placing scriptural parameters around the valid exercise of *ijtihād*. He adopts an epistemological framework from traditional *fiqh* that draws a distinction between norms or points of evidence (*adillah*, sing. *dalīl*) that are *qaṭʿī* (certain, definitive) and those that are *ẓannī* (conjectural, probable). *Ẓannī* norms or positions accept some interpretation or doubt, while *qaṭʿī* norms are unquestionable or inarguable. A *qaṭʿī* text is not simply from scripture, but explicit and unambiguous in its import and without any doubt in its authenticity: verses from the Qurʾān are therefore *qaṭʿī*, if clear, while most *ḥadīth* are *ẓannī*, even if straightforward in meaning. *Ijtihād* is possible only with matters that are *ẓannī*, whether that is how best to apply a *qaṭʿī* norm, extending a norm to an apposite case through analogy, or formulating a position on an issue about which scripture is silent. In virtually identical discussions in *To Be a European Muslim* and *Western Muslims*, Ramadan thus puts forward *ijtihād* as an essential part of the *sharīʿah*, but one which cannot supersede clear texts of scripture.[44]

These limits on *ijtihād* relate directly to Ramadan's understanding of *maṣlaḥah*, which, he argues, should guide the interpretation of *ẓannī* issues in order to serve the community. In *Western Muslims*, however, he emphasizes that concern for the common good, while fundamental to Islamic morality, is often used to justify otherwise religiously unfounded positions. Noting the prevalence of *maṣlaḥah* as a rationalization for sweeping reforms in economic and political spheres, he notes that revelation itself is oriented toward upholding the public interest, and therefore, God knowing best what is beneficial and harmful, clear (*qaṭʿī*) indicants from scripture cannot be contradicted "under the pretext that [practices violating scriptural norms] protect, or could or should protect, 'the common good'."[45] *Maṣlaḥah* serves as a guiding principle for the exercise of *ijtihād*, and it is thus subject to the same limitations as *ijtihād*, shaping legal formulations only regarding those issues that support scholars' interpretations. Moreover, *maṣlaḥah*, like *ijtihād*, should not be used in self-serving, arbitrary or capricious ways, but to truly benefit the community.[46]

ʿUlamāʾ must necessarily be vigilant of their own interpretations to avoid these pitfalls, but, Ramadan writes, they must also be aware of the significance—both practical and legal—of their *fatwā*s and the implications and ramifications they might have, to be certain that "the formulation of an injunction will avoid a difficulty and not do the opposite and increase problems in the context of the Islamic legal structure."[47] But *fatwā*s that approach *maṣlaḥah* in legitimate ways, formulated with due regard for the context and lived realities of Muslims, can lead to a meaningful reform of Islamic practices in a way that facilitates Muslims' integration into Western society as contributors and participants.

Reform by the "Two Books"

As Ramadan emphasizes in *Western Muslims*, as well as in *Islam, the West and the Challenges of Modernity* and *To Be a European Muslim*, the encounter with modern science and its products has represented a stumbling block for Muslims: "In industrialized and technologically advanced countries, Muslims seem to suffer from a malaise, wedged between their particular ethics and science, which sometimes seems to contradict, or more often to jostle, their faith and convictions." Faced with the secular, apparently valueless forms of knowledge that dominate Western society, Ramadan writes that Muslims are driven to question what association with the sciences they can hold as Muslims, if any; and the degree to which a potential clash or overlap between science and religion renders the former harmful: "What sort of relationship can be maintained among faith, the scriptural sources, ethics, and the human or hard sciences? . . . Are there aspects of the study of the sciences, or at least some of them, that have become 'non-Islamic' under the pressure of modernity?"[48]

As noted above, Ramadan himself believes in the compatibility of science with faithfulness, as a vehicle for insight into God's creation: "Science, from the moment it is a testimony of the attentive presence of conscience, is sacred. It is not at all a challenge to the Creator, it is the means of His continuing Revelation."[49] Noting the great history of scientific discovery in Islamic civilization, Ramadan argues that the past spirit of inquiry was driven by the fact that the acquisition of knowledge was encouraged in scripture, but also, and perhaps more significantly, that " the framework of reference [in classical Islamic civilization] was so nourished by religion that the connection between ethics and science was immediate and natural and necessarily less at risk at that time . . ."[50] Rather than disparate, much less conflicting, forms of knowledge or understanding, religion and science were part of single episteme—the Islamic intellectual tradition. Ramadan's point here is focused on the context for this knowledge and its attendant "framework of reference", presaging an aspect of his later reformism, discussed below. The encounter with Europe and modern ways of thinking, with their competing claims to scientific hegemony, threatened the entire edifice of Islamic thought. *'Ulamā'*, whose authority was directly tied to their mastery of scriptural subjects, defended those fields and "preferred to sacrifice 'the other knowledge,' rather than the norms of religion," consigning science to European predominance.[51]

The result was a narrowed scope for "Islamic" knowledge, which was limited to the religious sphere *sensu stricto*. Ramadan's reformist project, however, calls for renewing or reasserting Islam's comprehensive character, and thus he argues that no contemporary forms of knowledge are excluded from an Islamic purview. Underlying Islam's comprehensiveness is the divine unity (*tawḥīd*), which guarantees that God's moral injunctions permeate, and are situated within, His creation. Ramadan refers to these in *Western Muslims* as the "two books" which Muslims should study: one revelation, containing the message of the *sharīʿah*, the other the "book of nature". Just as scriptural sciences have been devised for understanding the former, appropriate methodologies have been crafted for approaching the latter. While these methodologies may be created by non-Muslims and be secular—or a-religious—in orientation, they are intended to discover the truth of the world, and they are therefore shaped by God's creation, rendering them inherently "Islamic". Moreover, the use of these methodologies and the study of nature is made "Islamic" through a conscientious regard for Islamic norms. Thus, all knowledge and research, regardless of its epistemological orientation or subject matter, is Islamic if it takes into account both books—that is, creation (in whatever guise as the object of study) and the moral norms of the *sharīʿah*.[52]

Ramadan posits that such research must abide by three "fundamental" moral criteria: that the intention (*nīyah*) behind it has "an active connection with *tawḥīd*;" that it must respect ethical boundaries "rationally connected with the scriptural sources;" and that its "ultimate objectives" are aligned with the *sharīʿah*—presumably, although not explicitly, by way of promoting *maṣlaḥah*. The fulfillment of these criteria serves a moral purpose; Ramadan in fact implicitly links such research with an act of worship, describing the study of the book of nature as a "faithful" action, guided by Islamic principles.[53]

Ramadan here presents a conceptual understanding through which modern science (and indeed all contemporary forms of knowledge) can be considered Islamic, while also incorporating the exercise of scientific research, when subordinated to an Islamic ethical frame. This argument plays an important role in his reformist project, particularly in terms of how it is situated within *Western Muslims*, in which it is included as part of the section on the *sharīʿah* and *ijtihād*. It immediately follows Ramadan's discussion of integration into Western society (made possible, of course, by the reform of Islamic legal practice), which makes sense, given that it deals directly with Western epistemologies, a potentially major obstacle to the engagement with the West and modernity that Ramadan so emphasizes. Nevertheless, it is a brief and minor part of the book, which does not return to the issue of science or the conceptualization of Islamic knowledge.

This would change with *Radical Reform*, published in 2008. Although the reformist project presented here builds significantly on Ramadan's previous work, the book signals a marked departure from his earlier approach to reform. It is important to note, to begin with, that many of the same premises for Ramadan remain: reform within Islam is both necessary and beneficial, such that Muslims' practices and thinking can be brought into line with their current context, and they can engage and contribute to modern society while remaining faithful to the unchanging foundation of the *sharīʿah* through a constant connection with scripture, maintained by way of the exercise of *fiqh*.[54] It is the precise method of reform, particularly in terms of *fiqh*, that breaks not only with his previous approach, but also with the conventional edifice of *fiqh* discourse.

Ramadan makes no secret of his goal. In *Western Muslims*, though acknowledging the self-consciously reformist tack of the book, he describes the approach presented as "anchored in the Islamic tradition and amplified within it: in this sense it is both deeply classical and radically new."[55] By contrast, *Radical Reform*—its title aside—begins with a general discussion of extant reformist projects (Ramadan's included) and their failure to bring about meaningful change. He writes that he could no longer simply, "as reformists had done in the past two centuries, question the productions of *fiqh*, but also its fundamentals, its sources, and the mother science (*uṣūl al-fiqh*)." Characterizing these earlier efforts as "inadequate" and "insufficient," he goes on, "Therefore I must go further and raise the issue of the sources of *uṣūl al-fiqh*, of the categories that organize them, of the methodologies that result from them and, finally, of the nature of the authority all those elements impart to text scholars (*'ulamā'* and especially *fuqahā'*)."[56]

At the heart of this new view is Ramadan's focus on context and how it drives (or rather should drive) reform. As he sees it, the disconnect between contemporary circumstances and *fiqh* practice had not been rectified or even satisfactorily addressed by his earlier attempts at reform because the degree of separation was so great and the steps toward reform so modest (at least in hindsight). Instead he puts forward two rationales for a more sweeping reformist *modus operandi* that questions "the modalities of [*ijtihād*] and of the methodologies brought into play to approach the texts and understand the context."[57] The first is that the context presented by modern society is too complex and too intricate for *fuqahā'* to comprehend sufficiently, much less to formulate *fatwā*s that serve to adapt *fiqh* to that context. The second argument, which follows from the first, is that *fiqh* should not adapt in a reactionary way to context, but must be used proactively to transform it.

In terms of the latter, Ramadan thus argues that *ijtihād* and the work of Islamic renewal should be aimed at "transformative reform," which is not simply a reform of *fiqh*, but rather of the broader environment in which Muslims live (that is to say, the world). He contrasts it with the "adaptive reform" of his previous works, as well as conventional reformist approaches (including *fiqh al-aqallīyāt* and the *maqāṣid* movement), which merely "means observing the world, noting its changes then coming back to the texts [of *fiqh*] to suggest new readings, alleviations, or exemptions in their implementation."[58] Such an approach is essentially reactive, and it has the effect of limiting and marginalizing its impact while also tacitly accepting and reifying the broader structure to which it reacts.[59] To give an example, *fatwā*s regarding a new financial practice serve as the vehicle by which *'ulamā'* take the practice into account and respond to its use. The relevant extant *fiqh* is thereby adapted to the changed circumstances, with these *fatwā*s representing part of the field of

Islamic finance, which will continue to change as more *fatwā*s are formulated in response to new practices. Islamic finance, however, only applies to Muslims, more accurately only those Muslims who choose to heed it; it therefore sits on the extreme periphery of the financial system, the constant evolution of which requires ever more *fatwā*s. Ramadan presents this situation as a kind of legal triage, in which *'ulamā'* are perpetually outpaced by circumstances and thus forced to react defensively, altering *fiqh* norms on the grounds of necessity (*ḍarūrah*) rather than engaging with the function of the financial system directly.[60]

This critique fits in with Ramadan's larger reformist project. If his aim is to incorporate Islamic moral values into broader society, then relegating those values to a distinct, marginal sphere only serves to undermine that goal. Not only does it exclude non-Muslims, but it restricts Muslims' participation and hinders their contributions, particularly in terms of ethics. Ramadan emphasizes throughout his works that Muslims have much to offer the valueless aspects of secular modernity through an Islamic critique of their premises and operation, which they can do by introducing a frame of reference based on *sharī'ah* principles.[61] The broader impact of that frame is lessened, if not negated entirely, by the link with an 'Islamic' field.

Ramadan's position here—that Islamic reform should strive to transform its environment rather than merely adapt to it—is not particularly radical in and of itself. As noted, it has been present throughout his works, and it does not actually alter the practice of *fiqh*. Indeed, on the face of it there is little that is objectionable, beyond the sheer scale of its ambition. But Ramadan argues (quite reasonably) that such reform requires a deep and extensive knowledge and mastery of the context at work, thus necessitating the participation of specialists in the work of reform. In *Western Muslims*, he advocates cooperation between *'ulamā'* and experts and intellectuals from different fields in order to better serve the practical application of *fiqh* within society.[62] In *Radical Reform*, however, he goes a step further, stating that the complexity of contemporary knowledge necessary to understand the current context is such that *'ulamā'* could not feasibly possess it in addition to their technical expertise in *fiqh*. As it is, *fiqh* and religious subjects are so distinct from other areas of knowledge that *'ulamā'* can no longer be sufficiently knowledgeable of the context to take it into account in their formulations.[63]

Ramadan therefore argues that *fiqh* as a framework is incapable of producing real, meaningful reform, or rather that reform is not possible through *fiqh* alone. He writes, describing this reasoning in terms of the scope of transformative reform:

> It aims to change the order of things in the very name of the ethics it attempts to be faithful to, in other words, to add a further step going from the texts to the context to act on the context and improve it, without ever accepting its shortcomings and injustices as matters of fate (to which one would simply have to adapt). That further step requires that a fundamental condition be

> fulfilled: acquiring deep knowledge of the context, fully mastering all areas of knowledge including the human and exact sciences, which alone can make it possible to act adequately on the world and its order. The further step, down the line in the process, thus reveals an axial condition up the line: a reform aiming to change the world—as well as providing a new reading of the [scriptural] texts [through *ijtihād*]—cannot rely only on text expertise, but requires a full and equal integration of all available human knowledge.[64]

Ramadan's reasoning here is straightforward: Islamic reform must not simply react to the contemporary world, but shape it, a goal that requires extensive knowledge of the world. The *fuqahā'* charged with crafting that reform have extensive knowledge not of the world, but of scripture and its interpretation. If Islamic reform is to be successful, then it cannot be driven solely or even primarily by *fuqahā'*, nor can it be based only on the interpretation of scriptural texts through *ijtihād*. Rather, it must incorporate both knowledge of the world and the attendant forms of interpretation.

To accomplish this, Ramadan proposes a sweeping alteration of *uṣūl al-fiqh*, not in its sense of legal theory or jurisprudence, but in its more basic sense of the "roots of *fiqh*". Traditionally understood as the Qur'ān, *sunnah*, consensus and *qiyās* (analogical reasoning), the *uṣūl al-fiqh* stand as the four sources of Islamic law, from which all *fiqh* norms stem. To these four, Ramadan adds all of creation: "Like a revelation of its own—conveying universal laws, constant principles, specific rules, and indeterminate areas—the Universe [*sic*] must be considered as an autonomous and complementary source of legal elaboration."[65]

In making this argument, Ramadan returns to the notion of the "Two Books" mentioned above, that sees nature placed alongside scripture as objects for moral study. Although the discussion of this idea is cursory in *Western Muslims*, in it he presents the book of nature as decidedly secondary, with knowledge of it supplementing knowledge of the *sharī'ah* formulated by *'ulamā'*.[66] In *Radical Reform*, however, he presents the Two Books (now capitalized, incidentally) as both distinct and co-equal; creation represents a revelation in its own right, as imbued with God's message for humanity as the texts of scripture, and its interpretation is just as essential for people's benefit. Ramadan supports this view with numerous references to the Qur'ān and *ḥadīth* about signs of God embedded in nature and Muslims' duty to seek knowledge of creation and to be inquisitive as to its meaning.[67] Thus positioned as a source of revelation, it should accordingly be treated as such within a reformist project. Ramadan writes,

> . . . everything in the Quran suggests that the unfurled Revelation, the book of the world, should be considered with the same importance, the same spiritual depth, and the same analytical and rational thoroughness as dealing with scriptural sources requires. I must thus, by referring step by step to what was said earlier about nature, go on to produce the same work of analysis, typology, and categorization of orders for the Universe and the social and human context (*al-wâqi'*) as was developed for texts.[68]

So presented, Ramadan's approach regards the book of nature as a "scriptural" source in the same way as Qur'ān or *sunnah*, with its interpretation likewise necessary for the formulation of Islamic moral norms.

He describes this as the combining of Text and Context. "Text" represents the scriptural texts, primarily, but also texts from the Islamic tradition, in addition to the hermeneutical methods used to understand them. "Context" represents the environment in which Text exists and is operative—that is, almost literally everything: the universe, the natural world, and humanity and human society in all its facets. As sources of law, they both must be explored and analyzed and considered as part of the exercise of *ijtihād*. Ramadan argues that this was, in fact, the implicit view of the first generations of Muslims, who had such intimate familiarity with their own context that it only seemed natural that it would play a role in their legal thinking.[69] However, the complexity and variegation of the contemporary period necessitates the dedicated and formal integration of context into the understanding of the *sharīʿah* (and hence as part of the *uṣūl al-fiqh*).

Radical Reform presents a framework for doing so, in which the interpretation of context and interpretation of text operate together on equal standing toward the articulation of a new Islamic ethics. Ramadan envisions this as a partnership between scholars and experts, particularly in the natural and social sciences. He labels these groups (respectively) *ʿulamāʾ al-nuṣūṣ*—"Text scholars"—and *ʿulamāʾ al-wāqiʿ*—"Context scholars"—and they each operate autonomously with the ethical formulations stemming from the combination of their relevant work on a given issue.[70]

Because both sets of scholars operate equally and autonomously, neither is beholden or subordinate to the other, whether this is in terms of authority or, importantly, in terms of knowledge. The knowledge and methodologies of Context scholars are held entirely separate from those of Text scholars. As such, existing scientific and social scientific fields and their paradigms and epistemes, which have been duly designed and developed for the study of their subjects, are not directly affected by Ramadan's reform, which precludes influence by *fiqh* in their function. Nor, he takes pains to add, should *fiqh* be influenced by scientific paradigms.[71] Because Context scholars' knowledge is of nature and distinct from Text scholars and their knowledge of scripture, their work is not "Islamic" in the same way, and therefore they do not have to be Muslim to engage in Ramadan's project.[72]

Fiqh (strictly speaking[73]), as the purview of Text scholars, is thus left relatively unchanged from Ramadan's earlier works. As in those books, he does not in *Radical Reform* delve deeply into the intricacies of legal theory, but rather the discussion here focuses on the orientation and priorities of reformist *fiqh*. He criticizes other, narrowly *fiqh*-based reforms as too restricted and insular, overly focused on fidelity to the text in ways that hinder the practical application of the law or reliant on legal devices (such as the principle of necessity) that are solely pragmatic, and thus failing to engage with the underlying *sharīʿah* issue.[74] He instead argues for a broader approach, more attuned to the real environment and also (not incidentally) more amenable to his larger project of transformative reform.

Specifically, his treatment of *fiqh* calls for a synthesis of three different approaches to reasoning taken from the legal tradition, which he explicitly associates with a historical exemplar: the deductive reasoning of Imām al-Shāfiʿī (767–820), the inductive reasoning of the early Ḥanafīs, and Shāṭibī's *maqāṣid*. For Ramadan, each approach highlights a distinct but equally important aspect for his reformist project. The most straightforward of the three, Shāfiʿī's work toward the development of *uṣūl al-fiqh* as a formal methodology relies on deductive logic—the process of formulating particular points from general premises—emphasizing the need for the direct derivation of *furūʿ* (positive law) from the texts of scripture. By contrast, the early disciples of Abū Ḥanīfah (699–767) crafted their school's jurisprudential doctrine out of the collective body of Abū Ḥanīfah's *furūʿ*, which were inevitably linked to the context in which they were articulated. The Ḥanafīs' contribution thus lies in their use of inductive logic in the determination of the 'effective causes' (*ʿilal*, sing. *ʿillah*) underlying the *furūʿ* as general norms, the practical manifestation of which took a precise form contingent on real, changing circumstances. Finally, Shāṭibī's *maqāṣid* offers a framework of guiding principles for legal reasoning that promote a focus on the practical impact of *fuqahāʾ*'s work and the ends that *fiqh* interpretation must uphold, such that scholars do not lose sight of how their judgments operate in Muslims' lives.[75]

From these three approaches Ramadan forms a *modus operandi* for reformist *fiqh* through the renewed exercise of *ijtihād*, which he argues should involve the derivation of moral action from the texts of scripture, the rational analysis of practice and circumstances best to apply *ʿilal* in specific settings, and an adherence to the universal spirit of the *sharīʿah* and use of *fiqh* to promote its aims. These, of course, reflect recurring themes throughout Ramadan's body of work: the importance of *ijtihād*, fidelity to scripture, regard for the practical and real environment in legal reasoning, and the promotion of the *maqāṣid* as overarching priorities for *ijtihād*.

This approach to *fiqh* represents the methodology for Text scholars' interpretations, and as such it is grounded in the Islamic tradition of hermeneutics and interpretive strategies, which were designed for dealing with scripture and other religious texts. This approach has been adapted to take into account contextual concerns, as part of Ramadan's broader reformist project. But those concerns rely for their interpretation on the work of Context scholars, whose knowledge falls within epistemes entirely separate from *fiqh* and who therefore follow wholly distinct paradigms.

Nevertheless, Ramadan's project aims for comprehensiveness, and he articulates a further way to bring the Two Books—the knowledge produced by each type of scholar—together, ensuring a holistic character. He envisions "*equal-representation, egalitarian, and specialized* research and *fatwā* committees that are able to ally three essential requirements: global understanding of the Two Books' higher goals, awareness of the higher objectives and goals in their field of study (the texts or writings in a particular scientific field), and first-hand specialized knowledge in the said subject" with *fuqahā'* who are learned in that subject.[76] For these committees' operation, he describes a dual process of "*ijtihād*" (which he defines as "autonomous critical reasoning") carried out in parallel by both Text and Context scholars. First, *ijtihād* that "respect[s] and tak[es] into account the immutable and the changing" is carried out into "texts" and "social and human contexts," respectively, leading to "Critical reading interpretations, and strategies in the legal [or] practical field," which are formulated autonomously by each set of scholars. This is followed by the "Common (collaborative, specialized) *ijtihād* of applied ethics," performed collectively by all scholars involved, ultimately producing studies on the subject in question "aiming to determine ethical rules, the scope and modalities of their application, and the stages of their implementation" for that field.[77]

To facilitate the combination of the two (or more) disparate methodologies of Text and Context at work, Ramadan puts forward a schema for making apples-to-apples connections between the different spheres of knowledge, based on *fiqh* epistemology. Relying on the distinction between *qaṭ'ī* and *ẓannī* evidence, he proposes a categorization for different types of knowledge of Context. He presents certain laws of the natural world (gravity, for instance) as well as theories verified through the experimental sciences as *qaṭ'ī*, which must therefore be taken into account as fundamental parts of creation. Though not moral, these principles are nevertheless critical for any moral understanding as, he writes, the message of scripture "cannot be understood and respected if the laws of the book of the world are not similarly recognized and respected."[78] The humanities and social sciences, by contrast, are subject to greater intellectual diversity and multiplicity of interpretations and methodologies, leaving less certainty as to their knowledge. While particular aspects of society and human interaction are beyond doubt, and therefore *qaṭ'ī* (such as the fact of diversity among societies), they are very few. The overwhelming bulk of these types of knowledge are *ẓannī*, which does not lessen their importance or utility, but rather, because they are equivalent to judgments by *fuqahā'*, encourages *ijtihād*, critique and debate on these matters.[79] This schema allows for analogous treatment of very disparate pieces of knowledge and the problem of how to weigh scientific or social scientific evidence against scriptural proofs.

More importantly, Ramadan offers a revised understanding of the *maqāṣid* as a further orienting principle for parallel *ijtihād* into the Two Books. He argues for a more extensive understanding of the *maqāṣid* for this purpose, better suited than the conventional *fiqh* conception to incorporating contributions from Context. Accordingly, he proposes a hierarchy of objectives of narrowing scope. The primary *maqāṣid* from which all others are derived (and also those most directly connected to the divine) are *maṣlaḥah* (i.e. the good) and transcend life and death. Following from this are three fundamental and *a priori maqāṣid* for all of creation: life, nature and peace. Beyond these are *maqāṣid* specifically aimed at humans, and as such they are historically contingent and liable to change. This, he contends, should be part of the broader work of reformism he proposes:

> New scientific knowledge, shaping a new outlook on human beings or Nature, might lead us to extend that list [of *maqāṣid*], since this must always remain dialectical elaboration: starting first from what the texts say about higher objectives, then from what social and human contexts reveal (and sometimes impose), we must return to the texts with a renewed, deeper understanding about the meaning and implementation of the aforesaid rulings.[80]

He suggests as third-level objectives "Dignity (of humankind, living species, and Nature), Welfare, Knowledge, Creativity, Autonomy, Development, Equality, Freedom, Justice, Fraternity, Love, Solidarity, and Diversity." Finally, the fourth-level objectives serve to complement and particularize the more fundamental *maqāṣid*, and are thus divided into distinct categories: the Inner Being; the Being, the Individual; Societies and Groups.[81]

These more specific *maqāṣid* are important for the elaboration of ethical norms because they direct *ijtihād* and the interpretation of the Two Books toward discrete, precise ends that are reflective of the contemporary age and its concerns. In this way, they focus the work of the two sets of scholars in articulating ethical norms on a given topic by enumerating explicitly what the intended priorities are. Their universal character likewise allows for the creation of "a global, and thereby holistic, vision of contemporary Islamic ethics."[82]

This is the basic aim for Ramadan's entire reformist project: the elaboration of a new ethics, grounded in Islam, but universal in their applicability, which will be a source for the broad transformation of various aspects of modern society—the economy, politics, the sciences, *everything* practically—through the introduction of Islamic norms fashioned by scholars and experts into workable and practical ethical models. And ultimately, regardless of the interpretive or epistemic underpinnings of the reform, it is the drive for ethical and moral righteousness, for the foundational *maqāṣid*, that qualifies it as "Islamic":

> The heart's meditation about the origin, meaning, and higher objectives of the texts and contexts, as well as the conscience's formulation of ethical limits to human action in the Universe and toward humankind—those are the attitudes that underlie the "Islamic" dimension of the scientific approach and of ethical choices. It is not a matter of superficially "making science and knowledge Islamic," but rather, essentially and deeply, of establishing an *Islamic conscience* of objectives and an *Islamic ethics* related to human behavior and the qualitative use of knowledge.[83]

Enacting Reform

The very nature of this ethics calls for its manifestation within society, something that Ramadan has not always addressed in specific terms. Accordingly, he devotes the final section of *Radical Reform* to the application of his reformist project in particular areas. He focuses on six broad spheres, comprising different, adjacent topics of current social and political import—medical ethics; culture and the arts; women and the family; ecology and the economy; "society, education, and power"; and "ethics and universals". The organization of these chapters is indicative of how he understands context within his reformist framework. This is, of course, of critical importance: given the centrality of context as a concept for Ramadan, seeing a concrete example of reform that takes it into account is certainly illustrative. And context without question shapes the discussion here. The chapter on ecology and the economy is a good example. While these two topics are seemingly distinct, Ramadan frequently addresses environmental and economic issues in light of one another, such that a critique of capitalistic consumption references its toll on the environment, while a proposed dialogue over global warning and its effects on agriculture "requires developing a general ethical approach focusing as much on economy, solidarity, and overconsumption as on respecting nature and species, because all these dimensions are linked."[84]

While touching upon contextual issues in a fairly systematic and extensive way, Ramadan does not positively offer, or advocate, concrete reforms. He focuses instead on attitude and approach, arguing that Muslims should adopt a more critical posture in response to the pressing issues facing them. He frequently calls for reflection, for Muslims to question and discuss what is best for their societies—what kind of government, what forms of artistic expression, how to foster women's participation, etc. At the same time, he repeatedly argues against resorting to rigid literalism or knee-jerk anti-Westernism in response to the challenges presented by the contemporary age.

As with his reformist project in general, Ramadan makes continual reference to the *maqāṣid* as guiding principles, and the reflection that he urges is intended to keep these moral ends in mind and to lead towards practical reforms that uphold them. He writes, for instance, that medical ethics should be oriented around the promotion of human life, dignity, welfare, conscience, personal stability, physical integrity and health (*maqāṣid* taken from the list above). Thus controversial practices, such as female doctors treating male patients, contraception and abortion, and organ donation, should be approached with *maqāṣid* as primary considerations. But this is as far as Ramadan goes in addressing these questions. When discussing abortion, after describing some positions on the matter taken from the legal tradition, he notes the relevant *maqāṣid* that must be taken into account by the doctors and *fuqahā'* who address the issue, enjoining them to consider both the fetus and the mother as well as their particular context when reaching their decisions.[85]

This is not to say that Ramadan takes no definitive positions. In fact, a strong critique of capitalism and Western economic and cultural hegemony underlies much of the final section of *Radical Reform*, touching upon artistic and cultural production, the economy, and social and political forms. He also expresses unequivocal support for democracy, but he defines it as a generic system of organizational and institutional models, listing its essential components as the rule of law, equality, universal suffrage, government accountability, and the separation of powers. The precise form that a democratic government should take, however, is up to the leaders and people of each country to decide for themselves. Such a government and its function must be based on ethical principles taken from the *maqāṣid*, which it must uphold and defend.[86]

Indeed, he critiques what he sees as the reductive treatment of secularism in global political discourse in a way that reinforces his reformist goals. Noting the misleading but prevalent association of the West with secular government and the attendant belief that Islam has no distinction between religion and politics, he argues that such a dichotomous view wrongly characterizes both sides. It obscures the central place of Christianity and Christian heritage in Western societies, as well as the long history of distinct political and religious structures in Islamic ones. For Ramadan, this view merely complicates and hinders any effort at true reform by pitting would-be "secularists" and "Islamists" on necessarily opposing sides. Instead, his reformist project calls for a government that combines *'ulamā'* with political, social, economic and other experts and elites, while explicitly operating according to the *maqāṣid*: it thus precludes a "secular" character but also rejects "Islamic" politics as such.[87] It is roughly this line of reasoning—that the government should not be strictly secular but should incorporate religious values in a meaningful and non-reductive way—that underlies Ramadan's *Islam and the Arab Awakening*, written in the aftermath of the Arab Spring.[88]

Overall, Ramadan offers straightforward but vague expressions of his reformism, namely that any concrete reform must be inclined toward permissibility, open to critical thinking and broad acceptance of diversity and disagreement, and reliant on the *maqāṣid* to maintain a connection with Islamic moral and ethical norms.

Andrew March, one of Ramadan's most insightful academic critics, has noted the seeming discrepancy between the sweeping nature of his reform of *fiqh* and the "much more elusive and risk-averse" character of his applied ethics. Why, March wonders, go to the trouble of devising and advocating an explicitly radical theoretical reform programme only to then articulate a conservative, even banal vision for its application? While March doesn't propose a definitive answer, he does note the limitations presented by Ramadan's Muslim readers (or potential readers) and the controversy that would arise from Ramadan attacking prominent markers of Islamic religious identity or widely held beliefs head on. Such an approach (if it is in fact Ramadan's wish to do so) would surely provoke significant backlash against what is otherwise already a very controversial endeavor. March hypothesizes, then, that Ramadan avoids this backlash by avoiding these issues altogether; his reformist project is clearly aimed at profound, foundational reform of Islamic legal thinking, and thus it would necessarily bring about changes in the ways Islamic ethics are applied without confronting problematic practices directly. (As March puts it, Ramadan is less trying to solve such problems than dissolve them.)[89]

There is also the fact of the matter that *Radical Reform*, as March points out, is quite obviously not intended for a popular audience. Its rethinking of *uṣūl al-fiqh* and legal interpretation stand as evidence that the audience Ramadan has in mind is primarily comprised of those people doing the interpreting—that is, Islamic religious authorities—and indeed the frequent calls for reflection and openness are accompanied by references to the shortcomings of contemporary Muslim leaders. While for many his reform is a non-starter, its express role for *fuqahā'* and calls for their involvement on a broad range of issues mean that it isn't necessarily so. Indeed, Ramadan argues explicitly for authority to be concentrated in the hands of *'ulamā'*, stating that violent and extremist religious orientations are fostered by uninformed and uneducated interpretations of scripture outside of any established framework connected with the tradition.[90] Ramadan thus seeks to preserve (or reestablish) elite, learned religious authority, while expanding and resituating its definition.

The importance of *'ulamā'* here is significant for the practical effects of Ramadan's reformism and how he understands his own role and function. It also offers another possible answer to March's question. Simply put, Ramadan is not a *muftī*, and does not consider himself so. Rather, he argues that the work of reform is not the work of a single individual, but of the community.[91] His reformist project, as noted, relies on myriad committees of scholars and experts to address various and sundry issues. If there is any place for definitive answers within his project, they would come out from these committees. Moreover, the central importance of cooperation between Text and Context scholars precludes Ramadan from articulating concrete views, particularly on subjects such as medicine or politics, which he explicitly asserts need detailed, specialized understanding. Instead, the vague and often cursory discussion of the applications of his reform represents a jumping-off point, a small first step toward extensive, significant reform utilizing his radical theoretical framework.

Such a framework is the impetus behind the Center for Islamic Legislation and Ethics (CILE), which began operation in early 2012.[92] This organization focuses on formulating Islamic reform in the areas of arts, environment, economics, education, food, gender, media, bioethics, migration and human rights, politics and psychology. It uses a "methodology" that is based in the *maqāṣid* and the cooperation of religious and secular experts and which is broadly along the lines of Ramadan's reformist project as described in *Radical Reform*.

CILE's scholarly contributions to date are small in scope, limited mainly to lectures, a handful of publications, and frequent conferences and workshops.

One of its primary projects is the convening of regular "Text & Context Seminars", with the aim of bringing together both types of *'ulamā'* in equal numbers to discuss topics of significance and "propose answers and ideas for further research."[93] Its efforts have also been more conventional than Ramadan's reformist project. The latter is understandably quite controversial: the reconfiguration of Islamic legal reasoning that it proposes is unpalatable to many *'ulamā'*, even those who are engaged in the reform of *fiqh*. As David Warren notes, reformist scholars participating in CILE's first conference in 2013 understood the goal of the event—and the reform project in general—in decidedly narrower and less radical terms.[94] Warren argues that Qatar, which has positioned itself through government patronage as a center for Islamic legal reform in the Arab world, acts as a moderating influence on CILE, limiting to some degree its more controversial positions. CILE is not independent, but falls under the bureaucratic umbrella of the Qatar Faculty of Islamic Studies, which is itself part of the Qatar Foundation, backed by the royal family.[95] The Qatar Foundation represents a significant aspect of Qatari state policy, which, as Allen Fromherz writes, has made the promotion of education a main priority. Describing intellectual reform as one of the "greatest untapped resources in the Middle East," he notes that Qatar has used patronage of scholars and intellectuals to build up its stature and project influence abroad.[96]

CILE appears to be quite consciously connecting itself with the established reformist circles in Qatar, most notably Yusuf al-Qaradawi's International Union of Muslim Scholars (IUMS, *al-Ittiḥād al-'Ālamī li-'Ulamā' al-Muslimīn*).[97] Figures associated with this group, including Qaradawi himself, IUMS secretary general 'Ali Qaradaghi, and then-IUMS vice chairman 'Abd Allah Bin Bayyah, participated in CILE's first events in early 2013.[98]

Ramadan's legal thought has been deeply influenced by Qaradawi, particularly in terms of *ijtihād*.[99] Since the publication of *Western Muslims*, Ramadan has criticized some of Qaradawi's positions, but nevertheless Ramadan's legal thought remains indebted to the so-called "*maqāṣidī* school", pioneered by Qaradawi, and its associated work on *fiqh al-aqallīyāt*. Though unacknowledged, Ramadan's theory of the Two Books mirrors an argument made by the late scholar at the International Institute of Islamic Thought, Taha Jabir Al-Alwani, that there are two "readings"—the Qur'ān and the natural universe—which Muslims are commanded to understand.[100] A *fiqh* methodology that combines both readings can thus account for social reality and practical knowledge to serve Muslim minorities' legal needs.[101]

As Warren notes, based on interviews with CILE staff, Ramadan is not positioning CILE as a *fatwā*-issuing body (in other words, as an Islamic authority) in its own right, but rather as a contributor to on-going work in Islamic reform, "to enable the text scholars to perform their current role more effectively."[102] In this way, its efforts are conceived as a part of "collective *ijtihād*" (*ijtihād jamā'ī*)—a term taken from Qaradawi—which it supports, but does not engage in itself (or rather, that Ramadan himself does not engage in).[103] CILE's work thus far supports this point. The overwhelming majority of its publications and scholarly focus has fallen on the field of Islamic bioethics, which is the area of legal reform that perhaps contains the most extensive literature.[104] In fact, Mohammed Ghaly, part of the CILE faculty, published an article in 2015 in a themed issue of the journal *Die Welt des Islams* dedicated to the topic.[105] Ghaly at the time of writing is the most prolific scholar at CILE, authoring several articles on its website and hosting a regular podcast. While this accounts for the degree of attention directed toward bioethics and related issues—it is Ghaly's research focus—this topic also allows CILE to connect its work with a substantial body of literature, while building on previous works. Indeed, Ghaly's article in *Die Welt des Islams* argues for more equal cooperation between scientists and *'ulamā'* on bioethical issues, presenting this view as an explicit corrective to earlier approaches led by Islamic scholars.

CILE's limited output so far speaks to the ambition of Ramadan's reform project and its intended scale, but also to the decidedly cautious approach to its enactment. The radical reform that he envisions is undoubtedly a long-term endeavor, in contrast to CILE's short history. The essence of Ramadan's project lies in its sweep: the restructuring of the very sources of Islamic law and ethics, and the incorporation of outside epistemes into an Islamic legal framework. This is the scale of reform that he believes is necessary to meet the challenges and obstacles faced by Muslims today. He insists that significant intellectual work must be done to bring the texts and context in line with each other, so that Muslims can fit into Western modernity while remaining Muslims. This work requires new approaches to scripture, to determine through *ijtihād* what is timeless and immutable in Islam and what can be altered; and a new approach to the historical context, in order to bring Islamic morality to bear on modernity and transform it in a principled and ethical way. The immense scale of the problems that modernity presents for Muslims can only be met by an equally sweeping project of reform.

Notes

1. For an example of the type of attention Ramadan receives in European circles, see the problematic discussion in Paul Hollander, "Political Pilgrimages: Their Meaning, Aftermath, and Linkages," in *Politics of Memory in Post-Communist Europe*, ed. Mihail Neamtu, Corina Dobbs, and Marius Stan (Bucharest: Zeta Books, 2010), 21–34, esp. 32–3.
2. Tariq Ramadan, "A Call for a Moratorium on Corporal Punishment—The Debate in Review," in *New Directions in Islamic Thought: Exploring Reform and Muslim Tradition*, ed. Kari Vogt, Lena Larsen and Christian Moe (London: I. B. Tauris, 2011), 163–74, esp. 168.
3. The exchange is recorded in Aziz Zemouri, *Faut-il faire taire Tariq Ramadan?* (Paris: Archipel, 2005).
4. Tariq Ramadan, *Radical Reform: Islamic Ethics and Liberation* (Oxford: Oxford University Press, 2008).
5. Ibid., 78–86 and *passim*.

6. Alexandre Caeiro, "The Power of European Fatwās: The Minority Fiqh Project and the Making of an Islamic Counterpublic," *International Journal of Middle East Studies* 42 (2010), 435–49, esp. 443.
7. Tariq Ramadan, *To Be a European Muslim: A Study of Islamic Sources in the European Context* (Leicester: The Islamic Foundation, 1999); Ramadan, *Western Muslims and the Future of Islam* (Oxford: Oxford University Press, 2004).
8. Ramadan, *European Muslim*, 3.
9. Ibid., 3–4.
10. Ramadan, *Western Muslims*, 69, also 72–3.
11. Ibid., 63–77.
12. Ramadan, *European Muslim*, 131.
13. Ramadan, *Western Muslims*, 21–2; also Ramadan, *European Muslim*, 43.
14. Ramadan, *Western Muslims*, 63.
15. Ibid., 27.
16. Ibid., 54.
17. Ramadan, *European Muslim*, 62–5, 171–2.
18. Ramadan, *Western Muslims*, 33–7.
19. Ibid., 52–5, 80–5, also esp. 113–15.
20. Tariq Ramadan, *Islam, the West and the Challenges of Modernity* (Leicester: The Islamic Foundation, 2001 [1995]), 308.
21. Ramadan, *Western Muslims*, 144–52.
22. Ibid., 160.
23. Tariq Ramadan, *In the Footsteps of the Prophet: Lessons from the Life of Muhammad* (New York: Oxford University Press, 2007), 22; emphasis added.
24. Tariq Ramadan, *The Quest for Meaning: Developing a Philosophy of Pluralism* (London: Penguin, 2010).
25. Cf. Ramadan, *Radical Reform*, 294–5.
26. Ramadan, *Western Muslims*, 22–4.
27. Ibid., 24–9.
28. Ibid., 28.
29. Ibid., 24–5.
30. Ibid., 25, 27.
31. Ibid., 27–8.
32. Ibid., 24.
33. Ibid., 28–9, also 22.
34. Bernard Weiss, "Interpretation in Islamic Law: The Theory of Ijtihad," *The American Journal of Comparative Law* 26 (1978), 199–212 at 201.
35. Ramadan, *Western Muslims*, 24–5, 28.
36. Ramadan, *European Muslim*, 233.
37. Ibid., 60.
38. Ibid.
39. Ibid. 76–82; cf. Madjid Khadduri, "Maṣlaḥa," in *EI*²; Felicitas Opwis, "Maslaha in Contemporary Islamic Legal Theory," *Islamic Law and Society* 12 (2005), 182–223.
40. See Wael Hallaq, *A History of Islamic Legal Theories: An Introduction to Sunni Usul al-Fiqh* (Cambridge: Cambridge University Press, 1999), esp. 162–206.
41. Ramadan, *European Muslim*, 62–5.
42. Ibid., 87.
43. Ramadan, *Western Muslims*, 62; emphasis in the original.

44. Ibid., 43–6; Ramadan, *European Muslim*, 82–6.
45. Ramadan, *Western Muslims*, 41.
46. Ibid., 38–43, also 52.
47. Ibid., 41.
48. Ibid., 55.
49. Ramadan, *Islam, the West*, 232.
50. Ramadan, *Western Muslims*, 56.
51. Ibid.
52. Ibid., 58–61.
53. Ibid., 60.
54. Cf. Ramadan, *Radical Reform*, 12–25.
55. Ramadan, *Western Muslims*, 3.
56. Ramadan, *Radical Reform*, 2–3.
57. Ibid., 30.
58. Ibid., 33.
59. Ibid., 32–3, 35.
60. Cf. ibid., 35, 117–19.
61. Cf. Ramadan, *Western Muslims*, 162–5; also Ramadan, *Islam, the West*, 308.
62. Ramadan, *Western Muslims*, 163.
63. Ramadan, *Radical Reform*, 31–3 and *passim*.
64. Ibid., 33.
65. Ibid., 102.
66. Ramadan, *Western Muslims*, 57–60.
67. Cf. Ramadan, *Radical Reform*, 87–90, 98–100.
68. Ibid., 102.
69. Ibid., 85.
70. Cf. ibid., 109, 121, 131–2.
71. Ibid., 109.
72. Ibid., 132–3.
73. Ramadan is rarely consistent with his terms, and he uses "legal" and "*fiqh*", as well as linked terms, to refer both to conventional Islamic legal reasoning and the radical form of ethics that is at the forefront of *Radical Reform*. For clarity's sake, from this point forward in the present paper "*fiqh*" will be used specifically for the work of Text scholars within Ramadan's project, rather than referring more generally to the project itself or its potential outcomes.
74. Ramadan, *Radical Reform*, esp. 30–8, 110–11, 113–25. Indeed, these critiques are frequent in *Radical Reform*.
75. Ibid., 39–77.
76. Ibid., 132; emphasis in the original.
77. Ibid., 144, cf. figure 10.3.
78. Ibid., 105.
79. Ibid., 104–8, also 94–5.
80. Ibid., 139.
81. Ibid., 139–43. He enumerates for these three respective categories: Education (of the heart and mind), Conscience (of being and responsibility), Sincerity, Contemplation, Balance (intimate and personal stability), and Humility; Physical Integrity, Health, Subsistence, Intelligence, Progeny, Work, Belongings, Contracts, and our Neighborhoods; the Rule of law, Independence (self-determination), Deliberation, Pluralism, Evolution, Cultures, Religions, and Memories (heritage); cf. figure 10.2.

82. Ibid., 144.
83. Ibid., 111–12; emphasis in the original.
84. Ibid., 254.
85. Ibid., 171–3.
86. Ibid., 273, 278–85.
87. Ibid., 261–5.
88. Tariq Ramadan, *Islam and the Arab Awakening* (New York: Oxford University Press, 2012).
89. Andrew March, "The Post-Legal Ethics of Tariq Ramadan: Persuasion and Performance in *Radical Reform: Islamic Ethics and Liberation*," *Middle East Law and Governance* 2 (2010).
90. Ramadan, *Radical Reform*, 23–7.
91. Ramadan, *Radical Reform*, 153–4.
92. Habib Toumi, "Centre for Islamic Legislation, Ethical Thought Launched in Qatar," *Gulf News Qatar*, January 16, 2012, accessed May 9, 2016, http://gulfnews.com/news/gulf/qatar/centre-for-islamic-legislation-ethical-thought-launched-in-qatar–1.966634.
93. Center for Islamic Legislation and Ethics, "Center Activities," accessed May 6, 2016, http://www.cilecenter.org/en/center-activities/.
94. David Warren, "Doha—The Center of Reformist Islam? Considering *Radical Reform* in the Qatar Context: Tariq Ramadan and the Research Center for Islamic Legislation and Ethics (CILE)," in *Maqāṣid al-Sharī'a* [sic] *and Contemporary Reformist Muslim Thought: An Examination*, ed. Adis Duderija (New York: Palgrave, 2014), 73–100, esp. 89.
95. Center for Islamic Legislation and Ethics, "Vision & Mission," accessed May 13, 2016, http://www.cilecenter.org/en/vision-mission/.
96. Allen Fromherz, *Qatar: A Modern History* (London: I. B. Tauris, 2012), 24, 27–9, also 152; cf. Warren, "Doha—The Center of Reformist Islam?," 77.
97. See Muhammad Qasim Zaman, *Modern Islamic Thought in a Radical Age: Religious Authority and Internal Criticism* (Cambridge: Cambridge University Press, 2012), *passim*.
98. Center for Islamic Legislation and Ethics, "Press Release: CILE Bioethics Seminar," January 7, 2013, accessed May 13, 2016, http://www.cilecenter.org/en/press-release/press-release-cile-bioethics-seminar/; Center for Islamic Legislation and Ethics, "The Research Center for Islamic Legislation and Ethics concludes its first International Conference," March 9, 2013, accessed May 13, 2016, http://www.cilecenter.org/en/press-release/the-research-center-for-islamic-legislation-and-ethics-concludes-its-first-international-conference/. On Bin Bayyah and contemporary legal reform, see the relevant chapters in the present volumes.
99. Ramadan's early understanding of *ijtihād* is taken primarily from Qaradawi: Ramadan, *European Muslim*, esp. 94–98; cf. Yūsuf al-Qaradawi, *al-Ijtihād al-mu'āṣir: Bayn al-inḍibāṭ wa-al-infirāṭ* (Cairo: Dār al-Tawzī' wa-al-Nashr al-Islāmīyah, 1993); see also Rainer Brunner, "Forms of Muslim Self-Perception in European Islam," *Hagar: Studies in Culture, Polity and Identities* 6 (2005), 75–86, esp. 82.
100. Ṭaha J. al-Alwani, "The Islamization of Knowledge: Yesterday and Today," *AJISS* 12 (1995), 81–101, esp. 84–5.
101. Taha Jabir Al-Alwani, *Towards a Fiqh for Minorities: Some Basic Reflections* (London, International Institute of Islamic Thought, 2003). See also Chapter 3 in this volume.

102. Warren, "Doha—The Center of Reformist Islam?," 88.
103. Ibid., 87; cf. Ramadan, *European Muslim*, 97–8; Qaradawi, *al-Ijtihād al-mu'āṣir*, 97–9; also Zaman, *Modern Islamic Thought*, esp. 95–6.
104. Cf. Center for Islamic Legislation and Ethics, "Publications," accessed May 13, 2016, http://www.cilecenter.org/en/publication/. CILE's Arabic- and French-language pages list virtually no articles.
105. Mohammed Ghaly, "Biomedical Scientists as Co-Muftis: Their Contribution to Contemporary Islamic Bioethics," *Die Welt des Islams* 55 [*The Social Politics of Islamic Bioethics*] (2015), 286–311.

PART III

♦ ♦ ♦

NEO-CONSERVATIVES

This final part looks at a third kind of response, which might appear to be far more conservative in its reformist potential than the previous two, but which is in reality equally dynamic. This comprises the adjustments and adaptations which can be observed among some representatives from the most conservative of Muslim scholarly traditions, namely Salafism and Deoband. Chapter 5 focuses on the work of Yasir Qadhi, an influential young Muslim scholar in the U.S.A. After years of study at Islamic University of Medina (IUM) in Saudi Arabia, Qadhi initially identified as a Salafi. But today, having been back in America for some years and having studied for a Ph.D. at Yale, he is revisiting many of his previously hard line positions to advance a much more nuanced reasoning of how Muslims can best practice their faith when living in a Western context. Chapter 6 in turn reviews current debates within two reformist Deobandi platforms in the West: Darul Qasim in Chicago and Ebrahim College in London. While respecting the Deobandi *fiqh*, both show a clear departure from the narrowly defined process of *taqlīd* still dominant within Deobandi circles in South Asia (Volume 1, Part III).

CHAPTER
5

YASIR QADHI AND THE DEVELOPMENT OF REASONABLE SALAFISM

Christopher Pooya Razavian

Yasir Qadhi has recently become one of America's most influential Muslim public figures. He has brought new life to Salafism in America by reforming the movement away from its conservative core, arguing that it offers no solutions for the modern age. His defence of same-sex marriage laws in America, approach to liberal citizenship, and his views about Islamic law are alien to many mainstream Salafis. Yasir Qadhi, it is argued here, has developed a new *Reasonable Salafism* whereby greater emphasis is placed on the lived realities of modern Muslims. This move towards reasonable Salafism was prompted by his own dissatisfaction with mainstream Salafism. He uses various conservative historical *fatwās*, such as the ban on the printing press, to highlight the negative effect that such rulings can have on Muslim life. Ultimately, his position on the necessity of incorporating modern context serves as a foundation for his position on Muslim citizenship in liberal societies. It is a type of citizenship that echoes Rawls' position on "reasonable citizenship"[1]: Muslims should consider other citizens as free and equal and endorse liberal laws that grant freedoms for other minorities even if these laws go against moral Islamic principles.

Born in Houston, Texas, Yasir Qadhi, who is of Pakistani origin, spent his early years in Jeddah, Saudi Arabia where his parents had temporarily relocated. He returned to the United States to attain his B.Sc. in Chemical Engineering though only to later travel back to Saudi Arabia to study at the Islamic University of Medina (IUM), where he received multiple degrees. He has a diploma in Arabic, a B.A. from the Faculty of Hadith and Islamic Sciences and an M.A. in Islamic Theology from the Faculty of Da'wah and Islamic Belief. He then returned to the United States in 2005 to pursue a Ph.D. degree in Religious Studies at Yale University. His dissertation was on Ibn

Taymīyah and it was submitted in 2013.[2] It is difficult to know exactly what Yasir Qadhi studied during his time at IUM given that there are no historical records of the curriculum; moreover, it is common practice for IUM students to augment their university studies by studying with teachers outside of the university. Nonetheless, most Islamic studies programmes follow a general path of progression and a review of the current curriculum reveals that the courses at IUM do not steer too far from that path. The Faculty of Hadith and Islamic Sciences has designed a programme dedicated primarily to the study of *ḥadīth*. This includes courses on the historiography of *ḥadīth* (*tadwīn al-sunnah*), *ḥadīth* terminology (*muṣṭaliḥ al-ḥadīth*), as well as criticism of the chain of narration (*al-jarḥ wa-al-ta'dīl*). More general subjects are offered as well, such as a course on the history of the Prophet, another on the history of Saudi Arabia, and courses on Islamic law and Arabic grammar.[3] The Faculty of Da'wah and Islamic Belief also follows a standard path of progression. The interests of this college are much broader with courses ranging from Islamic law and principles of jurisprudent (*uṣūl al-fiqh*) to issues relating to theology and Qur'ānic exegesis.[4]

Qadhi's Ph.D. dissertation is focused on Ibn Taymīyah and it is titled "Reconciling Reason and Revelation in the Writings of Ibn Taymiyyah (d. 728/1328): An Analytical Study of Ibn Taymīyah's *Dar' al-Ta'āruḍ*.[5] The dissertation is an examination of Ibn Taymīyah's attempt to reconcile reason and revelation, specifically as outlined in Ibn Taymīyah's ten-volume *Dar' al-Ta'āruḍ* which was written in response to Ash'arī theology, specifically Fakhr al-Dīn al-Rāzī's (d. 606/1209) *Ta'sīs al-Taqdīs*.

In the dissertation, Qadhi stays engaged with the academic debates and does not explain the relevance of this work for contemporary Muslims though he does attempt to do so in a lecture given at the International Institute of Islamic Thought (IIIT) about his dissertation. He believes that although Ibn Taymīyah's book was written about God's attributes, and the issue of God's attributes is of little relevance to the lives of contemporary Muslims, the broader implications of the issue are relevant. It is about the balance between revelation and reason. The issue of God's attributes was used by Fakhr al-Dīn al-Rāzī to develop his "*al-Qānūn al-Kulī*", the Universal Rule, which states that if reason conflicted with revelation then precedence is to be given to reason.[6] This does not mean that revelation is rejected, but that the text is understood in a way that it conforms to reason. Ibn Taymīyah wrote a ten-volume refutation to al-Rāzī's short treastise in order to refute this universal claim.[7]

Qadhi states that one of the attributes that separated Ibn Taymīyah from previous Ḥanbalī scholars is that Ibn Taymīyah read the books of his intellectual opponents. Previous Ḥanbalī scholars believed that reading the books of philosophers or other theologians would lead them astray. Ibn Taymīyah instead read the works of these scholars including the works of the Greek philosophers. Thus, previous Ḥanbalī scholarship on theology was rather simplistic, whereas Ibn Taymīyah's scholarship was much more philosophically grounded. Qadhi use this as the pretext to claim that today those who claim to be the followers of Ibn Taymīyah are not truly following in his footsteps.[8] Qadhi argues that the topical debates during the time of Ibn Taymīyah were related to issues of theology and not to issues of Islamic law. That has been reversed today. While it is no longer relevant to discuss the issues of theology that Ibn Taymīyah discussed, Ibn Taymīyah's approach to these issues, and the way he harmonises revelation and reason, is still relevant to many contemporary issues. He argues that anyone that is arguing for change in Islamic law today, must understand Ibn Taymīyah and the reason his views are so attractive.[9] Ibn Taymīyah managed to redeem *'aql* (reason) while keeping *naql* (text) supreme. For Ibn Taymīyah, *'aql* follows *naql*.

Qadhi states that this is an important point, given that some progressive Muslims push the rational aspect of Islamic law too far. He gives a particular example of same-sex marriage. He says that the Qur'ān is clear that same-sex marriage is forbidden, yet, there are Muslims that argue that the Qur'ān has been misinterpreted on this subject. If we find the issues of homosexuality in the Qur'ān to be problematic, then people will find other parts of the text to be problematic and they will interpret it as they see fit.[10] Qadhi believes that while we do need to adapt Islam to its time and place, we do not need a complete overhaul in the sense of changing the fundamentals of the Qur'ān and *sunnah*. Calling for a complete overhaul makes the Qur'ān and *sunnah* superfluous.[11]

Qadhi is also a faculty member of the AlMaghrib Institute, where he is the Dean of Academic Affairs and an instructor. Founded in 2002, the goal of AlMaghrib "is to make learning Islam in a quality fashion as easy as possible." They were driven by answering "how could we teach you Islam in a way that was fun, social, quality, spiritual, and oh yeah, academic?" Grewal comments that the AlMaqhrib institute has "almost single-handedly revived the Salafi movement in the U.S. among Sunni American Muslim college students, and its success is demonstrable in its high student enrolment."[12]

AlMaqhrib focuses on conducting seminars all over the world, this includes the United States, Canada, United Kingdom, Australia, and even a few Gulf States such as Kuwait and the United Arab Emirates. These seminars consist of a variety of social and religious issues. In 2016, Yasir Qadhi went on a seminar tour titled "No Doubt: God, Religion and Politics in the Modern World." The seminar is focused on securing one's faith in the existence of God, but it covers a wide variety of other topics. The seminar profile describes the seminar as such:

> This class aims to tackle some of the most difficult and controversial topics head on, whether the rise of militant atheism, or the evolution issue, the existence of evil, political allegiances, rebellion against dictators, secular feminism,

> the conflict between citizenship and the support for armed forces pressing forwards with their own agenda regardless, and just so much more.[13]

The institute also offers a bachelor's degree, but this does not seem to be accredited by any governing body. AlMaghrib consists of four departments: Islamic Theology and Ethics, Islamic Law and Legal Theory, Qur'ānic and Ḥadīth Sciences, and Islamic History and Homiletics.

Many of the faculty at AlMaqhrib are graduates from Saudi universities, especially the Islamic University of Medina. The president and founder of AlMaqhrib is Shaykh Muhammad Alshareef. Alshareef is a graduate of IUM and received his degree in Islamic law in 1999.[14] Shaykh Waleed Basyouni, the Vice President and Head of the 'Aqīdah and Adab Department received both his bachelor's and master's degree from the al-Imam Muhammad University in Saudi Arabia. He then travelled to Indiana to gain his Doctorate in Theology from the Graduate Theological Foundation.[15] Shaykh Yaser Birjas is the head of the Islamic Law and Theory Department, and he received his bachelor's degree from the IUM in the Faculty of Shariah in 1996. He also studied under popular scholars within mainstream Saudi Salafism such as Shaykh Muḥammed al-Amin Al-Shanqiṭi and Shaykh Al-Uthaymin.[16] Shaykh Abdullah Hakim Quick is an African American convert and one of the first two students from the West to receive his degree from IUM. He graduated from the Faculty of Da'wah and Islamic Beliefs in 1979.[17] Not all of the staff are graduates of Saudi Universities. Dr. Reda Bedeir is an Egyptian scholar who has attained two Ph.D.s from al-Azhar University and also teaches as a professor at al-Azhar.[18]

There have also been some notable controversial figures associated with the institute. Shaykh Anwar al-Awlaki was an American citizen that became the most notable English-speaking cleric in al-Qaida, and became the first U.S. citizen to be targeted and killed by a drone strike.[19] Grewal comments that although al-Awlaki was never formally affiliated with AlMaqhrib, recordings of his speeches were sold at AlMaqhrib events. His recordings were still sold even after the faculty at AlMaqhrib declared a ban on his tapes following al-Awlaki's praise of the 2009 Fort Hood shooting.[20] Yasir Qadhi has given speeches against al-Awlaki's views while being critical of his extrajudicial assassination.[21] Moreover, the institute has come under criticism for teaching to the infamous underwear bomber, Umar Farouk Abdulmutallab. Qadhi has said that he barely knew him, that they fully corroborated with the FBI investigation, and that ultimately Abdulmutallab was exposed to radical jihad through al-Awlaki.[22]

On the other hand, AlMaqhrib has come under criticism from other Salafi groups that consider the institute to be too liberal.[23] It was due to these criticisms that the institute moved away from the label "Salafi", although Grewal reports that many of the faculty still describe their approach to Islam as such.[24] It is interesting to note that Yasir Qadhi has stated that he believed Hamza Yusuf had so effectively appropriated the "traditionalist" label that it forced the institute to find a different brand in order to compete.[25]

Qadhi and Mainstream Salafism

Yasir Qadhi embodies this transition from mainstream Saudi Salafism to a more liberal Salafism. He is quite forthcoming about his own transition. If AlMaqhrib has revived Salafism within America, as Grewal has claimed, then it is a Salafism that is alien to that very tradition: Yasir Qadhi defends democracy, the legality of same-sex marriage (albeit among non-Muslims) in secular societies, and one that understands that Islamic laws change depending on context. This is not to say that there have never been different strands within Salafism, or that Qadhi and the AlMaghrib Institute have left Salafism as it is formally defined (see Volume 1, Chapter 6). It is to say, however, that it is a very specific type of *American Salafism*. It is a Salafism that understands that context matters and that American Muslims require American and not foreign scholarship.

It is difficult to piece together Qadhi's earlier views because they are scattered about on the internet. He himself has shown no interest in archiving his older views, and there is no central archiving authority. Most of the content that is available on Qadhi's earlier views is from his critics. There are several controversial points that Qadhi has commented on.

One of the issues that haunt Qadhi are his statements on the Holocaust. His old comments have led some bloggers to give him unflattering names, such a "Holocaust-denying anti-Semitic Hitler-sympathizing extremist fundamentalist radical Muslim preacher."[26] In one of his early lectures that delved into the history of Judaism, Qadhi had said that "Hitler never intended to mass-destroy the Jews" and he had urged Muslims to read *The Hoax of the Holocaust*.[27] He sums up his views by saying that "We're not defending Hitler, by the way, but the Jews, the way that they portray him, also is not correct."[28] Qadhi has tried to distance himself from the views expressed in this lecture. He writes that:

> I was a young, budding, twenty-something undergraduate at Madinah when I gave that talk, during my very first cross-Atlantic da'wah trip . . . It's been almost a decade since that one-time mistake; I admit it was an error and an incorrect "fact" was propagated. But even in that talk, I did not deny the actual occurrence of the Holocaust, or express any support or admiration for Hitler, or claim that all Jews were worthy of being despised or hated.[29]

He states that "the Holocaust was one of the worst crimes against humanity that the twentieth century has witnessed."[30] He adds that "[p]eople change over time. Views develop, are modified, or discarded outright. Simplistic notions, especially those held in younger years, are typically shown to be stereotypical and false."[31]

In regards to his views towards democracy, Qadhi again in the past took the more extreme Salafi line. Many Salafis believe that democracy promotes man-made laws and that these laws are in conflict with the Divine Law, as was discussed in the previous volume. Supporting these man-made laws is tantamount to denying God's sovereignty.[32] Although it is difficult to find Qadhi's writings on the issue, if any such writings exist, there is a short video clip of him passionately defending this opinion:

> It is not my right to legislate or your right to legislate . . . Can you believe a group of people coming together and voting, and the majority vote will then be the law of the land. What gives you the right to prohibit something and allow something. Who gave you this right? Are you creators? Are you all knowledgeable? Do you understand the repercussions, the implications of the laws that you're going to pass?[33]

It is clearly visible in the video that Qadhi was much younger at the time and the description in the video states that this clip was recorded in Egypt in 2001. Many of the commentators on this video clip mention that they miss the old conservative Qadhi and some mention that Qadhi has now become a *munāfiq* (hypocrite).[34] As it will be shown below, Qadhi no longer holds these beliefs, but instead argues in favour of supporting liberal democracies in non-Muslim countries. He has changed his stance from one in which he believed secular laws denied God's sovereignty, to his current position whereby he believes that liberal secular laws actually grant Muslims the freedom required for personal worship, and for this reason these laws require the support of the Muslim community.

Qadhi has also held extremely negative views towards the Shi'a. He followed the standard Salafi formula of painting the Shi'a as polytheist lying fornicators that curse the wives and companions of the Prophet.[35] He has said the Shi'a are "the most lying sect of Islam" and that "it is their religion to lie." This is in reference to the concept of *taqīyah*, a concept that allows a Muslim to conceal their faith when they are in mortal danger. Although many Sunni scholars support the concept of *taqīyah*, it has become associated with Shi'ism because of their suppressed minority status.[36]

Qadhi also criticized the Shi'a for allowing *mut'ah* (time based marriage contracts), and labels it as prostitution and fornication. He states the Shi'a believe that the more that one fornicates, the higher their spiritual status. Moreover, Qadhi also stated that Shi'i beliefs were tantamount to *shirk* (polytheism). This is in reference to the Shi'i belief of *al-wilāyah al-takwīnīyah*, the belief that with the permission of God the prophets and *imāms* can bring about change within the material world. The Shi'a defend this position stating that it is an explanation of how Prophets perform miracles.[37]

Qadhi has formally renounced his old views towards Shi'ism. In a recent interview on the Iranian English news channel, Press TV, Qadhi has stated that:

> What I said about Shi'as, probably around 17–18 years ago, was in fact quite inflammatory and stereotyping an entire segment of people. And yes I do regret the language that I used, I do regret what I said, and I do believe that I have moved on from that, and I have given enough lectures and videos publicly and, you know, interviews which demonstrates that I am now a different person. We all go through phases in our lives, and at a younger age I kind of took what was taught to me from a certain methodological background and accepted it without verification. And I was also a bit more fiery person in my early 20s. And I think, you know, age and wisdom, and experience really, and interacting with people tempers went down . . .[38]

When asked specifically about why he changed his position he attributed it to age, experience, and simply being with people. He also attributed his earlier views to a "cut and paste job", where he would find one quote and generalize from that one quote. He compares how he discussed Shi'ism as similar to how Islamophobes take Islamic text out of context.[39]

Qadhi constantly refers to the fact that he has changed his views, but he rarely delves into the historical progression of his ideas. His criticisms of mainstream Salafi beliefs are clear, but the story of his personal development has not been fully told. In an interview with Interfaith Voices in 2013 Qadhi partially explains why he no longer identifies with Salafism. From the interview, as well as other sources, it seems that the main impetus that drove Qadhi away from traditional Salafism is that Salafi thought was in his view unable to address modern issues. He states this point twice in this interview and reiterates this position in his other works.

The interview begins by Qadhi stating that he would have identified with the Salafi movement 20 years ago, but he has now grown out of the movement. The interviewer pushes him to clarify what he means by that statement. He replies that:

> I found the movement is not as intellectually stimulating as I would like it to be. I think that it is not really capable of addressing modern issues. It's very intransigent in the way it views certain ideas. It's also very hostile to any that disagree with its interpretation. So I find myself disagreeing with quite a lot of the methodological issues associated with the Salafi movement.[40]

What attracted Qadhi to the Salafi movement was the empowerment of being able to understand the religion straight from the text of the Qur'ān and *ḥadīth*:

> There is a sense of liberation where you're not dependent on a group of clerics and you have no idea why they're saying what they're saying. The Salafi tradition always challenged people to think about why particular clerics are saying their particular positions, and they challenged people to find the evidences for every single Islamic opinion. And therefore what it did is, it allowed Muslims to reconnect to their tradition. It also allowed Muslims to separate a lot of what was culture from religion. So lot of things were dismissed for being cultural. For example certain dress codes, or treatment of women, or other things of this nature could be dismissed as being cultural practices, and people were told to embrace a more authentic, or a more pure, or a more pristine understanding of the faith.[41]

When he was asked, "What would that look like in the modern world?" He replied that:

> Frankly, I think that is a question that no Salafi has answered in a very realistic manner. And this was one of the main reasons that I myself found myself distancing myself from the movement. That, this type of clichéd rhetoric that we want to go back to the first three generations. What exactly does that mean in a modern world? I don't think that any Salafi really has a concrete clue as to how that will take place.[42]

Qadhi has written a more recent article titled *On Salafi Islam*. In this article, he goes into depth about the various trends of Salafism and what he believes are the positive and negative aspects of Salafi thought. He begins the section on criticisms of the movement by highlighting a flaw in the Salafi method:

> Additionally, there is a methodological flaw in attempting to extrapolate a *salafi* position (meaning: a position that the *salaf* would hold) about a modern issue that the *salaf* never encountered. The "Salafi position" (meaning one that is held by some scholars of the modern Salafi movement) with respect to questions on citizenship in nation-states, democracy, the role of women in today's society, the permissibility of voting, and the issue of *jihād* in the modern world, etc., are merely personal opinions (*fatāwā*) of the scholars who pronounce them and cannot be representative of the views of the first three generations of Islam.[43]

In regards to the issue just mentioned above, about the lack of any coherent understanding of what Salafi Islam would look like in the modern world, Qadhi fiercely criticizes the lack of attention that Salafis give to *fiqh*. In the comments section of the same article he writes: "There is no such thing as 'Salafi fiqh'. It is a myth propagated by the hard-core Jordanian branch of Salafism."[44]

In his article *On Salafi Islam*, Qadhi criticises Salafis for simply engaging in theological disputes of the past that have no relevance to the lives of the modern Muslims: "modern Salafīs are, for the most part, unwilling to venture outside of the territories and ideas that Ibn Taymīyah wrote about seven hundred years ago and face the challenges of *our* day."[45] He argues that he is not alone in his criticism of Salafism, and believes that he is a part of a growing trend of younger generation students: "More and more intelligent students of knowledge, in Madinah and elsewhere, are realizing this. One of the goals of the article was to make them feel that they are not alone, and take active measures to correct these mistakes."[46]

Towards a Reasonable Salafism

Qadhi's move away from mainstream Salafism is followed by a move towards reasonable Salafism. As stated above, reasonable here indicates towards the necessity of scholars to give rulings and present an interpretation of Islam that is appropriate to the lived experiences of Muslims. Qadhi's move towards a reasonable Salafism is built on his critique of overly conservative interpretations of Islamic law. He argues that overly conservative interpretations harm Muslim life and Islam in general. This echoes many of the same concerns of Salman al-Ouda and Bin Bayyah that were discussed in Volume 1 (see Chapter 6 and Chapter 3 respectively). It is therefore not surprising that Yasir Qadhi considers Salman al-Ouda to be his mentor.

As it will be shown below, Qadhi begins his criticism by showing the detrimental effects of unreasonable interpretations of Islamic law through practical historical examples, specifically the ban on the printing press in the Ottoman Empire. Moreover, he urges Muslims to follow scholars that have had similar life experiences as themselves. Ultimately, his position that Salafi scholars do not have any coherent plan about applying Islamic law to contemporary times has led him to argue for a greater degree of dynamism in terms of Islamic law. Furthermore, Qadhi's conception of reasonableness extends to the issue of science specifically the theory of evolution. Qadhi is a defender of the theory of evolution, and argues that evolution is compatible with Islamic thought. He urges Muslims to not follow in the footsteps of Evangelical Christians but to look back to their own heritage where there was a greater balance between science and religion.

Qadhi's movement towards reasonable Salafism begins with a criticism of conservatism. He defines conservatism as the "reluctance to change Islamic law."[47] He states that he does not want to give a negative impression of conservatism, but that he is simply referring to the reluctance of some scholars to adapt to changing circumstances. There are two lectures in which he delves deeply into this topic. The first is a lengthy lecture on the history of the printing press in Muslim lands.[48] In this lecture Qadhi discusses the reason it took over 300 years for Muslims to adopt the printing press. The first printing press was created by Johannes Gutenberg in 1440. Qadhi argues that it was only after Napoleon's invasion of Egypt, and Muhammad Ali Pasha's attempt at modernization that the first indigenous printing press was established. This allowed printing for Muslims in Arabic in 1822.

The reason for this delay, argues Qadhi, is because of the conservative mind-set that governed the Muslim world during that time period. Qadhi begins his lecture by discussing the history of paper. He tells the story of the Abbasid Caliph who captured two Chinese papermakers as prisoners of war. The Caliph ordered these two Chinese workers to teach Muslims how to make paper in exchange for their freedom. He uses this as an example of the open-mindedness of the earlier Muslims, which in his view was central to shaping the "Golden Age" of Islam. Qadhi then describes how paper manufacturing travelled to Europe via Muslims and how it were the Europeans who in turn developed paper mills leading to the invention of the printing press. While Muslims had been one of the first civilizations to understand the importance of paper they were now falling behind. There were two reasons for the apprehension of incorporating the printing press. The first is that Muslims were weary of anything foreign. The second is that scholars feared that the layperson would be led astray if they read books without the guidance of scholars.

It was for these reasons that the Grand Mufti of Istanbul declared that it was unlawful to own and operate a printing press. Printing presses were thus according to Qadhi banned throughout the Ottoman Empire. Special concessions were given to religious minorities that lived within the Empire, but they were to print in their own languages and could not print anything related to Islam. Printing presses were banned until Muhammad Ali Pasha established the *Bulaq* Printing Press in Egypt in 1822. Qadhi laments that while literacy had flourished in Europe and people were reading the classics written by Charles Dickens, the Muslim world was predominantly illiterate. The banning of the printing press in his view effectively stunted literacy, innovation, and cultural growth within the Muslim World.

Qadhi builds on this lecture in another lecture that further clarifies his stance towards change in Islamic law.[49] Qadhi describes this lecture on his YouTube as being a "highly controversial and paradigm-shifting talk".[50] In this lecture, Qadhi is much more direct about the importance of finding scholars that understand the needs of contemporary Muslims. He believes that Muslims today are facing problems that do not have solutions in the classical text. This requires a type of scholarship that is in tune with the lived experience of the people. Otherwise, he believes that people will simply ignore the *fatwās* of the scholars and live life as they see fit.

In order to highlight this point he refers to the recent controversy over the production of the *Omar* television series.[51] This television series, which is based on the life of the second Caliph, 'Umar ibn 'Abd al-Khattāb, had attracted the criticism of various *sharī'ah* councils including at al-Azhar and in Saudi Arabia. Given 'Umar's revered status in Sunni Islam, his depiction on screen has been controversial.[52] Qadhi comments that even though various *sharī'ah* councils gave *fatwās* against this TV series, it was still one of the most highly watched shows in the Muslim world. For Qadhi, this shows the disconnectedness between the scholars and the masses. The religious opinions of these scholars were irrelevant to the producers of the TV show and also to the millions of Muslims that were watching. Nonetheless, there were many forward thinking scholars that helped in the production of this programme. One of which was Shaykh Salman al-Ouda, who was also on a committee to review the historical accuracy of the series.[53]

Salman al-Ouda's thought has had an impact on Qadhi's own intellectual development, and Qadhi praises him highly in this lecture. Elsewhere, Qadhi has commented that: "Sh. Salman is someone whom I know personally, and consider a mentor."[54] He also praised Salman al-Oua on social media for "making a concerted effort to make Islam more relevant to the people," and has stated that "it is scholars like Sh. Salman that I take as my role models in my own endeavors in the West."[55]

Qadhi presents Shaykh al-Ouda as someone who understands contemporary Muslim life and society, and this is reflected in al-Ouda's approach and religious rulings. Qadhi defends al-Ouda's position on the production of the *Omar* television series due to the fact that his rulings are more in line with the way that people live their lives. He praises al-Ouda for being reasonable, and that this reasonableness is one of the key aspects that religious scholars should keep in consideration: "One of the jobs of an *'alim* is to get a sense of the pulse of the people, to see what is better than the status quo. Not necessarily what is ideal."

Qadhi also argues that religious scholars require more than a pragmatic approach towards religious rulings, and that they must also have real life experience. These experiences will affect a scholar's viewpoint towards social issues. Qadhi's emphasis on the fact that scholars must have real life experience drives him to say that Muslims should seek out scholars that have similar experiences as them. In essence, this means that Muslims should seek out religious scholars that are living in the West, because their experience in the West will change how they view religious rulings:

> Choose a scholar who's living your life, in your land, in your culture and society . . . One of the biggest problems of all of our, these movements, and has caused Islam to not spread as well as it should, was that we outsourced our *fatwās* to back home . . . But the fact of the matter is, that those people [scholars], with all great respect to them, they are great for their societies, they know their societies, but you cannot get a *fatwā* about living in a secular democracy from somebody who has never lived in a secular democracy. You cannot get a *fatwā* about how to interact with your homosexual neighbor when a person has never met a person who is a homosexual in his life. There has to be a human element. Experience, wisdom, most of it comes from life, not from books. Take this as a rule of thumb. Most experience comes from living and not from reading books.[56]

This lengthy quote captures the essence of Qadhi's critique. Religious scholars might have a good deal of book knowledge, and even a good understanding of their own social surroundings, but they do not have the lived experience necessary to comment about life in the West. He then urges Muslims to find scholars that are living in the West and to follow the religious interpretations of these scholars.

Overall, Qadhi believes that Islamic law needs to take into context the lived experience and contemporary context of the people. This is precisely the reason that he left traditional Salafi thought: he found Salafism to be too concerned with impractical debates of theology and unable to offer a practical vision for how best to live Islam in contemporary times. Islamic law in his view does not need a complete rethinking, but simply needs to take the social context into greater appreciation.

The issue of reasonableness is also extended to science. A common debate in American culture is the issue of evolution and religion. Qadhi is a firm believer in the theory of evolution, and considers the debate about evolution amongst Muslims to be more the effect of Muslims importing the Christian clash between religion and science into their own thought. He believes that evolution in general is true, but God intervenes through the creation of Adam. God's intervention was in line with evolution such that an outside observer would not be able to tell the difference. In one video, he begins his presentation on evolution and the Qur'ān by stating that:

> We as Muslims, we need to understand that the theory of evolution pretty much has been accepted as much as a fact as any scientific theory. We need to stop deluding ourselves and saying that "Oh it is only a theory" it is not a very academic way to phrase this.[57]

He states that evolution is based on certain facts that develop into a broader theory. This includes for example human and humanoid bones, and microevolution. He then argues that many Muslims simply have not spent the time to properly study the issue noting that "the theory of evolution from a scientific standpoint makes a lot of sense," and that the major "issue is how to reconcile when the book says X and modern science says Y." And ultimately "no other theory has challenged the Quranic paradigm more than this."[58]

He states that reconciliation between theory of evolution and Qur'ānic understanding of creation is possible because Muslims do not have an antagonistic history towards science. It is Christianity that has had conflict with science. To support his case, he presents examples such as the Christian Evangelical position that the world is only 6,000 years old, as well as the popular retelling of the trial of Galileo. Muslims, in his view, on the other hand have had a long positive history with religion and science such that the Muslim empire during its peak was the centre of scientific progress.

Qadhi's impression of the conflict between Christianity and science is unfortunately skewed by the dominant positions of Evangelical Christians. The Catholic Church, the Church of England, and various mainline Protestant denominations accept the theory of evolution. Many Christians believe in what is normally labelled as "theistic evolution": God set evolution in motion.[59] Pope Pius XII issued a papal encyclical, "Humani Generis", in 1950 that affirmed the fact that there is no conflict between Christianity and evolution.[60] The Church of England also supports the notion of evolution, and even has a section of their official website dedicated to the issue.[61] In America, there is a nationwide movement, The Clergy Letter Project, which has gathered in the region of 14,000 clergy members that support evolution, including the United Methodist Church.[62] Although this project includes members of different faiths, the majority of clergy members are Christian. Even Qadhi's understanding of the Galileo affair is influenced by contemporary American sentiments of the events: a closer examination would reveal that the event did not pan out the way it is presented in the popular American imaginary and that of Yasir Qadhi.[63]

Qadhi's position on theistic evolution therefore has many partners within the Christian world. It would seem even beneficial to study the works written by Christian intellectuals on the issue to see if it can inform his own position on the debate. More interestingly, Qadhi's stance on evolution differs from that of Tim Winter. As we saw in Chapter 2, he does not believe that the theory of evolution has been fully proven.

Reasonable Citizenship

By arguing that Islamic scholars must take into consideration the lived experiences of modern Muslims, Qadhi is able to set the stage for advancing the notion of reasonable citizenship. Liberal secular societies in his view are a modern construction and the way in which Muslims should live in these societies requires novel solutions: Muslims "cannot get a *fatwā* about living in a secular democracy from somebody who has never lived in a secular democracy."[64]

Qadhi's understanding of how Muslims should live in secular liberal societies echoes much of John Rawls' sentiments. The concept of "reasonable citizen" was popularised by John Rawls specifically in his book *Political Liberalism*. Rawls clarifies his stance on "reasonable citizen" in his article *The Idea of Public Reason Revisited*.[65] Rawls' theory of political liberalism tries to tackle two main problems within liberal thought: legitimacy and stability. What constitutes legitimate coercive power by the state and why would citizens agree to it? For Rawls, legitimacy and stability in turn rely upon public reason. Legitimacy and stability are attained if political ideas go through a process of public deliberation whereby there is an exchange of ideas and justifications that are understandable to groups adhering to different comprehensive beliefs. A justification for a law that is solely based on one's religious views would fail this test of public reason.

This concept of public reason has various aspects that make the process of public reason possible. One of these aspects is the concept of "reasonable citizens". Citizens are considered reasonable when they view one another as being free and equal, and they believe in the criterion of reciprocity. The criterion of reciprocity requires that citizens offer one another fair terms of cooperation, and they agree to act on those terms even if it comes at a cost in a particular situation given that other citizens also act on those terms.[66] Reasonable citizens, therefore, understand that each individual has her own comprehensive doctrine of beliefs and do not believe that it is legitimate to impose one's comprehensive beliefs on others.

Qadhi echoes this understanding of reasonable citizenship. He argues that all citizens are free and equal to pick and choose their own comprehensive doctrines and moral norms. This will become apparent in his discussion about apostasy and homosexuality. He also defends the criterion of reciprocity by arguing that Muslims should be willing to support rights for other minority groups because those rights can be used in favour of Muslims as well, even if that particular right comes at a cost to Islamic values. This is the argument that he makes as to why Muslims should support same-sex marriage laws.

Intertwined with this understanding of reasonable citizenship is Qadhi's compartmentalization of Islamic law. He separates issues that he believes are applicable to the Islamic state from issues that are applicable to the believer. This is the strategy he uses when discussing issues of apostasy. As an extension of that, Qadhi separates the concept of law from morality when dealing with issues of law in a secular society. The validity of the law in secular societies does not depend on its moral status. Separating laws that apply to an Islamic state from laws that apply to a secular state in the West, gives Qadhi greater room to put forward his own ideas without coming into conflict with religious scholars abroad.

The issue of apostasy highlights how Qadhi defends freedom of conscience by compartmenting Islamic law. In a question and answer session he is asked about the issue of apostasy, and the implementation of various punishments. Qadhi quickly states that this is an issue that the religious bodies of Muslim-majority countries must tackle. It is not in an issue that concerns him; it is an issue for those sitting on *sharīʿah* councils. Apostasy is not an issue for Muslims in the West because they cannot carry out any of the punishments since they must abide by the laws of the land:

> The modern nation state has to discuss this . . . What is going to be the case? Let the Islamic states decide. I as an American Muslim I have no problems legally with an atheist, a homosexual, with a person who is a Satan worshipper, this is the reality of this country. You are free to do as you please. I might morally disagree, but legally they are free to do as they please.[67]

In a separate speech, Qadhi argues that the issue of apostasy has always had a different application in Muslim lands from non-Muslim lands. He gives the story of ʿUbayd-Allāh ibn Jahsh as evidence. ʿUbayd-Allāh converted to Islam during the time of Prophet Muhammad but converted to Christianity when he emigrated to Abyssinia.

> If you become *murtad* (apostate) in a land that is not ruled by the *sharīʿah*, this is your freedom. You cannot do anything. So the whole question, and I'm saying this now because our religion is being attacked. "You guys have a blasphemy law, if somebody leaves the religion you have to cut his head off." That's what we're told. The response is very simple: No. Our *sharīʿah* tells us that in lands that are not ruled by Islam—ʿUbayd-Allāh ibn Jahsh converted back to Christianity. Nobody harmed a hair on his head. This is the land of Negus, the land of Najāshī do as you please. It's not the land where the *sharīʿah* is going to be implemented.[68]

Qadhi defends freedom of conscience by stating that apostasy laws do not apply to Muslims living in the West. Apostasy laws are only applicable to Muslim-majority countries, and even then it is a debated issue. Moreover, Qadhi is against any coercive application of Islamic beliefs and norms. He makes this stance quite clear when he discusses the issue of homosexuality. He argues that it is not permissible for Muslims to forcefully coerce others to adhere to Islamic norms on homosexuality:

> But hey, at the end of the day, all we have is the right to speak and to believe. And we do not have the right to force other people to conform to what we believe is ethical and moral. You ask us, we'll tell you. But at the same time, at the end of the day, it's your business and you have to answer to, you know, God on the day of judgement. And that's basically between you and your Creator. All we can say is tell you what we believe.[69]

Not only does he argue against coercive means, but he also argues against harboring hatred towards those who do not adhere to Islamic norms. This is quite far from the concept of *al-walāʾ wa-al-barāʾ* that has shaped the mainstream Salafi thinking (see Volume 1, Chapter 6). Continuing his discussion on homosexuality Qadhi argues the worst sin in Islam is idol worship, but the Qurʾān allows Muslims to show compassion and love towards idol worshippers. If Muslims are allowed to show love towards the worst sinners, then they are allowed to show love towards those who are less sinful. He argues that "In Islam we are not required, we are not obliged, to hate people that disagree with us. The fact of the matter is we would disagree and we don't like this action, but that doesn't mean we have to treat or mistreat or dehumanise anybody."[70]

So far we have seen how Qadhi considers other citizens as free and equal. They are able to pick and choose their own comprehensive doctrines and ethical norms. Muslims are not allowed to enforce coercive measures whether it is in regards to beliefs, such as issues relating to apostasy, or practices, such as homosexuality. Moreover, Muslims should not harbour hatred or ill will towards those have decided to live a life different than theirs.

Yet for Rawls, not only was the issue of equal citizenship important, but so too was the issue of reciprocity. Interestingly, this issue of reciprocity finds importance for Qadhi in his discussions of same-sex marriage. The underlying reason that he defends the legality of same sex-marriage in America is that he believes that freedoms that are granted to other minority groups translate into greater freedoms for Muslims as well. Underlying this debate about reciprocity is Qadhi's distinction between what is legally allowed and what is morally acceptable. He delves into this subject in depth in a blog post titled *God's Law and Man-Made Laws: Muslims Living in Secular Democracies*. This post tackles a variety of issues that Muslims deal with as minorities in non-Muslim countries especially in regards to "the question of navigating a relationship between Shariah and the laws of the land where they live."[71]

Qadhi begins the article by describing the various ways in which the Divine Law and secular law may or may not conflict. He states that God has revealed laws on many issues which are also regulated by the state, such as family issues, and business transactions. On many issues the divine law and secular law do not clash. He gives examples in which there is no precedent in the divine law, and which he sees as areas where the divine law allows human legislation, such as traffic laws and civic regulations. In reverse, there are certain areas in which Western liberal democracies avoid legislation, such as personal religious laws. In these areas the individual is free to follow one's own religious beliefs. This is why many Muslims prefer to live in secular democracies as opposed to religiously repressive regimes in Muslim-majority countries.[72]

There can be, theoretically, certain laws that do clash with divine laws. Such as the state passing a law that requires Muslims to drink alcohol, or worship idols. In these areas Muslims "would not be obliged to follow such a law" and in certain circumstances they "would be required to immigrate to other lands."[73] Given the examples that he is presenting, and their hypothetical nature, it seems that Qadhi does not believe that the United States has currently passed any laws that would require Muslims to undertake actions that go against their religion. It would have been interesting if he included the banning of headscarves in France in this category.

The rest of the article is dedicated to the third group of laws, those that do not fall to the two extremes cited above. These are laws that make room for certain actions that the divine law prohibits, although he does not clearly state it as such. One example that he does give is abortion. He turns to the history of the Christian and Jewish views within the United States about abortion to help guide Muslims on this issue: "Practicing Muslims many times overlook that they are not alone in this dilemma. We need to realise that the situation in which we find ourselves is not much different from that of Orthodox Jews, or, to a certain extent, conservative Christians."[74]

He uses the precedent set by Christian and Jewish religious thinkers to help support the view that there is a difference between moral obligation and legal permission. He argues that Christians do not believe that the laws of the land are necessarily moral, thus if "Christians are told that the law of the land allows it, or that the Supreme Court itself has ruled in favour of it, they would not acknowledge the moral right of the Supreme Court to legislate in such a manner."[75] He uses this to not only show how Muslims can navigate between the Divine Law and secular law, but also to show that this attempt is not alien to the American lifestyle. It is in fact a continuation of how many religious groups have approached this issue:

> For many Muslims, the exact same sentiments that conservative Christians and Jews have about the law of God also ring true. No man has the right to morally challenge what God has decreed to be good and evil, and if someone does so, it should come as little surprise that religious people will always choose the law of God over the law of man. There is nothing wrong or illegal in saying this—this is quintessential manifestation of being American, even if certain agencies with well-known agendas try to spin it otherwise.[76]

In his lectures, as it will be shown below, Qadhi builds on this notion and states that while it is permissible for the government to legally permit same sex-marriage, apostasy, and the consumption of alcohol, this does not mean that these actions are moral. Muslims have a right to state that these actions are immoral, while respecting that they are legally permissible. This separation between legality and morality is maintained by many legal positivists, and has been the topic of lengthy debates within legal philosophy. That is not to say that legal positivists do not believe that legality and morality have no relationship, but that morality is not a necessary condition of legal validity.[77]

Qadhi continues his paper by critiquing the term "*jāhilī* law". The term *jāhilī* law was coined by Islamist thinkers, such as the two globally influential Islamists Abu A'la Mawdudi (d. 1979) and Sayyid Qutb (d. 1966). Although the concept of *jāhilīyah* (ignorance) was used in the classical literature to mean the pre-Islamic era, Qutb began to use it for anything that went against God's rule. Khatab describes Qutb's understanding of *jahilīyah* as "a condition of any time and place where Allah is not held to be the highest governmental and legal authority."[78] For these Islamist thinkers, all man-made laws were considered *jāhil* (ignorant) because they did not conform to the Divine Law.

It is quite clear that he himself was influenced by these views, as is evident by the statements quoted above from his earlier years. This current article can therefore be seen as how Qadhi has moved away from these conceptions. Qadhi warns that these ideas quickly lead to *takfīr* (the excommunication of Muslims) by "claiming all those who oppose one's understanding of Shariah are *kafirs* [infidels] because they have rejected *hakimiyyah* [God's sovereignty]."[79] He considers this idea to be dangerous especially in consideration of the fact that no Muslim country is completely ruled by the *sharī'ah*. This would then mean that all Muslim rulers would be *kāfirs*. He writes that this is not just a theoretical debate, but that the concept of *takfīr* has real consequences in modern political movements.

Beyond the issue of *takfīr*, Qadhi also criticizes these Islamist views for considering all non-Islamic ideas as a unified whole and not understanding that there are great differences amongst them. This, in his view, makes it difficult to incorporate aspects of non-Islamic political philosophy into Islamic thought: "Hence, if someone were to take even parts of such a system and adopt it for use within some type of Islamic model, it would be easy for simplistic followers to label such a model as being *jahili*."[80] He adds that there are many Islamic intellectuals that are trying to incorporate democracy into Islamic thought, and that such quick and simplistic accusations of *jāhilī* are a barrier to their developments.[81]

Qadhi's related critique is that these Islamist ideals do not provide any practical solutions for Muslims living in the West. He wonders if these Islamist thinkers would consider Muslims to be *kāfir* simply because they are living in non-Muslim lands. In order to ground his argument Qadhi considers the position of a Muslim who falls victim of a robbery or murder: should the Muslim, or their heirs, suffer in silence or should they prosecute through the courts?

In order to help answer this question about Muslims in non-Muslim lands, Qadhi turns to the works of Andrew March, Professor of Political Science at Yale. March has written a book titled *Islam and Liberal Citizenship: The Search for an Overlapping Consensus*. Although Qadhi refers readers to March's book, the material that he is citing is actually from March's article *Theocrats Living under Secular Law: An External Engagement with Islamic Legal Theory*.[82] In this article March puts forward a new paradigm of a "thick social contract model" through the use of the political philosophy of John Rawls. It is possible that Qadhi became acquainted with March during his period of study at Yale, and in the comments section of the article Qadhi remarks that March is a personal friend.[83] In his article *On Salafi Islam* Qadhi remarks that March "has done admirable work, and we need to benefit from such works wherever they come from."[84]

Qadhi references March's categorization of the five ways in which Muslims see their relationship with the secular state. These four are the thin social contract model, the internal retreat model, the self-governance model, the temporary modus vivendi model, and the thick social contract model.[85] The first (thin social contract) and the last (thick social contact) models deem attention: the first model has support amongst Muslim thinkers and Qadhi himself, and the last model is the model that March is putting forward as an alternative. Qadhi describes the thin social contract model as thus:

> This model posits that when the wider community (in our case, the American Constitution) guarantees certain rights of security and religious freedom, and when Muslims have agreed to take advantage of these rights, in return they will consent to obey laws even if they do not derive from Islamic principles.[86]

He adds that this is the dominant view amongst modern Sunni scholars, including Yusuf al-Qaradawi and Abdullah ibn Bayyah, and that he himself presents his own arguments from within this model. He adds that this model has its own particular set of problems and that he will address these problems in a future article. However, it does not seem that he has written such an article yet.

The thick social contract model is the model defended by March and is developed on Rawls' concept of an overlapping consensus. Qadhi understands the model as such: "In this model, religious constituents would acknowledge and agree that while the existing system of government is not divine, it is sufficiently just or acceptably legitimate in many areas, and thus may be actively endorsed."[87] March argues that Muslims should engage Western law through the paradigm of *maqāṣid*, or what he labels as complex purposiveness. If a secular law is sufficiently protective of the five main essential goals of the *sharīʿah* then Muslims should endorse the system based on religious grounds.[88] The difference between this model and the thin social contract model is that Muslims are not simply agreeing to follow secular laws but they are instead endorsing them through religious reasons. This would in turn promote a larger degree of participation and enthusiasm.

Qadhi considers the thick social contract model to be a novel approach to the relationship between Muslims and non-Muslim states. Yet, it is due to this novelty that he is still hesitant to support or critique it. Qadhi believes that it seems that this model works well when it comes to certain laws (such as prosecuting criminals) but harder in other areas, such as divorce. Although Qadi finds it difficult to endorse the thicker social contract model presented by March, he does endorse views that echo the criterion of reciprocity presented by Rawls. This is most evident in his lectures on same-sex marriage. Qadhi's stance on the issue of same-sex marriage is derived from this separation between legal validity and morality. He argues that simply because Muslims believe that homosexuality is a sin does not necessitate that same-sex marriage should be illegal. He believes that Muslims must strike a balance between their morals and the law of the land. In a short video clip on homosexuality, he says that Muslims easily manage this balance and have done so for a long time. There is a list of sins which are allowed legally, but Muslims still consider them to be immoral:

American Muslims have done this easily when it comes to let's say alcohol. We all know alcohol is legal, we all know Islamically it is illegal for us, in the ethical, in the religious sense. The same applies for pre-marital, and extra-marital [sex], and the same should also apply for same-sex relations.[89]

Thus, similar to how Muslims in America accept that alcohol is legal, they should also accept that homosexuality, and same-sex marriages are legal. Moreover, the freedom that is given to others through the fact that the state is not trying to enforce its understanding of morality, also grants Muslims many of their own freedoms. If Muslims defend the freedom of people to pick and choose their own course of life this will translate to greater freedoms for Muslims as well.

Freedoms for any one group, translates as more freedoms for us. The more free any group is the more free we are. The same freedom that allows them [homosexuals] to do what they are doing allows us to do what we are doing. If the dominant majority had the power to ban an alternative lifestyle they could also have the power to ban our lifestyle.[90]

This echoes Rawls' position of reciprocity. Qadhi is willing to accept the freedom granted to homosexuals, even though it comes at a cost to his own moral beliefs, because he expects a reciprocal endorsement of freedom for Muslims. If Muslims were to defy this criterion of reciprocity for homosexuals, it could in turn be used to justify coercive means against Muslims.

A further topic that has arisen from Qadhi's discussion about reciprocity is the concept of "Islamic hypocrisy". Given that many Muslims can practice their religious beliefs openly, because of the freedoms granted by the state, it would be hypocritical of Muslims to want these freedoms for themselves but not want it for other people. The AlMaghrib Institute has posted a video online that includes one interviewer and three students that had just participated in one of Yasir Qadhi's seminars. The video is titled *Liberalism, Gay Marriage, and Islamic Hypocrisy*, and the title aptly summarizes the various topics that are discussed in this short video clip. In this video one of the students begins to discuss this notion of Islamic hypocrisy that came up during Qadhi's seminar:

Student: "One of the things that we were noting in the class with Yasir Qadhi is that it [liberalism] puts us in a black and white situation. We as the youth, the current youth, they see the generation before them as hypocrites almost, because they're completely against liberalism . . . We're kind of living the hypocrisy in a sense where we want our religious freedom we do want . . ."

Interviewer: "But we don't want the freedom for other things . . . that don't agree with us . . ."
Student: "Yeah."

Thus, it is not only reasonable for Muslims to support current approaches to liberal laws, but choosing not to support these laws can be seen as a form of hypocrisy. It is a rather interesting turn of events where the moral position is to defend laws that seem to go against Islamic beliefs and practices. It makes it seem more Islamic to defend same-sex marriage in the United States than to oppose it.

Yasir Qadhi quite clearly supports a Rawlsian understanding of reasonable citizens. He defends the fact that other citizens are free and equal, and he also supports the criterion of reciprocity. He denies the implementation of any coercive practices by Muslims in the West and defends the freedom of others based on a notion of reciprocity. This also presents the practical means by which an overlapping consensus can be reached by examining the thought of contemporary Western Muslim thinkers.

Notes

1. John Rawls, "The Idea of Public Reason Revisited," in *Political Liberalism* (New York: Columbia University Press, 1993), 446.
2. "Shaykh Yasir Qadhi [Instructor Profile]," *AlMaghrib Institute*, accessed March 19, 2016, http://almaghrib.org/instructors/yasir-qadhi.
3. "Al-Khaṭah Al-Dirāsiyyah," Kulīyah Al-ḥadīth Al-Sharīf wa-al-Dirāsāt Al-Islāmiyyah, accessed March 18, 2016, http://www.iu.edu.sa/colleges/Hadith/Pages/Plan.aspx.
4. "Al-Khaṭah Al-Dirāsiyyah," Kulīyah Al-Daʿwa wa-Uṣūl al-Dīn, accessed March 18, 2016, http://www.iu.edu.sa/colleges/DaFund/Pages/Plan.aspx.
5. Yasir Kazi, "Reconciling Reason and Revelation in the Writings of Ibn Taymiyya (d. 728/1328): An Analytical Study of Ibn Taymiyya's 'Dar' Al-Ta'arud'," (Ph.D. thesis, Yale University, 2013).
6. Fakhr al-Dīn al-Rāzī, *Asas al-Taqdīs,* ed. Ahmad Ḥijāzī al-Saqqā (Cairo: Maktabat al-Kullīyāt al- Azharīyah, 1986), 220-221; Kazi, "Reconciling Reason and Revelation," 88–9.
7. Yasir Qadhi, "Ibn Taymiyya: A Summary of Dr Yasir Qadhi's dissertation at Yale University" [Video], *YouTube*, March 22, 2013, accessed February 19, 2015, https://www.youtube.com/watch?v=hn0QbNUbh7I.
8. Ibid.
9. Ibid.
10. Ibid.
11. Ibid.
12. Zareena Grewal, *Islam Is a Foreign Country: American Muslims and the Global Crisis of Authority* (New York: New York University Press, 2014), 330.

13. "No Doubt: God, Religion and Politics in the Modern World [Information]," *AlMaghrib Institute*, accessed May 21, 2016, http://almaghrib.org/seminars/islamic-theology/no-doubt#info.
14. "Shaykh Muhammad Alshareef [Instructor Profile]," *AlMaghrib Institute*, accessed March 17, 2016, http://almaghrib.org/instructors/muhammad-alshareef#profile.
15. "Shaykh Waleed Basyouni [Instructor Profiles]," *AlMaghrib Institute*, accessed March 17, 2016, http://almaghrib.org/instructors/waleed-basyouni#profile.
16. "Shaykh Yaser Birjas [Instructor Profiles]," *AlMaghrib Institute*, accessed March 19, 2016, http://almaghrib.org/instructors/yaser-birjas#profile.
17. "Shaykh Abdullah Hakim Quick [Instructor Profiles]," *AlMaghrib Institute*, accessed March 19, 2016, http://almaghrib.org/instructors/abdullah-hakim-quick#profile.
18. "Dr Reda Bedeir [Instructor Profile]," formerly available from *AlMaghrib Institute*, accessed March 17, 2016, http://almaghrib.org/instructors/reda-bedeir#profile.
19. Frank Gardner, "Islamist Cleric Anwar Al-Awlaki Killed in Yemen," *BBC News*, September 30, 2011, accessed March 17, 2016, http://www.bbc.co.uk/news/world-middle-east-15121879.
20. Grewal, *Islam Is a Foreign Country*, 331.
21. Yasir Qadhi, "An Illegal and Counterproductive Assassination," *The New York Times*, October 1, 2011, accessed November 4, 2016, http://www.nytimes.com/2011/10/02/opinion/sunday/assassinating-al-awlaki-was-counterproductive.html.
22. Yasir Qadhi, "Salafi Muslims: Following the Ancestors of Islam." *Interfaith Voices*, February 21, 2013, accessed November 4, 2016, http://interfaithradio.org/Story_Details/Salafi_Muslims__Following_the_Ancestors_of_Islam.
23. Grewal, *Islam Is a Foreign Country*, 331.
24. Ibid.
25. Ibid.
26. David T, "Sheikh Yasir Qadhi: 'I Became a Racist . . . by Mistake!'" *Harry's Place*, November 13, 2008, accessed November 4, 2016, http://hurryupharry.org/2008/11/13/sheikh-yasir-qadhi-i-became-a-racist-by-mistake/.
27. In his lecture, Qadhi states that the title of the book is *The Hoax of the Holocaust,* but given that there is no book by that title he is mostly likely referring to Butz's influential *The Hoax of the Twentieth Century*: Arthur R. Butz, *The Hoax of the Twentieth Century* (Richmond, Surrey: Historical Review Press, 1976).
28. Yasir Qadhi, "2001 Tafsir of Surah Yusuf Part 8 (Yasir Qadhi's Anti-Semitic Rant" [Audio], *YouTube*, November 19, 2015, accessed November 4, 2016, https://www.youtube.com/watch?v=2bSxOmcyl18.
29. Yasir Qadhi, "GPU '08 with Yasir Qadhi: When Islamophobia Meets Perceived Anti-Semitism," *MuslimMatters.org*, November 10, 2008, accessed November 4, 2016, http://muslimmatters.org/2008/11/10/gpu-08-with-yasir-qadhi-when-islamophobia-meets-perceived-anti-semitism/.
30. Ibid.
31. Ibid.
32. Quintan Wiktorowicz, "Anatomy of the Salafi Movement", *Studies in Conflict & Terrorism* 29, no. 3 (2006): 209, 234,
33. Yasir Qadhi, "Qasir Qadhi Talks about Democracy and Voting" [Video], *YouTube*, March 18, 2011, accessed November 4, 2016, https://www.youtube.com/watch?v=oSQW-NQ6-9A.
34. Ibid.

35. Yasir Qadhi, "Shia (Shiite) Islam is not Islam, it is KUFR (disbelief)" [Audio], *YouTube*, October 21, 2011, accessed November 4, 2016, https://www.youtube.com/watch?v=4wnNjyNzNpY.
36. R. Strothmann and Moktar Djebli, "Taḳiyya," *EI*².
37. Jafar Subhani and Muhammad Muhammad-Riza'i, "Pajuhishī dar Bāb Vilāyat-i Takvīnī-i Insān az Dīdgāh-i Qur'ān", *Insān Pajuhī-i Dīnī* 24, no. 7 (2011): 5–18.
38. Roshan Muhammed Salih, "Sunnism & Shi'ism: Press TV Interview Dr Yasir Qadhi" [Video], *YouTube*, June 24, 2014, accessed November 4, 2016, https://www.youtube.com/watch?v=HLvsQA1oaCg.
39. Ibid.
40. Yasir Qadhi, "Salafi Muslims."
41. Ibid.
42. Ibid.
43. Yasir Qadhi, "On Salafi Islam," *MuslimMatters.org*, April 22, 2014, accessed November 4, 2016, http://muslimmatters.org/2014/04/22/on-salafi-islam-dr-yasir-qadhi/. A more readable PDF version of the text can be found at http://cdn.muslimmatters.org/wp-content/uploads/On-Salafi-Islam_Dr.-Yasir-Qadhi.pdf.
44. Ibid.
45. Ibid., emphasis in the original.
46. Ibid.
47. Yasir Qadhi, "Looking Back as We Look Forward—Change & Modernity [Detroit, Michigan, 7th December 2013]" [Video], *YouTube*, December 13, 2013, https://www.youtube.com/watch?v=jJmrPh2sRuw.
48. Yasir Qadhi, "The Printing Press and Fall of the Muslim Ummah [Memphis, TN, 2012–01–04]" [Video], *Memphis Islamic Center (MIC)*, *YouTube*, August 28, 2013, accessed November 7, 2016, https://www.youtube.com/watch?v=Rg1c62x0NYk.
49. Yasir Qadhi, "Looking Back."
50. Ibid.
51. Ola Salem, "Scholars Split on Ramadan Series," *The National*, July 20, 2012, accessed November 7, 2016, http://www.thenational.ae/news/uae-news/scholars-split-on-ramadan-series.
52. Ola Salem, "Scholars Split on Ramadan Series," *The National*, July 20, 2012, accessed November 7, 2016, http://www.thenational.ae/news/uae-news/scholars-split-on-ramadan-series; Mahmood Habboush, "Ramadan TV show stirs argument across Arab world," *Reuters*, August 14, 2012, accessed November 7, 2016, http://www.reuters.com/article/us-media-islam-drama-idUSBRE87D0LR20120814.
53. "The Prophet Mohamed's companions are biggest drama hit this Ramadan," *Al Bawaba*, August 12, 2012, accessed November 7, 2016, https://www.albawaba.com/entertainment/omar-tv-ramadan-437995.
54. Salman al-Oudah (with Yasir Qadhi et al.), "Standing United against Terrorism & Al-Qaeda," *MuslimMatters.org*, October 12, 2009, accessed November 7, 2016, http://muslimmatters.org/2009/10/12/standing-united-against-terrorism-al-qaeda-salman-al-awdah-with-yasir-qadhi-and-yaser-birjas/.
55. Yasir Qadhi's *Facebook* page, last modified November 29, 2013, accessed May 21, 2016 https://www.facebook.com/yasir.qadhi/posts/10151872642653300.
56. Yasir Qadhi, "Looking Back."
57. Yasir Qadhi, "The Quran and Evolution" [Video], *877–Why–Islam?*, *YouTube*, July 11, 2013, accessed November 7, 2016, https://www.youtube.com/watch?v=DPuoGVlCjZ0.

58. Ibid.
59. Francis S. Collins, *The Language of God: A Scientist Presents Evidence for Belief* (New York–London: Free Press, 2006), 199-201; See also "Building Bridges [Editorial]," *Nature* 442 (July 13, 2006), 110.
60. Pope Pius XII, "Humani Generis (August 12, 1950)", *The Holy See Website (Encyclicals)*, accessed November 7, 2016, http://w2.vatican.va/content/pius-xii/en/encyclicals/documents/hf_p-xii_enc_12081950_humani-generis.html.
61. "Darwin," *The Church of England Website (Medical Ethics & Health & Social Care Policy)*, accessed May 21, 2016, https://www.churchofengland.org/our-views/medical-ethics-health-social-care-policy/darwin.aspx.
62. Michael Zimmerman, "Evolution Weekend: An Example of Reasoned, Civil Discourse," *The Huffington Post*, February 11, 2016, accessed November 7, 2016, http://www.huffingtonpost.com/michael-zimmerman/evolution-weekend-an-exam_b_9206764.html.
63. Maurice A. Finocchiaro, "Science, Religion, and the Historiography of the Galileo Affair: On the Undesirability of Oversimplication," *Osiris* 16 (2001), 114–32.
64. Yasir Qadhi, "Looking Back."
65. John Rawls, "The Idea of Public Reason Revisited".
66. Ibid, 446.
67. Yasir Qadhi, "Does Islam Respect the Right of Someone Not to Believe in a God? [Hartford, CT, 26th May 2012]" [Video], *YouTube*, December 19, 2012, accessed November 7, 2016, https://www.youtube.com/watch?v=vQMxkLR7ZTY.
68. Yasir Qadhi, "Apostasy in Non Muslim Countries" [Video], *YouTube*, March 23, 2015, https://www.youtube.com/watch?v=In6EwVMzyTo.
69. Yasir Qadhi, "What Should be the Muslim Response to Gay Marriage?" [Video], *AlMaghrib Institute (No Doubt), YouTube*, July 23, 2015, accessed November 7, 2016, https://www.youtube.com/watch?v=o0oxJ-wfJZo.
70. Ibid.
71. Yasir Qadhi, "God's Law and Man-Made Laws: Muslims Living in Secular Democracies," *MuslimMatters.org*, March 1, 2010, accessed November 7, 2016, http://muslimmatters.org/2010/03/01/gods-law-and-man-made-laws-muslims-living-in-secular-democracies/.
72. Ibid.
73. Ibid.
74. Ibid.
75. Ibid.
76. Ibid.
77. Leslie Green, "Legal Positivism," in *The Stanford Encyclopedia of Philosophy*, ed. Edward N. Zalta (Fall 2009 edition), accessed November 7, 2016, http://plato.stanford.edu/archives/fall2009/entries/legal-positivism/.
78. Sayed Khatab, *The Political Thought of Sayyid Qutb: The Theory of Jahiliyyah* (London: Routledge, 2006), 3.
79. Yasir Qadhi, "God's Law."
80. Ibid.
81. Ibid.
82. Andrew F. March, "Theocrats Living under Secular Law: An External Engagement with Islamic Legal Theory", *Journal of Political Philosophy* 19 (2011), 28–51.
83. Qadhi, "God's Law."
84. Qadhi, "On Salafi Islam."

85. Within political philosophy, especially in Rawls' terminology, the terms 'thick' and 'thin' refer to level of modularity of a concept. A thin concept is one that is not deeply embedded in a comprehensive doctrine.
86. Qadhi, "God's Law."
87. Ibid.
88. March, "Theocrats Living under Secular Law."
89. Yasir Qadhi, "What Should Be the Muslim Response to Gay Marriage?"
90. Ibid.

CHAPTER
6

NEW DEOBANDI INSTITUTIONS IN THE WEST

Christopher Pooya Razavian and Nathan Spannaus

The growth of South Asian Muslim communities in the West over the last forty years has brought with it not only the spread of Deobandi Islam, but also the emergence of a new type of Deobandi institution, connected religiously and culturally to the mainstream Deobandi movement but also more inclined to seek connections outside these communities, with other Muslims and more broadly with non-Muslims. Two such institutions are Darul Qasim in Chicago and London's Ebrahim College. This chapter will argue that these two Deobandi institutions should be considered as "second wave" institutions because they are attempting to adjust Deobandi *fiqh* to the needs of Western Muslims. Both Deoband-inspired schools are staffed in large part by graduates of Deobandi *madrasahs*, and have sought to break with the mould of conventional *dār al-ʿulūms* by incorporating new kinds of educational practices and expanding the scope of their activities beyond the South-Asian Deobandi community.

The two schools are quite similar in their basic function and history. Darul Qasim was founded in 1998 by its current head Shaykh Mohammed Amin Kholwadia, a British-born scholar who studied at Deobandi *madrasahs* around India. Kholwadia moved to Chicago in 1984, becoming very active in the local Muslim community, particularly the sizable Pakistani population, which is concentrated on the far North Side and the city's northwest suburbs. Although Darul Qasim has had several physical headquarters during its existence, it is now located in one such northwestern suburb, Glendale Heights, Illinois.[1]

Darul Qasim today has a range of academic programmes: a doctoral programme in *iftāʾ*; a master's in Islamic law and theology; a bachelor's in Islamic studies; the "Shaykh al-Hind"[2] pre-collegiate prerequisite programme, which prepares students for the linguistic challenges of Islamic scholarship; introductory Arabic classes; an extracurricular programme in Islamic studies aimed at high school students; and classes in Qur'ānic recitation.[3] The lower-level classes, particularly the high school programme and introductory Arabic, are intended as popular courses for members of the community broadly. The upper-level programmes, on the other hand, including the "Shaykh al-Hind", are intended to produce graduates prepared for work as *imāms* and *'ulamā'*. The school has also since 2009 opened satellite chapters teaching primarily Arabic and Qur'ānic recitation in Cleveland; Louisville, Kentucky; Knoxville, Tennessee; and Newark, California, outside San Francisco.[4]

Ebrahim College likewise offers a rich diversity of educational offerings. It began in 2003 as an *imām*-training seminary and a sixth-form school. The seminary programme was transformed several years later into a four-year undergraduate *ālimīyah* degree, while Ebrahim Academy and Rashidun School were formed as a full-time high school and primary school, respectively under the under the auspices of the college. In addition, Ebrahim College offers Arabic language classes and short-term classes in different areas of Islamic Studies, as well as online courses in Arabic and an array of religious subjects.[5]

Deobandi *Dār al-'ulūms*

Both Ebrahim College and Darul Qasim are what could be termed "second wave" Deobandi institutions. Unlike the pioneering Deobandi *madrasahs* and seminaries in the West that date from the 1970s to 1980s and adhere more closely to the Deobandi educational model, to say nothing of religious outlook, these later schools are more open to adaptation and reform in education and, as we will see below, more explicitly oriented toward adjusting to their immediate societal context.

In the U.K., Deobandi education has been led by the Darul Uloom Bury, founded in 1979, and the Institute of Islamic Education (IIE) in Dewsbury, founded in 1982. Subsequently *dār al-'ulūms* were established in cities around the country. These schools are located in areas with large South Asian populations and are overwhelmingly insular in their operation, training Deobandi students to serve as Deobandi *imāms* and teachers in Deobandi mosques and schools in Deobandi communities.[6] Ebrahim College, by contrast, is located in a relatively diverse section of London, with the college itself taking great pains to forge connections broadly, outside of the Deobandi milieu. Hafiz Mushfiq Uddin, Ebrahim's chief executive, has stated that he views the school's relationship to the Deobandi movement to be primarily academic, rather than sectarian or political.[7]

That is not to say that the older Deobandi institutions bear no influence on Ebrahim College. Many of its current leadership, including Ad Duha and Mushfiq Uddin, studied at Dewsbury, as well as Deobandi schools in South

Asia, but many also have degrees from Western universities and a significant number have studied at institutions in the Middle East (Syria and Egypt, recent political instability notwithstanding) that are not affiliated with the Deoband tradition.[8]

The environment in the U.S. is quite different. Unlike in Britain, where Deobandi *dār al-'ulūms* form a plurality of Islamic schools (45 per cent, according to John Bowen)[9]—which certainly accounts somewhat for their inward focus—Deobandis (and South Asians in general) make up a much smaller share of a much more diverse Muslim population. The first Deobandi *madrasah* in America was the Darul Uloom al-Madania, which opened its doors in Buffalo, New York in 1990. Given the different religious context in America, it has a broader student body. This is perhaps tempered by its proximity to Toronto, with its large South Asian population and concentration of Deobandi *madrasahs*.[10] Nevertheless, Darul Uloom al-Madania has stuck strongly by the Deobandi religious and educational tradition to the exclusion of outside influences, which has led to some friction with the Buffalo Muslim community.[11] The school has also been linked with global Deobandi networks, such as Darul Ishaat in Karachi, a publisher of Deobandi texts that Darul Uloom al-Madania distributes.[12] A similar Deobandi residential primary school was opened in Elgin, Illinois, a suburb northwest of Chicago, in 1991. Called the Institute of Islamic Education, it was founded and led by Shaykh Abdullah Saleem, who himself studied in Darul Uloom Deoband.[13]

Both of these institutions have exerted some influence on Darul Qasim, particularly the IIE, for obvious reasons, and a number of scholars have moved between them. Like Ebrahim College, however, Darul Qasim's faculty is staffed by teachers who have received training in Western academia (the University of Chicago in particular) as well as in the Middle East. Indeed, Darul Qasim's faculty is more markedly non-Deobandi, with many teachers who have not studied in Deobandi schools.[14]

These schools also place considerable influence on accommodating their respective national educational systems. In contrast to more conventional Deobandi schools like the Darul Uloom al-Madania and IIE Dewsbury, which fulfill state curriculum requirements only as necessary, both Ebrahim College and Darul Qasim work to fit into—or at least work with—mainstream academic structures, the former with GCSE and A-level curriculum, the latter with high-school and pre-college programmes.[15]

The primary goal of both of these institutions is an Islamic education that is simultaneously grounded in Islamic tradition and scripture and suited to the modern, Western context. The objectives of Ebrahim College include producing religious leaders who "understand and respond to *the needs of modern society*, to make traditional Islamic education accessible and relevant, [and] to deliver outstanding *mainstream education* that enriches people's lives underpinned by an Islamic ethos . . ."[16] Darul Qasim in turn describes itself as "ha[ving] a unique ability to offer classical Islamic knowledge in a very vibrant, contemporary context, and to a very contextually aware audience," while describing its programmes as combining the content of the Islamic sciences with the context of contemporary society.[17] Moreover, in terms of their seminary-style programmes, both schools emphasize training *imāms* and scholars who understand contemporary circumstances.

Curriculum and Tradition

It is critical to note, however, that Ebrahim College and Darul Qasim also ground themselves and their educational offerings within the Deobandi religious and intellectual tradition. This tradition is based on the combination of a focus on scripture and a reliance on, and deference to, the views of authoritative *'ulamā'* from the past, primarily from the Ḥanafī and Māturīdī schools. Accordingly, the *madhhab* and the structures of *taqlīd* that underpin the Deobandi tradition (see Volume 1, Chapter 8) have particular relevance in both institutions, shaping their approach to instruction. Although they do differ slightly in this regard: at Ebrahim College, all teaching in *fiqh* is done through the Ḥanafī school, whereas Darul Qasim allows students to study any of the four *madhhabs*, even if Ḥanafism is the default.[18] Adherence to the *madhhab* is not implemented through the study of strictly Ḥanafī-Māturīdī texts, but rather—and quite significantly—through the progression of the curriculum, which begins with positive law (*furū' al-fiqh*) before proceeding to matters of legal theory (*uṣūl al-fiqh*).[19] This progression follows the traditional organization of legal education historically in the madrasa, in which a student became familiar with the *corpus juris* of his school through the study of authoritative commentaries (sing. *sharḥ*) and summaries (sing. *mukhtaṣar*), before moving on to the jurisprudential and interpretive theory according to which those points of positive law were formulated.[20] For Ḥanafīs, one of the primary *furū'* texts was the eleventh century *Mukhtaṣar* of Qudūrī, which forms the basis for the first year of Islamic law at Darul Qasim.[21] Ebrahim College unfortunately does not specify the text for its equivalent course.

The purpose of *taqlīd* in this respect is to act as parameters for acceptable religious discourse, to limit the possibility of aberrant or anomalous interpretations by making students dependent upon positions that have been already validated within the tradition. Accordingly, there is a marked difference in the texts and approach used at Darul Qasim between the bachelor's and master's levels, with the latter focused on scriptural interpretation and evaluation. The study of *furū'* here is subordinated to *uṣūl*, which is explored through engagement with *ḥadīth* texts. As the website describes:

> The Master's level program elucidates the link between the derivatives (*furu'*) of Islam and their primary sources (*uṣūl*) . . .

> The connection between the Qur'ān and Islamic Law will be discussed through *Tafsīr al-Aḥkām* (Exegesis of Islamic Law). The understanding of Islamic Law will be shown through an in-depth study of the six authenticated, canonical books of Hadith, along with the *Muwaṭṭa'* of Imām Muḥammad and Imām Mālik. Further comparative *fiqh* in light of Hadith will be discussed through Imām Ṭahāwī's *Sharḥ Ma'ānī al-Āthār.*[22]

This higher-level study is aimed at understanding the relationship between *madhhab* doctrine and jurisprudential methodology and the sources of scripture, which represents a markedly different scope of inquiry and study than for the bachelor's programme, yet one that still operates within the *madhhab* as a religious frame. Ebrahim College for its part offers a slightly different approach, incorporating *ḥadīth* sciences into the undergraduate programme in later years.[23]

These schools have each built their programmes around the distinctively Deobandi form of the *Dars-i Niẓāmī*, the foundational curriculum in South Asian scholarly circles since the seventeenth century, with an emphasis on *ḥadīth* study and textual interpretation supplemented with philosophical and logical subjects.[24] This is more pronounced at Darul Qasim, which includes more advanced logical and *kalām* texts than Ebrahim, which seems to limit theological study to more basic matters of belief[25] (see the respective curricula below).

Both institutions also, however, incorporate pedagogical practices from modern academia, which they employ alongside the textual study of the *madrasah*. Darul Qasim employs formal assignments, including a thesis for master's students. Ebrahim College requires a thesis as well for undergraduates, but more significantly its *Dars-i Niẓāmī*-derived curriculum also includes several courses that are organized as modern classes. They are not, however, "secular" subjects—e.g. math, science—which are often added to Deobandi *madrasahs*, but rather religious and humanities courses organized around academic subjects, such as philosophy of religion, critical thinking, Islamic history and Arabic literature.[26] Darul Qasim, for its part, has courses that are not text-based, but they are focused on a particular aspect of Islamic scholarship (for instance, a specific concept in *fiqh* reasoning).

A comparison of the *alimiyyah* curriculum for each shows both the similarities and differences in their use of the *Dars-i Niẓāmī*. Darul Qasim divides its curriculum into several subjects (law, theology, *Qur'ān*, etc.), enumerating the texts to be studied and in what order.[27]

As is evident, the curriculum at Darul Qasim is overwhelmingly text-based, as in the case of a conventional *madrasah*, with subjects taught through authoritative works from the scholarly tradition. Courses that do not rely on a particular text, namely the intermediate *fiqh* sequence, are few. This stands in contrast to Ebrahim College's approach, which not only has far more classes, with a credit hour system, but many that are not focused on a text or, as noted, are organized thematically like modern university courses.[28]

Table 6.1 Curriculum of Darul Qasim

Subjects	Year 1	Year 2	Year 3	Year 4
Arabic and the instrumental Islamic Sciences	*Iẓhār al-Asrār*, *Hidāyat al-Naḥw* and *Ādāb*	*Jāmi' al-Durūs al-'Arabīyah*, *al-Balaghāt al-Wāḍiḥah*	*Mukhtārāt min Ādāb al-'Arab*	
Qur'ānic studies and recitation	*al-Muqaddamāt al-Jazārīyah*, *Ḥifẓ* with introduction to the evolution of *tajwīd*	*Tarjumāt al-Qur'ān*, *Ṣafwāt al-Tafāsīr*	*Al-Fawẓ al-Kabīr fī Uṣūl al-Tafsīr*, Themes of the *Qur'ān*	*Tafsīr al-Jalālayn*
Islamic law	*Mukhtaṣar al-Qudūrī*	*al-Zād min Uṣūl al-Fiqh*, Intermediate *Fiqh* I and II, *Sharḥ al-Manār*	Intermediate *Fiqh* III and IV, *Sharḥ al-Manār*	*al-Hidāyah*
Hadith	*Riyāḍ al-Ṣāliḥīn*		*Bayqūnīyah*, *Nuzhat al-Naẓar*	*Mishkāt al-Masābīḥ*
Theology	*al-'Aqīdah al-Ṭaḥāwīyah*, *Badā' al-Āmālī*			*Īsāghūjī* and *Sharḥ al-'Aqa'id al-Nasafīyah*

Source: Darul Qasim website (transliteration kept as original)

Table 6.2 Curriculum of Ebrahim College

Year 1	Year 2	Year 3	Year 4
Tafsir al-Tahlili (3 modules)	Tafsir al-Tahlili (3 modules)	Tafsir al-Tahlili (3 modules)	Tafsir al-Mawdhu'i (3 modules: Understanding Tafsir and the Mufassirun)
Tajwid (3 modules)	Tajwid (3 Modules)	Hadith (3 modules: *Mishkāt al-Maṣābīḥ*)	Tafsir al-Tahlili (3 modules)
Hadith (1 module – *Riyāḍ al-Ṣāliḥīn*)	Hadith (3 modules: *Mishkāt al-Maṣābīḥ*)	Fiqh (3 modules)	Hadith (3 modules)
Islamic History (1 module - Prophetic Biography)	Fiqh (3 modules)	*Qur'ān*, Hadith and the Orientalist (1 module)	Fiqh (5 modules)
Arabic Language and Grammar (3 modules)	Arabic Language and Grammar (3 modules: *Sharḥ Ibn Aqīl*)	Ulum al-Hadith (*Nukhbat al-Fikr*) [*sic*]	Ulum al-Hadith (1 module – Understanding Takhrij and its Application)
Arabic Literature (3 modules)	Ulum al-Hadith (1 module)	Usul al-Fiqh (3 modules)	Usul al-Fiqh
Fiqh (3 modules)	Usul al-Fiqh (1 module)	Aqidah (1 module- Understanding Muslim Sects)	Aqidah (1 module: Understanding World Religions)
Philosophy of Religion (3 modules)	Aqidah (3 modules)	Arabic Literature (3 modules)	History of Ideas (2 modules)

Continued

Table 6.2 Curriculum of Ebrahim College *(continued)*

Year 1	Year 2	Year 3	Year 4
Aqidah (1 module - *al-'Aqīdah al-Ṭaḥāwīyah*)	Philosophy of Religion (3 modules)	Balaghah (1 module)	Philosophy of the Shariah (1 module: Hujjatullah al-Bālighah)
	Arabic Literature (3 modules)	Speaking & Composing in Academic Arabic (1 module)	Islamic Activism and Leadership (3 modules)
	Academic Writing and Research Skills (1 module)	Academic Skills (1 module – Developing Effective Translation Skills)	Critical Thinking (1 module)
	Islamic History (1 module – The Rightly Guided Khalifahs)	Islamic History (1 module – History of Muslim Dynasties)	Islamic History (1 module – History of Islam in Britain)
		Optional Languages: Urdu (3 modules) Bengali (3 modules)	Dissertation 1 (English) Dissertation 2 (Arabic)
			Optional Languages: Urdu (3 modules) Bengali (3 modules)

Source: Ebrahim College website (transliteration kept as original)

Ebrahim College organizes its curriculum in a rather different way than Darul Qasim, yet the shared intellectual lineage is apparent. Virtually all of the texts listed for its courses here appear in Darul Qasim's curriculum. One seeming discrepancy, the *Nukhbat al-Fikr*, is in fact a different version of the *Nuzhat al-Naẓar*, studied at Darul Qasim, with the latter being a commentary on the former by the same author, the fifteenth century Cairene scholar Ibn Hajar Asqalani.

Despite their differences, it is noteworthy that neither school employs the sequential learning that was characteristic of the traditional *madrasah*, wherein one subject is mastered before moving onto the next (Arabic > Qur'ān > grammar > rhetoric > logic > theology > *fiqh*, and so on). Instead, different subjects are taught simultaneously, as would be found in a modern school. Zaytuna College, which offers a close point of comparison for explicitly tradition-based Islamic education, also organizes classes this way, with its curriculum most resembling Ebrahim College's (see Chapter 1). That said, both school's preparatory programmes preceding the *alimiyyah* consist largely of *tajwīd* (Qur'ānic recitation), which functionally teaches literacy in the Arabic script and proper pronunciation of Arabic letters—distinct from an Arabic language class—which was traditionally the beginning stage of Islamic education. Indeed, at Darul Qasim this initial course teaches pronunciation and recitation through the vocalization of the names of the Arabic letters, which is historically a very old approach.[29]

In sum, each institution's curriculum shows it to combine elements of Deobandi *madrasah* education—and versions of the *Dars-i Niẓāmī*—with modern, Western educational practices and structures, whether through altered pedagogical methods or adapting Deobandi educational content into A-levels and high school programmes.

A worthwhile point of comparison here is Darul Uloom New York, founded in Queens in 1997, the entirety of whose faculty studied overseas in Deobandi *madrasahs* (primarily in Pakistan and South Africa).[30] Its seven-year *alimiyyah* programme is overwhelmingly text-based, with most courses associated with a classical work from the *Dars-i Niẓāmī*, though unfortunately the sequence of courses is not given.[31]

Notwithstanding the length of the course of study, which is more extensive in terms of both time and number of texts, Darul Uloom New York's curriculum is more conventional than that of Darul Qasim or Ebrahim College. There remains however extensive overlap in terms of the texts utilized among the three schools, and the common grounding in the *Dars-i Niẓāmī* is evident. But this comparison also makes it apparent the degree to which Darul Qasim and Ebrahim College have adapted the content of Deobandi schooling to fit into an altered educational model, Ebrahim College in particular. Their curricula are not only shorter, but also condensed, treating the same subjects with less time and fewer texts. Moreover, the way the texts are taught and discussed in class—an issue often ignored when focusing simply on lists of the courses being offered—plays a significant role in shaping the

Table 6.3 Curriculum of Darul Uloom New York

***Qur'ānic* Studies**	
Tajwīd I	Tajwīd for Beginners
Qira'a	Marifat al-Waquf
Tajwīd II	Tashīl al- Tajwīd
Introduction to *Qur'ān* Translation	Miftāḥ al-*Qur'ān*
Tajwīd III	Jamāl al-*Qur'ān*
Qur'ān Translation I–III	Tarjumat al-*Qur'ān*
Qur'ānic Exegesis	Tafsir Jalalayn
Hadith Studies	
Hadith Memorization I–II	Mazād al-Ṣāliḥīn
Introduction to Hadith	Zād al-Ṭālibīn
Hadith Comprehension	Riyād al-Ṣāliḥīn
Hadith Memorization II–IV	Ḥifẓ al-Ḥadīth
Principles of Hadith I	Khaīr al-Uṣūl
Principles of Hadith II	al-Bayqūniyyah
Advanced Hadith Methodology I	Mishkat Masabih
Principles of Hadith III	Nukhbat al-Fikar
Advance Hadith Methodology II	al-Sihah al-Sittah, Muwatta Mālik, Muwatta Muhammad, Shamā'il al-Tirmidhī, Sharh Ma'āni al-Āthār
Arabic Language Studies	
Introduction to Arabic Morphology	Miftāḥ al-Ṣarf
Introduction to Arabic Grammar	Miftāḥ al-Naḥw
Introduction to Arabic Conversation	al-Lughat al-'Arabiyyah

Continued

Table 6.3 Curriculum of Darul Uloom New York *(continued)*

Beginner Arabic Morphology	Tamrīn al-Ṣarf
Intermediate Arabic Morphology	ʻIlm al-Ṣarf
Beginner Arabic Grammar	Tamrīn al-Naḥw
Intermediate Arabic Grammar	ʻIlm al-Naḥw
Beginner Arabic Conversation	al-Tariqat al-ʻAsriyyah
Advance Arabic Morphology	ʻIlm al-Ṣīghah
Intermediate Arabic Grammar I	al-Naḥw al-Wāḍiḥ
Intermediate Arabic Grammar II	Sharḥ Miʾat ʿĀmil
Advanced Arabic Grammar I	al-Naḥw al-Wāḍiḥ
Advanced Arabic Grammar II	Ḥidāyat al-Naḥw
Arabic Rhetoric I–II	al-Balāghat al-Wāḍiḥah
Arabic Literature Studies	
Arabic Literature I–IV	Qasas al-Nabiyin
Arabic Literature V	Ṣuwar Min Ḥayāt al-Ṣaḥābah
Islamic Studies	
Islamic Manners I	Taʻlīm al-Muta'allim Tarīqa al-Taʻallum
Islamic Beliefs & Practices	Taʻlīm al-Islām
History of Islam	Ḥayāt al-Ṣaḥābah
Supplication I	Masnūn Duʻain
Islamic Manners II	Mufīd al-Ṭālibīn
Introduction to Islamic Theology	ʻAqā'id al-'Islām

Continued

Table 6.3 Curriculum of Darul Uloom New York *(continued)*

Supplication II	Ḥiṣn al-Muslim
Sects in Religion	Ikhtilāf Ummat Aur Sirāt Mustaqīm
Introduction to Logic	Āsān Manṭiq
Islamic Theology	al-'Aqīdah al-Ṭaḥāwiyyah
Islamic Inheritance	Sirājīyyah
Islamic Jurisprudence Studies	
Introduction to Islamic Jurisprudence	al-Fiqh al-Muyasar
Beginner Islamic Jurisprudence I–II	Mukhtaṣar al-Qudūrī
Intermediate Islamic Jurisprudence	Sharḥ al-Wiqāyah
Principles of Islamic Jurisprudence I	Uṣūl al-Shāshī
Advanced Islamic Jurisprudence I–II	al-Hidayah
Principles of Islamic Jurisprudence II	Nūr al-Anwār

Source: Darul Uloom New York website (transliteration kept as original)

character of education: Darul Qasim's and Ebrahim College's emphasis on teaching the content of Islamic tradition in ways that can better relate it to the context, will almost certainly foster different understandings of the same texts between the *madrasahs*.

Educational Reform and Social Outreach

The contrast in curricula of Darul Uloom New York compared to that followed at Darul Qasim or Ebrahim College is indicative of the more socially oriented outlook of the latter two. Darul Qasim and Ebrahim College are committed to the project of educational reform within the Deobandi tradition, and to training religious students so that they may learn to apply their tradition to contemporary circumstances especially in the minority contexts. There are many similarities between the two institutions in this regard. They are focused on training *imāms* and *'ulamā'* who are learned in Islamic tradition but also familiar and engaged with their broader social environment, and who can also contribute to academic research on Islam and Islamic issues.[32] Nevertheless, there are also substantial differences in how each institution approaches educational reform.

For Ebrahim College, its academic mission clearly states its reformist project. As an institution, it appears set firmly against the insularity and inward focus of the British Deobandi community and strives to have greater engagement with Britain, a prominent theme in Ad Duha's speeches and sermons, as will be shown below. Education, accordingly, is Ebrahim's College main vehicle for its contributions to British society. Moreover, it has been working for the past several years, at least since 2010, to form a partnership with a British university to transform the *alimiyyah* programme into a full-fledged bachelor's degree.[33] Successfully doing so would effectively reorient the *Dars-i Nizāmī* into a modern academic frame, which would stand as a perfect manifestation of adapting Islamic tradition to fit into contemporary society in order to "deliver outstanding mainstream education that enriches people's lives underpinned by an Islamic ethos."[34]

The reformism of Darul Qasim, though scholarly, is best characterized as intellectual. More so than Ebrahim College, Darul Qasim is closely linked with mainstream American academia; its associated teachers and scholars have contributed to the scholarly debates through extensive publications. Leading this work has been Shaykh Kholwadia himself, who has written a number of works dealing with practical and currently socially relevant issues from an Islamic perspective. He is a contributing co-author of a book on ethical Islamic finance and banking, for instance, published in 2010.[35] Most significantly, Kholwadia has done extensive work in bioethics employing a framework from Islamic tradition (this will be discussed in detail below).

These efforts are representative of the kind of institution Darul Qasim aims to be and the type of impact and contribution it aspires to make. Ebrahim College likewise seeks to play a productive part in contemporary British society, beyond the confines of the Deobandi community, though following a different approach.

Shams Ad Duha and Shaykh Amin Kholwadia

The leading figures of Ebrahim College and Darul Qasim are Shaykh Shams Ad Duha and Shaykh Kholwadia respectively. A key difference between the two shaykhs is that Shams Ad Duha is more involved with direct engagement in the public sphere by tackling issues such as the face veil, *sharīʿah* patrols and *madrasahs*, whereas Kholwadia primarily addresses more conceptual issues about Muslims' life in the West with a particular academic interest in Islamic bioethics. Ad Duha's approach is based on a concept of *ikthilāf* (disagreement), whereby as in case of Yasir Qadhi (see Chapter 5) he expects Muslims to be tolerant of different beliefs and for Western non-Muslims to be tolerant of conservative Islamic belifs. He also has argued that the Conservative government's attempt to undermine this tolerance during the premiership of Prime Minister David Cameron will lead to a hermeneutics of suspicion and increased radicalization amongst British Muslim youth. Darul Qasim also puts forward a concept of the *responsible citizen*, although this is referenced in a public statement from the institution and not discussed in detail in Shaykh Kholwadia's personal writings. Kholwadia's academic articles on Islamic bioethics discuss some of the difficulties presented by modern medical practice for traditional Islamic law.

Shams Ad Duha and Public Engagement

Ebrahim College has a strong social media presence. They are active on YouTube, Twitter, Facebook, and even run an online magazine called *Islamique*. This active presence on social media is reflective of their active engagement with the public sphere. Ad Duha, one of Ebrahim College's founders and its most prominent lecturer, engages with many topics that are controversial in the United Kingdom. His lectures have been viewed by thousands on YouTube and he has even debated the firebrand extremist Anjum Choudary on the popular British current affairs programme, *Newsnight*.[36]

Ad Duha was born and raised in East London.[37] He has studied at various *dār al-ʿulūms* in England before traveling to South Asia. He began his religious training by memorizing the Qur'an and completed his memorization at the Darul Uloom in Dewsbury, were he also studied various Islamic sciences such as Arabic, Qur'ānic recitation, and Islamic law. He continued his education at the al-Jamia al-Islamia in Nottingham. There he furthered his studies in the field of Islamic law, principles of jurisprudence, *ḥadīth* sciences, and Qur'ānic exegesis. In 1997 he travelled to Bangladesh in order to complete his *dār al-ʿulūm* studies. His biography is unclear about the contents of his study. After his studies in Bangladesh, Ad Duha returned to England where he finished a master's degree in Islamic Studies from the University of London. Ad Duha's primary focus has been on Islamic education especially for children. He has worked with various institutions in pursuit of this goal. He has worked with the Safar Academy in North London as well as helping found the Mazahirul Uloom secondary school in 2000. In 2002, along with other shaykhs he founded Ebrahim College where he is currently Founding Director and Principal. Ad Duha has authored his own original Islamic creedal work (*ʿaqīdah*) that is used in courses at the college but is as yet unpublished.[38] He has also produced translations of a number of classical Islamic texts.

Ad Duha's views can be found in his lectures and sermons delivered mainly at Ebrahim College, which are then uploaded to YouTube. Parts of his classroom lectures are also available, but none of the uploaded material resembles an entire lecture series. The majority of these videos have to do with issues of spirituality and faith. This includes speeches entitled "Reconnecting with the Qur'an," "Perils of Procrastination," and "God Consciousness and Good Character."[39] This is to be expected given that one of the primary goals of an

Islamic education is spiritual development. Ad Duha has also given multiple speeches that directly tackle issue of Islam in Britain. Some of these speeches discuss how Muslims should live in Britain, and others challenge British attitudes towards Islam.

As described earlier, Ebrahim College stays within the *taqlīd* framework. In his talk about "Following Saheeh Hadith vs Taqleed," Ad-Duha defends this *taqlīd* approach against Salafi critics.[40] He argues that those calling to eschew *taqlīd* and only follow authentic *ḥadīth* are themselves following blindly. The only justification they have as to why one must follow only authentic *ḥadīth* is that someone else told them to do so. They are only imitating the views of others, as it is not a conclusion that they have reached by themselves through some process of academic investigation.

Ad Duha echoes a common criticism against Salafism that the ability to understand and abide by authentic *ḥadīth* requires proficiency in the principles of jurisprudence. This proficiency is only gained through a mastery of the debates found in the works of the scholars of the *madhhab*. He compares those that try to understand *ḥadīth* by foregoing this training to an Urdu saying that translates as "the frog in the well": the frog assumes that what it sees in the well is all that there is. Similarly, those who try to understand Islamic law simply by referring to authentic *ḥadīth*, mistakenly assume that all they know is all there is. By ignoring the vast tradition of Islamic scholarship they also ignore the vast debates that have been held about these very *ḥadīth*. This person ends up following issues in Islamic law more blindly than those that follow traditional schools of Islamic law. To engage in these types of discussions is, in his view, compound ignorance, meaning that one is ignorant about one's ignorance. He quotes Shaykh al-ʿUthaymīn, the prominent mainstream Salafi scholar, on this issue; it is necessary to follow the way of the *Salaf* (pious forbearers) but it is not necessary to follow the group that labels themselves as Salafi. Ad Duha then argues that all Muslims believe that they are following the Qur᾽ān and *sunnah*, and that this is not a privileged status of Salafism.

Although Ad Duha calls for the adherence to *taqlīd* and the *madhhab* this does not mean that he is calling for a single interpretation of Islam. He argues that any detailed understanding of the *madhhab*s will reveal the deep-rooted historical debates both within the *madhhab* and between the various *madhhab*s. This difference of opinion in religious law is called *ikhtilāf*. Ad Duha makes use of these debates in order to argue for a reasonable degree of pluralism.

The term reasonable pluralism was popularized by the political philosopher John Rawls. Rawls argued that our religious and moral differences are not simply a matter of history such that we can achieve a consensus sometime in the future. They are instead the natural outgrowth of reasonable deliberation within a liberal environment. They are therefore a permanent feature of our democratic culture.[41] Ad Duha echoes these same views in regards to religious opinions, although through the use of *ikhtilāf*. Moreover,

Ad Duha's debate on reasonable pluralism is limited to Islamic practice and not Islamic belief.

The issue of *ikhtilāf* has a long history within Islamic thought, and Ad Duha's usage of the term brings this history to the fore. *Ikhtilāf* refers to the differences of opinion in issues of religious law, but does not include issues regarding the core tenets of faith such as the oneness of God, *tawhīd*.[42] The genre of *ikhtilāf* literature began quite earlier in the history of Islamic thought with the earliest existing work belonging to Abū Ḥanīfa's student, Abū Yūsuf (d. 789/ 182).[43]

Thus, through the use of the concept of *ikhtilāf* Ad Duha is able to make an argument for reasonable pluralism without having to necessarily detail its philosophical premises. Similar to Rawls' argument, the concept of *ikhtilāf* assumes that reasonable people will develop differing opinions about issues of religious law. *Ikhtilāf*, however, is much more limited in that it pertains only to religious law and Rawls' reasonable pluralism covers all types of comprehensive doctrines. This issue of *ikhtilāf* finds importance for Ad Duha in his discussion on voting.[44] The issue of voting tends to spark debates within Muslim communities. The crux of Ad Duha's argument is that voting is an issue of *ikhtilāf*, disagreement; some scholars say it is permissible other scholars say that it is not. By arguing that voting is a matter of *ikhtilāf*, Ad Duha maintains that there is no single ruling for all people. For some people, voting is a sin, for others it is not. Therefore it is not permissible to judge others based on criterions which one has accepted but others have not. Because one believes that voting is a sin, does not mean that for someone else voting is a sin as well.

Ad Duha strengthens his argument by appealing to cases of *ikhtilāf* in the past. He gives an example of reciting the *Fātiḥah*. For Ḥanafīs, remaining silent behind the *imām* and not reciting the *Fātiḥah* is obligatory. On the other hand, Shāfi'īs say that it is obligatory to recite the *Fātiḥah*. It is therefore not justified to enforce the rulings of one school of law to those who adhere to another school of law. For Ad Duha, unity is developed amongst Muslims despite these differences: "The question isn't let's unite on these issues. You unite despite your disagreement. It isn't possible to unite the minds."[45] There always has been and always will be a reasonable pluralism within religious law. Muslims should respect these differences and not coerce others to act or believe in one's own understanding of religious law.

However, Ad Duha does put limitations on the scope of reasonable pluralism ruling it out in cases where it can lead to causing harm to another person. Although this is a rather quick comment that he gives towards the end of his lecture, it is quite interesting given that it follows John Stuart Mill's argument about the harm principle. Mill argued that the "only purpose for which power can be rightfully exercised over any member of a civilized community, against his will, is to prevent harm to others."[46] This is not to say that Ad Duha is a liberal similar to Rawls and Mill, mainly due to the fact that they are discussing a different subject: Ad Duha is discussing pluralism within Islamic law while Rawls and Mill are discussing political philosophy. Yet it is interesting to see that they are grappling with similar types of problems and come to similar types of conclusions. They all broadly agree on the notion of reasonable pluralism as well as to its limits in regards to harm.

As it will be shown, Ad Duha extends this concept of reasonable pluralism to non-Muslims as well. Although one disagrees with their religious viewpoints, it is not moral to coerce them to adhere to Islamic beliefs or actions. This, he maintains, holds true regardless of whether one lives in a Muslim or non-Muslim-majority country.

Shams Ad-Duha clarifies his views about the interaction between Muslims and non-Muslims in a speech about *sharīʿah* patrols.[47] In 2013 a group of men who labeled themselves "Muslim Patrol" started to demand that all those living in their area of East London adhere to Islamic norms. A description on one of their YouTube videos stated: "From women walking the street dressed like complete naked animals with no self respect, to drunk people carrying alcohol, to drunks being killed in the middle of the road, we try our best to capture and forbid it all."[48] Three of the members were jailed for harassment, intimidation and assault.[49] Ad Duha was concerned about these events given that they occurred so close to Ebrahim College, in the London Borough of Tower Hamlets.

Ad Duha was upset that this issue about Muslim street patrols was not approached from the perspective of the *sharīʿah*. He makes the argument that "this is actually wrong Islamically."[50] The idea of implementing *sharīʿah* has, he argues, to be governed by the *sharīʿah* itself going on to criticize "Muslim Patrol" for their "bad boy" attitude towards Islam: "I was a bad boy yesterday and now become practising so I need to be a bad boy as a Muslim as well."[51] He states that it is a delusion to consider this area of London as "Islamic" and stated that it is a British area, and that they are all Muslims of Britain.

Nonetheless, had it been an "Islamic" area it would, in Ad Duha's view, have to be governed by the norms of the *sharīʿah*. Ad Duha begins by explaining what a traditional understanding of *sharīʿah* itself has to say about implementing *sharīʿah* in an Islamic state, and then builds on that to describe the implementation of *sharīʿah* for non-Muslims in non-Muslim-majority countries. He states that a large number of non-Muslims were ruled according to Ḥanafī law, and cites several examples of how non-Muslims should be treated according to Ḥanafī law from traditional Ḥanafī texts. He cites specifically from the influential Egyptian Ḥanafī jurist Imām al-Kamāl ibn Humām (d. 861/457) and his *Sharḥ Fatḥ al-Gadīr ʿAlā al-Hidāyah Sharḥ Bidāyah al-Mubtadī*. Ibn Humām's book is a commentary on *al-Hidāyah* written by Burhān al-Dīn al-Marghinānī (d. 1197/593). *Al-Hidāyah* has been one of the key texts of legal studies in South Asian *madrasahs*.[52]

The text that Ad Duha is quoting from can therefore be seen as coming from within the heart of the Ḥanafī tradition. The section that Ad Duha quotes in particular deals with the issue of Muslims forcefully taking possession of alcohol or swine from non-Muslims. Ibn Humām maintains that if a Muslim causes any damage to the wine stock or swine then he has to pay damages.[53] Ad Duha notes that this issue of compensation itself is interesting, for these goods are as per Islamic law generally not seen as goods that have *māl* (intrinsic value). Thus, if these goods belong to a Muslim and they were destroyed, there would be no damages to pay because these goods did not have any value. However, if they are the property of a non-Muslim then it has value and one must pay damages. Ad Duha states that: "We can't judge them [non-Muslims] according to the principles that bind us in our *sharīʿah*."[54] Thus pork for non-Muslims is like lamb for Muslims, and wine for non-Muslims is like vinegar for Muslims. Islam celebrated this pluralism that allowed non-Muslims to live according to their own religions. Ad Duha then discusses the issue of *dhimmah*, whereby non-Muslims pay tax in order to have their rights protected. Due to this arrangement it becomes the duty of the state to protect the non-Muslims' right to drink alcohol.

By giving these examples, Ad Duha thus expresses his extreme frustration with the actions of the *sharīʿah* patrols: "It's just, it's some kind of problem. I don't know if it's a psychological problem or what, that people think that just because, you know, I've now become practicing so on and so forth I've got to go around and behave like a complete bigot."[55] Ad Duha reiterates that the behaviors of a Muslim towards others must also be governed by the *sharīʿah*: on the day of judgment these *sharīʿah* patrols will, he argues, be held accountable and responsible for pushing people away from the religion, for damaging the image of Islam, and for misrepresenting the *sharīʿah*. Moreover, he argues that these street patrols destroy the attractiveness of Islam. There is only one duty that Muslims have in regards to non-Muslims, and that is to spark an interest in non-Muslims so that they ponder about their place in religion and in the world, and might come towards Islam: "And in that context, the only thing a Muslim can be obliged to do is to take that message to that person in the best possible manner."[56] He also adds that: "Islam will come to people when they choose it, our responsibility is to present it." He eschews any attempts to force people to convert to religion arguing that the use of *ḥikmah* (wisdom) entails the most effective means of propagating Islam. These street patrols are clearly not the most appropriate way of convincing people to come to Islam in his view; rather he holds them responsible for doing a lot of harm, even though they are a very small minority.

Ad Duha's commitment to reasonable pluralism means that he expects the same level of tolerance to be granted to Muslims living in the West. Yet, he feels that the concept of reasonable pluralism is not evenly applied to all citizens within the U.K. and that Muslims in particular are excluded. In one of his lectures Shams Ad Duha critiques David Cameron's address at the 2015 annual Conservative Party Conference. In that speech, Cameron tackled the issue of extremism and targeted the *madrasah*s in the U.K. specifically.[57] This obviously struck a nerve with Ad Duha and Ebrahim College because of their affiliation with *madrasahs*.

Cameron's speech was a response to the increased worry and suspicion about *madrasahs* stirred by various undercover documentaries and government studies that highlighted instances of child abuse as well as teaching of extremist and racist ideas.[58] In this address, Cameron puts forward a plan to tackle extremism, especially within the *madrasahs*. Cameron began his address by highlighting the extremist behavior of some British Muslims and stated that reading about the atrocities that they were committing abroad made him sick to his stomach. He added that this "ideology, this diseased view of the world, has become an epidemic—infecting minds from the mosques of Mogadishu to the bedrooms of Birmingham."

Cameron then put forward an action plan on how to remedy this problem. The first step is to "tear up the narrative that says Muslims are persecuted and the West deserves what it gets." He added that no one "should get away with this politics of grievance anymore." The second step is to "take on extremism in all its forms, the violent and non-violent." The final step is the "need to tackle segregation."

It is in discussing this third step that Cameron singles out the *madrasahs*. He stated that there are areas of Britain were one can live without ever speaking English or encountering a person from a different culture. He blames this segregation on several institutions in the U.K.: "Zoom in and you'll see some institutions that actually help incubate these divisions." He then quickly adds: "Did you know, in our country, there are some children who spend several hours each day at a Madrasa?" The implication being that it is the *madrasahs* that are incubating divisions. He adds a disclaimer that he is not against faith-based schools such as "Madrasas, Sunday Schools or Jewish Yeshivas." Yet, he suggests that there is something occurring particularly in some of these *madrasahs*:

> These children should be having their minds opened, their horizons broadened . . . not having their heads filled with poison and their hearts filled with hate. So I can announce this today: if an institution is teaching children intensively, then whatever its religion, we will, like any other school, make it register so it can be inspected. And be in no doubt: if you are teaching intolerance, we will shut you down.[59]

Following this speech the U.K. government announced that they are requiring all out-of-school settings that provide intensive education to register and to also be open for inspection.[60] This would then allow the government to intervene in cases of corporal punishment or teachings that promote extremism. Many mosques have since opposed these new rules. The Northern Council of Mosques, a council that represents roughly 400 British mosques, rejected the government's proposal stating that it encroached on their religious freedoms.[61]

Ad Duha's reflection on Cameron's speech was given a few days later, as is evident by the upload date on the YouTube video.[62] Ad Duha views segregation and ghettoization as a general problem that affects a variety of communities. Moreover, he does not believe radicalization exists in the *madrasah*s as Cameron had stated. The issue of English is faced by all communities—not just Muslims. He finds fault with Cameron for singling out Muslims on issues that other communities are dealing with as well. He states that by doing so, Cameron has himself segregated the Muslim community from other communities.

Ad Duha states that the *madrasah* is more fundamental to the Muslim community than mosques, and that Cameron has no understanding of the aims of *madrasah*s since they began in the 1970s. Ad Duha adds that rather than understanding the many challenges that *madrasah*s face—such as poverty, lack of aspiration, crime, and curriculum—Cameron is making the *madrasah*s the subject of national suspicion, and this will lead to more segregation. The madrasa, Ad Duha believes, is where Muslims learn the basics of their beliefs, where they learn their humanity, and were they learn to be better students in school. He comments that teachers from regular schools have commented that students that attended *madrasah*s are better students in the classroom. Moreover, the *madrasah*s keep the children out of trouble.

Ad Duha states that segregation is a top-down problem and that it is often created from the top and blames Cameron for creating a new demon called the *madrasah* whereby the problems associated with a minority of *madrasah*s will be attributed to all. This will bring all *madrasah*s under suspicion.

Ad Duha also adds that this issue of segregation is tied in closely to the problem of radicalization, and that Cameron's course of action will inflame the problem whereby even Muslim children will now be suspicious of the government. They will question why aspects of their religion had to be toned down. Ad Duha concedes that there are issues of belief that are taught that do not put non-Muslims in the best of light, but these ideas are balanced by other ideas within the faith: "There are things Christians learn about Muslims and Jews, these aren't always positive but it's a part of their theology. Other aspects of the faith, however, will often temper these ideas. The same is true of the Jewish tradition and the same is true definitely of the Muslim tradition."[63]

Moreover, Ad Duha believes that Cameron's attempts will put pressure on *madrasah* scholars to conceal aspects of their religion, and that this will cause many Muslims to bottle in mainstream aspects of their faith. And when they bottle it in they will become an object of suspicion and scorn of their own children. He believes that children will ask why they were not taught these aspects of their faith, and when they find out why then they will in turn be more suspicious of the government. This will ultimately plant the seeds of radicalization. This in turn means that when there is a genuine threat of radicalization it is difficult for the Muslim community to deal with these issues. The child is suspicious of not only the government but also the leaders of the *madrasah* who they view as being in line with the government.

Ad Duha scorns Cameron for not reaching out to the Muslim community but rather dictating to them their problems and solutions. He states that if segregation is the issue than racism should receive a greater mention and share of the Prime Minister's speech. Ad Duha argues that under existing policies hatred is going to increase towards the Muslim community and that this in turn is going to lead to greater segregation.

Ad Duha not only defends the *madrasahs*, but also many of the conservative practices found within the Deoband tradition, such as wearing the *niqāb* (the face veil). Ad Duha defends this practice even though he does not believe that it is obligatory. Following the ban on the *niqāb* in France, the issue of *niqāb* has also become the topic of debate in the United Kingdom. Some Members of the Parliament (MPs) have stated that the *niqāb* is against British values.[64] Ad Duha tackles the issue of the banning of the *niqāb* head on. He states that his mother and his mother-in-law have worn the *niqāb* for many years in Britain. He argues that those who propose banning the *niqāb* in defence of British values are actually going against British values:

> In our current situation, we live in Britain as British people. This is our country. For everybody is this room, everybody upstairs, downstairs, for all of the sisters in this building, we don't really know any other place as home. And so we are part and parcel of this land, and therefore part and parcel of British culture, of Britishness, of whatever it is that is this ever changing ever evolving identity that is deemed to be British.[65]

Ad Duha also highlights how Britishness changes through history. What is considered British now would have been alien to Britons in the past. He adds that immigration has played a large role in defining Britishness. Muslims can, therefore, play a positive role in defining Britishness, and the issue of *niqāb* and the *ḥijāb* is "the contribution of Muslims to Britishness with a new flavor."[66] It is important in his view that MPs and members of British societies come to understand the *ḥijāb* and the *niqāb*, rather than calling for out-right bans. It is also important for Muslims to engage with the broader the society on this issue.

Ad Duha is keen to state that wearing the *niqāb* is not simply a cultural practice but also a religious practice.[67] The very existence of the debate on religious grounds makes it a part of religion. He quotes various *ḥadīth* that support the wearing of the *niqāb*, and argues that the female companions of the Prophet wore the *niqāb*. He explains that there are differences about the necessity of wearing the *niqāb* within the traditional Islamic schools of law. The Shāfiʿīs and Ḥanbalīs stated that it was obligatory, but the Ḥanafīs and

Mālikīs did not. The later Ḥanafīs changed their opinion and stated that even though the original position was that wearing the *niqāb* is not obligatory, the conditions of the modern era currently require women to wear the *niqāb*. By this they mean the fact that they see infidelity and immoral behavior as ever increasing. Thus the majority of South Asian Ḥanafīs now state that it is obligatory to wear the *niqāb*.[68]

Due to these scholarly opinions, Ad Duha is then critical of those that state wearing the *niqāb* is simply cultural. Ad Duha argues that just because one scholar says that the *niqāb* is cultural does not deprive the *niqāb* of its religious status, and criticizes scholars from al-Azhar who have taken this position.[69] He argues that stating that the *niqāb* is a cultural issue is to deny the religious importance it has to some Muslims. His argument again is based on reasonable pluralism: "While I hold an opinion for myself, I fight for the right for the other person to see their own opinion to be the correct opinion. And this is a fundamental aspect of Islamic scholarship that is really lost on some of these people."[70]

Ad Duha's lectures highlight various issues about life in Britain. The first is that Islamic law makes room for reasonable pluralism. There are various issues in which Muslims disagree about, and that is understandable. It would be incorrect to try and impose one's beliefs on others. At the same time, there are limits to this reasonable pluralism, and it is here that Ad Duha evokes the harm principle: clearly if one is going to harm another person than that it is not a valid interpretation. He then goes on to argue for extending the practice of reasonable pluralism to allow for accommodating conservative practices as well. He thus finds it upsetting that several Muslims publicly disavow the wearing of the *niqāb* as being only a cultural issue; this to him amounts to denying him and various other conservative Muslims their right to practice an essential aspect of their faith. Moreover, he is critical of the way that the current British government is approaching the issue of radicalization, and argues that their current method will increase and not decrease radicalization.

Furthermore, Ad Duha has not applied the criterion of reciprocity in the manner that Yasir Qadhi has. As discussed in Chapter 5, Yasir Qadhi defends the freedoms of other minority groups, specifically homosexuals, based on the argument that it translates into greater freedoms for Muslims as well. So far, we have not seen similar argumentation from Ad Duha: he does indeed defend the rights of Muslims to observe their religious practices in liberal democracies, but does not necessarily do so by presenting a defence of rights of other minority groups.

Shaykh Mohammed Amin Kholwadia and Islamic Bioethics

The leadership of Darul Qasim is under Shaykh Mohammed Amin Kholwadia. Kholwadia was born and raised in England, and traveled to Deoband,

India to pursue his Islamic education. On return to England he began work as a translator and book reviewer. In 1984 he moved to Chicago where he performed several community leadership roles for Muslim communities.[71] Shaykh Kholwadia has also translated a book by a leading Pakistani Deobandi scholar, Taqi Usmani (See Volume 1, Chapter 9), on the importance of *taqlīd* and adherence to the *madhhab*.[72]

Darul Qasim has no social media presence, and in turn neither does Kholwadia. Unlike Ebrahim College that actively uses social media to both promote its events and its ideas, Darul Qasim does no such thing: it presence on the internet is limited to a well structured website. The website provides a good overview of the institution such as its history, academic programmes, upcoming events, and even has a section for media. Audio recordings of Kholwadia's Friday lectures are also available on the website, but there are hardly any videos whether on the official website or YouTube. Reflective of Darul Qasim's and Kholwadia's lack of social media presence is their lack of broader public engagement. One cannot find the same level of engagement with broader social issues as illustrated in case of Ad Duha and Ebrahim College. Kholwadia undertakes more general spiritual and religious discussions with a particular focus on contributing to academic debates especially on the topic of Islamic bioethics.

There is, interestingly, a public statement about sexual harassment on Darul Qasim's website.[73] Through the topic is on sexual harassment, the statement also discusses the position of Muslims in liberal democracies. It reveals Darul Qasim's approach towards law and the definition of a responsible citizen. The statement begins by declaring that it is in response to a particular incident that has been brought to the attention of the institution. No description is further given, although it seems that this statement is in response to the sexual harassment case brought against Mohammed Abdullah Saleem, the founder of the Institute of Islamic Education in nearby Elgin.[74]

The intention of the statement is to offer Muslims a general guideline on how to deal with cases of sexual harassment. The statement begins by stating a few preliminary points. The first is that all Muslims have a general duty to command good and forbid evil (*al-ʿamr bi-al-maʿrūf wa al-nahy ʿan al-munkar*). It then quotes the *ḥadīth* in which the Prophet says: "Each one of you are shepherds and each one of you is responsible for your (own) flock."

The statement ties this notion of forbidding evil to the notion of citizenship arguing that Muslims are required to be responsible citizens. The way one becomes a responsible citizen is through enacting the principle of forbidding evil. Thus, if one witnesses an evil act one should try to stop that act by one's own hand, by speech, or by disliking the said act in the heart. Furthermore, in a Muslim-majority country it is the duty of the state to enact Islamic law and administer punishment. It is the combination of forbidding evil and the administration of justice through the state that "absolves the whole Muslim community from its moral and legal obligation in such matters." It seems then that in non-Muslim countries half of this issue is unresolved. Muslims are still duty bound to perform the obligation of forbidding evil. The use of physical means to stop the evil act "is limited to what is allowed by the law of the land." If the state does not allow it, it is not permissible. Yet, one is still required to fulfil the legal obligations imposed by the state.

The statement explains this in these words: "This means that if the law of the land requires a citizen to report sexual crimes to any state authority, Muslims must do so. However, if the state does not require them to report or take any action, then Muslims, like their non-Muslim counterparts, have the discretionary prerogative that the law of the land offers them—even though the Muslims must believe that the crime or sin is abominable."[75]Deferring to the law of the land then becomes necessary for Muslims in order to fulfil the legal component of their Islamic obligation. The statement urges Muslims to "not do anything that may obstruct the course of justice." This would include blaming the victim for the incident or pressuring her to not exercise her legal rights.

Although this statement is focused on only one particular incident, it highlights how Darul Qasim views the relationship between Muslims and the law of non-Muslim-majority countries. Muslims are required to be responsible citizens and this includes not only the traditional practice of forbidding evil but abiding by the laws of the land as well. Muslims should try to stop sinful actions and they should not do anything that would be against the law nor should they hinder the process of justice.

The Darul Qasim website hosts a series of Shaykh Kholwadia's Friday sermons.[76] These sermons touch on general Islamic beliefs and practices. On a speech given on April 15th, Kholwadia discusses the issue of atheism. He discusses the issue not in terms of Islamic law but as a social practice. He praises the fact that the Muslim community has grown, but states that even with this growth more young Muslims recently are leaving the religion than are entering the religion. Kholwadia then outlines a framework through which the subject of atheism should be addressed. In another lecture, Kholwadia touches on the issue of communal unity. His approach is rather unorthodox: what makes a community a civilization is its ability to unite despite having differences. He states that since Muslims in the West are seen as one community, the Muslims should in turn internalize this conception and understand that they are in fact one community. Despite all of their differences Muslims, he argues, can be seen as one shared group. In another lecture Kholwadia discusses the necessity of commitment to *waḥī* (divine revelation). He states that one should not simply give in to scientific and empirical ideas about the world but that it is through the Divine truth and revelation that one can witness a change for the better.

Kholwadia's lectures touch on the very general necessities of religious life in the modern age. He lectures about the fact that adhering to divine revelation is important for success in both this life and the hereafter, that it is important to aid those in need, and that Muslims should unite despite their differences. He does not, however, engage with the particular problems of practicing Islam in the West. Unlike Ad Duha, Kholwadia does not engage in the public sphere on specific issues such as Ad Duha does as illustrated through the case of *sharīʿah* patrols, the wearing of the *niqāb*, or the issue of voting. Ad Duha comments on specific events and quotes specific speeches that have been brought to the public and in turn engages directly with these issues, and in certain cases presents alternative understandings. It is for this very reason that his lectures on YouTube have so many views. The more controversial the issue is within the public sphere the more views his discussion of that topic has received. Kholwadia's speeches, on the other hand, have no direct engagement with the public sphere. They do discuss general trends within the Muslim community of North America but do not engage with the public sphere in the direct manner that Ad Duha does.

Kholwadia's academic engagement focuses on Islamic bioethics. Collaborating with Aasim Padela of the University of Michigan Medical School and Ahsan Arozullah of the University of Illinois-Chicago School of Medicine, Kholwadia has co-produced a handful of papers on the subject. He has also participated in conferences at several locations in the U.S. and Canada and at Ankara University in Turkey in recent years.[77] Kholwadia also serves in an advisory capacity on various projects at the University of Michigan and University of Chicago.[78]

The fact that he has co-authored papers makes it difficult to know Kholdwadia's opinions precisely. Still, it is clear that Kholwadia's works are in line with the *madhhab* framework. Moreover, Kholwadia himself never presents any explicit solutions, but his works are summaries of what various *sharīʿah* councils have written on these issues and the difficulties that they face. His co-authored paper titled *Wilāyah (authority and governance) and its implications for Islamic bioethics: a Sunni Māturīdi perspective* simply argues that Muslims living in non-Muslim states do not have political or legal *wilāyah*, and must therefore rely on academic *wilāyah*. The term *wilāyah* is translated as authority and governance. Simply put, Muslims living in non-Muslim states must seek out the opinions of religious scholars on issues that have to do with Islamic bioethics: "For Muslim healthcare providers and patients living in the absence of political *wilāyah*, academic *wilāyah* still requires believers to seek authentication of uncertain actions through scholarly opinions."[79] No framework or approach is, however, discussed as to how scholars are to come to conclusions about bioethics.

One of the issues raised in that paper is about the use of medication derived from pork. Pork is considered to be religiously impure (*najis*) which makes its use in medicine problematic for Muslims. In that paper, the authors do not directly address the issue about the permissibility of porcine products, and simply state that medical professionals must rely on the opinions of religious scholars. In a separate paper, co-authored by various academics, this issue is addressed in more detail. Again here it is difficult to know what exactly is Kholwadia's position, especially since this paper is co-authored with the influential reformist thinker Ebrahim Moosa. The paper is, however, an overview of the opinions of the Islamic Organization for Medical Sciences (IOMS) about the use of porcine products. The IOMS is an influential transnational council that gives religious rulings on medical issues.

The paper, therefore, is an examination of traditional jurisprudence as it is applied to the issue of porcine proteins in medicine. The authors purposely put aside reformist approaches towards Islamic bioethics and are interested in highlighting "where scientific expertise and insights may inform the traditional *usul*-based ethico-legal assessment and thereby create a platform for enhanced collaboration between medical scientists and traditional jurisconsults and councils."[80] The paper is interested in how the traditional concept of *istiḥālah* (transformation) can be applied to the issue of porcine medical products. *Istiḥālah* is a term used to define when one object is transformed into another object. One such example is the process of wine turning into vinegar. The paper examines how *istiḥālah* can be used to argue that although the medical products under discussion originally started out as pork products, they have subsequently transformed into something else, the same way that wine transforms into vinegar.

Kholwadia also has an edited chapter about brain death, a rather difficult and technical subject. This chapter, however, is an overview of the various approaches towards the issue of brain death as outlined in the publications of various Muslim thinkers and organizations. The chapter itself offers no definitive stance on the issue but merely highlights the shortcomings and difficulties that Islamic jurisprudence must grapple with.[81] This is similar to another chapter co-authored by Kholwadia in the same book about surrogate motherhood. This chapter discusses the role of *fatwās* in religious life, and analyses *fatwās* issued by various *sharīʿah* councils on surrogate motherhood.[82]

Kholwadia's works on Islamic bioethics have consisted of mostly summaries of the opinions of *sharīʿah* councils, commenting on some of the difficulties they face on these issues. Till now, he himself has not offered any definitive stances, nor has he offered a definitive approach towards answering these questions. It would be interesting to see if his research on Islamic bioethics leads to any further advancement in this way. This should not however undermine the type of work that Kholwadia himself has done. His publications can help to bridge the gap between the requirements of medical practice and Islamic ethics: they can help medical practitioners better understand the hesitations and religious requirements of Muslim patients. These publications also help to spread awareness about the rulings of *sharīʿah* councils, many of which are unknown to medical practitioners in the West.

Neo-conservatism

Thus, both Darul Qasim and Ebrahim College can be labelled as *second wave* Deobandi institutions because they are more open to adaptation and reform in terms of education, and are more engaged with the broader societal context than the traditional *dār al-'ulūms*. Both institutions are still conservative, in the sense that they are more willing to adhere to traditional rulings and a traditional approach to *madhhabs*, especially in comparison to the various other scholars and institutions discussed in this volume. This conservatism should not be confused with disengagement from politics, or intolerance for the beliefs of others. For as we have seen, they not only argue for tolerance and pluralism within Islamic thought, but in relation to the broader society as well. In return they also expect the same tolerance to be applied to them. They have been able to use traditional concepts such as *ikhtilāf* to defend the reasonable pluralism found in modern society. Moreover, their approach towards education stresses that a religious leader should be able to understand and respond to the needs and changes of modern society. This underpins their willingness to reform their educational programmes. Each institution is engaged with debates on the notion of citizenship and how Western Muslims should relate to it. Both in their own way advance the concept of a "responsible citizen" whereby they encourage Western Muslims to respect the secular laws while also defending their right to freely practice even the most conservative aspects of their faith.

Notes

1. "Leadership," *Darul Qasim*, accessed May 19, 2016, https://darulqasim.org/aboutus/leadership.
2. So named in honor of Mawlana Mahmud al-Hasan (1851–1920), one of the first students of Darul Uloom Deoband and a major Indian religious and political figure.
3. "Programs of Study," *Darul Qasim*, accessed May 19, 2016, https://darulqasim.org/programs.
4. "Chapters," *Darul Qasim*, accessed May 19, 2016, https://darulqasim.org/chapters.
5. *Ebrahim College Website*, accessed May 19, 2016, https://ebrahimcollege.org.uk/.
6. Cf., recently, Innes Bowen, *Medina in Birmingham, Najaf in Brent: Inside British Islam* (Oxford: Oxford University Press, 2014); John Bowen, *On British Islam: Religion, Law, and Everyday Practice in Sharia Councils*, (Princeton: Princeton University Press, 2016); also Peter Mandaville, "Islamic Education in Britain: Approaches to Religious Knowledge in a Pluralistic Society," in *Schooling Islam: The Culture and Politics of Modern Muslim Education*, ed. Robert Hefner and Muhammad Qasim Zaman (Princeton: Princeton University Press, 2007): 224–41.
7. Bowen, *Medina in Birmingham*, 20, 25.
8. *Ibid*., 20; "Faculty," *Ebrahim College*, accessed November 8, 2016, https://ebrahimcollege.org.uk/faculty/.
9. Bowen, *British Islam*, 35.

10. Four of the five Deobandi schools in Canada are located in southern Ontario; cf. Marcia Hermansen, "South Asian Sufism in America," in *South Asian Sufism: Devotion, Deviation, and Destiny*, ed. Clinton Bennett and Charles Ramsey (London: Continuum, 2012), 247–68 at 263.
11. See the anthropological account in Akbar Ahmed, *Journey into America: The Challenge of Islam* (Washington, D.C.: Brookings Institution Press, 2010), 216–21.
12. E.g. Ali ibn Abi Bakr Marghinani et al., *The Hidaya: Commentary on the Islamic Laws* (Karachi: Darul Ishaat, n.d.), vol. 2, ii.
13. Asad Husain and Harold Vogelaar, "Activities of the Immigrant Muslim Communities in Chicago," in *Muslim Communities in North America*, ed. Yvonne Yazbeck Haddad and Jane Smith (Albany: State University of New York Press, 1994), 231–57 at 245; *Institute of Islamic Education (IIE) Website*, accessed May 19, 2016, http://www.iieonline.org. Zareena Grewal and David Coolidge offer slightly different dates for the founding of the two schools, placing IIE's in 1989 and Darul-Uloom al-Madania's in 1992: Zareena Grewal and David Coolidge, "Islamic Education in the United States: Debates, Practices, and Institutions," in *The Cambridge Companion to American Islam*, ed. Juliane Hammer and Omid Safi (Cambridge: Cambridge University Press, 2013), 246–65 at 253–4. IIE Elgin continues to operate, though it appears to have limited its educational functions in the wake of Saleem's arrest for sexual abuse in 2015 and civil lawsuits filed against the institution; cf. George Houde and Stacey Wescott, "Elgin Islamic Leader Now Accused of Sexual Abuse of Former Student," *Chicago Tribune*, October 7, 2015, accessed November 8, 2016, http://www.chicagotribune.com/suburbs/elgin-courier-news/news/ct-elgin-imam-new-charge-met-20151007-story.html.
14. Cf. "Faculty," *Darul Qasim*, accessed May 19, 2016, https://darulqasim.org/aboutus/faculty.
15. Cf. Bowen, quoting Mushfiq Uddin's personal characterization of education at Dewsbury: Bowen, *Medina in Birmingham*, 16; also Grewal and Coolidge, "Islamic Education in the United States", 254.
16. "About Us (Our Aims & Objectives)," *Ebrahim College*, accessed May 19, 2016, https://ebrahimcollege.org.uk/about-us/; emphasis added.
17. "Programs of Study," *Darul Qasim*, accessed May 19, 2016, https://darulqasim.org/programs.
18. "Bachelor's Level Program," *Darul Qasim*, accessed May 19, 2016, https://darulqasim.org/ba.
19. Ibid.; "Alimiyyah Full Time," *Ebrahim College*, accessed May 19, 2016, https://ebrahimcollege.org.uk/alimiyyah-programme/alimiyyah-full-time/.
20. See Norman Calder, "Al-Nawawī's Typology of *Muftīs* and its Significance for a General Theory of Islamic Law," *Islamic Law and Society* 3 (1996), 137–164; Mohammed Fadel, "The Social Logic of *Taqlīd* and the Rise of the *Mukhtaṣar*," *Islamic Law and Society* 3 (1996), 193–233; also Wael Hallaq, *Authority, Continuity and Change in Islamic Law* (Cambridge–New York: Cambridge University Press, 2001).
21. "Bachelor's Level Program," *Darul Qasim*, accessed May 19, 2016, https://darulqasim.org/ba.
22. "Master's Level Program," *Darul Qasim*, accessed May 19, 2016, https://darulqasim.org/masters-level-program.

23. Cf. "Alimiyyah ," *Ebrahim College*.
24. On the *dars-i niẓāmī*, see the chapter on Deoband in Volume One.
25. Nevertheless, Ebrahim College's website explicitly states that the school uses the *dars-i niẓāmī*: "Frequently Asked Questions," Ebrahim College, accessed May 19, 2016, https://ebrahimcollege.org.uk/alimiyyah-programme/alimiyyah-faq/.
26. "Alimiyyah", *Ebrahim College*.
27. "Bachelor's", *Darul Qasim*.
28. "Alimiyyah," *Ebrahim College*.
29. "Qur'an Recitation Program," *Darul Qasim*, accessed May 19, 2016, https://darulqasim.org/quran. In this method, the student learns to pronounce the name of each Arabic letter, rather than its phoneme, so e.g. the letter *dāl* is "dāl" rather than "d", and the word *dīn* is broken down for the learner as "dāl-yā'-nūn" rather than "d-ī-n".
30. "Alim Course Instructors," *Darul Uloom New York*, accessed May 19, 2016, http://darululoomny.org/alim-course-instructors/.
31. "Alim Course Catalog," *Darul Uloom New York*, accessed May 19, 2016, http://darululoomny.org/alim-course-catalog/. Some titles have been edited for clarity and some courses using the same texts have been condensed here.
32. "Our Mission & Method," *Darul Qasim*, accessed May 19, 2016, https://darulqasim.org/aboutus/our-mission; "About Ebrahim College," *Ebrahim College*, accessed May 19, 2016, https://ebrahimcollege.org.uk/about-us/.
33. Bowen, *Medina in Birmingham*, 20.
34. "About," *Ebrahim College*.
35. Tarek El Diwany et al., *Islamic Finance: What It Is and What It Could Be* (Bolton: 1st Ethical Charitable Trust, 2010).
36. Kirsty Walk, "Discussion with Anjum Choudary, Shams Adduha Muhammad and Julie Siddiqi on the Woolwich Attack" [Video], *BBC Newsnight, YouTube*, May 23, 2013, accessed November 8, 2016, https://www.youtube.com/watch?v=JiWOC1MpD7Y.
37. Shams Ad-Duha Muhammad, "About Me," *Shamsadduha.com*, accessed May 19, 2016, http://shamsadduha.com/about-us/; "Teachers," *Ebrahim College*, accessed May 19, 2016, https://ebrahimcollege.org.uk/teachers/.
38. "Faculty," *Ebrahim College*.
39. Shams Ad Duha, "Reconnecting with the Qur'an" [Video], *Ebrahim College, YouTube*, December 11, 2015, accessed November 10, 2016, https://www.youtube.com/watch?v=mXhUarNszes; Shams Ad Duha, "Perils of Procrastination" [Video], *Ebrahim College, YouTube*, January 15, 2016, accessed November 10, 2016, https://www.youtube.com/watch?v=7nBumpSiBXM; Shams Ad Duha, "God Consciousness and Good Character" [Video], *Ebrahim College, YouTube*, October 16, 2015, accessed November 10, 2016, https://www.youtube.com/watch?v=gqwldY6qG64.
40. Shaykh Shams Ad Duha, "Following Saheeh Hadith vs Taqleed" [Video], *Ebrahim College, YouTube*, April 19, 2012, accessed November 8, 2016, https://www.youtube.com/watch?v=-SlkbM182Ro.
41. John Rawls, *Political Liberalism*, new ed. (New York–Chichester: Columbia University Press, 1996), 36.
42. Mohammad Hashim Kamali, "The Scope of Diversity and 'Ikhtilāf' (Juristic Disagreement) in the Sharī'ah," *Islamic Studies* 37 (1998), 315–37.
43. Joseph Schacht, "Ikhtilāf," *EI*².

44. Shaykh Shams Ad Duha, "Voting in Islam" [Video], *Ebrahim College, YouTube*, May 23, 2014, accessed November 8, 2016, https://www.youtube.com/watch?v=OKhgpeLEsWs.
45. Ibid.
46. John Stuart Mill, *On Liberty* (London: Longmans, Green, and Co, 1865), 6.
47. Shams Ad-Duha, "An Islamic Response to 'Muslim Street Patrols'" [Video], *Ebrahim College, YouTube*, January 18, 2013, accessed November 9, 2016, https://www.youtube.com/watch?v=fpDJTBBwrKM.
48. The YouTube video itself has been taken down; quoted from "Muslim 'Vigilantes' Confront Londoners in Name of Islam," *The Daily Telegraph*, January 17, 2013, accessed November 9, 2016, http://www.telegraph.co.uk/news/uknews/law-and-order/9808539/Muslim-vigilantes-confront-Londoners-in-name-of-Islam.html.
49. Sam Jones and agency, "Muslim Vigilantes Jailed for 'Sharia Law' Attacks in London," *The Guardian*, December 6, 2013, accessed November 9, 2016, http://www.theguardian.com/uk-news/2013/dec/06/muslim-vigilantes-jailed-sharia-law-attacks-london.
50. Ad-Duha, "Islamic Response to 'Muslim Street Patrols'."
51. Ibid.
52. Muhammad Qasim Zaman, "Tradition and Authority in Deobandi Madrasas of South Asia," in *Schooling Islam: The Culture and Politics of Modern Muslim Education*, ed. Robert W. Hefner and Muhammad Qasim Zaman (Princeton: Princeton University Press, 2007), 64.
53. Although Ad Duha attributes this text to Ibn Ḥumām this section of the commentary was completed by Qāḍī Zādih. Moreover, the actual text he cites in his speech is a section that is quoted verbatim from al-Hidāyah and is not from of the commentaries. See Qāḍī Zādah, *Natā'ij al-Afkār fī Kashf al-Rumūz wa-al-Asrār*, Vol.9 (Beirut: Dār al-Kutub al-'Ilmiyyah, 2003), 364.
54. Ad-Duha, "Islamic Response to 'Muslim Street Patrols'."
55. Ibid.
56. Ibid.
57. "Tory Party Conference 2015: David Cameron's Speech in Full," *The Independent*, October 7, 2015, accessed November 9, 2016, http://www.independent.co.uk/news/uk/politics/tory-party-conference-2015-david-camerons-speech-in-full-a6684656.html.
58. Jeremy Vine, "British Schools, Islamic Rules," *BBC Panorama*, November 22, 2010, formerly available at http://www.bbc.co.uk/programmes/b00w8kwz; Fran Abrams, "Madrassas," *File on 4*, *BBC Radio 4*, October 23, 2011, accessed November 9, 2016, http://www.bbc.co.uk/programmes/b015zpf1.
59. "Tory Party Conference 2015: David Cameron's Speech in Full."
60. Branwen Jeffreys, "Plans to Regulate Madrassas Published by Government," *BBC News*, November 26, 2015, accessed November 9, 2016, http://www.bbc.co.uk/news/education-34933970.
61. Sean Coughlan, "Mosques Oppose Madrassa Registration," *BBC News*, January 7, 2016, accessed November 9, 2016, http://www.bbc.co.uk/news/education-35252469.
62. Shaykh Shams Ad Duha, "A Response to David Cameron's Comments About Madrasahs," [Video], *Ebrahim College, YouTube*, October 9, 2015, accessed November 9, 2016, https://www.youtube.com/watch?v=7tUmUgZUiLk.
63. Ibid.

64. Michael Wilkinson, "Tory MP Calls for Complete Veil Ban as it 'Stops Women from Enjoying British Values of Smiling and Saying Hello'," *The Telegraph*, January 27, 2016, accessed November 9, 2016, http://www.telegraph.co.uk/news/politics/12124345/Tory-MP-calls-for-complete-veil-ban-as-it-stops-women-from-enjoying-British-values-of-smiling-and-saying-hello.html.
65. Shaykh Shams Ad Duha, "The Niqab (Face Veil) and its Place in Britain" [Video], *Ebrahim College, YouTube,* September 24, 2013, accessed November 9, 2016, https://www.youtube.com/watch?v=djhCTisKWKM.
66. Ibid.
67. Shaykh Shams Ad Duha, "Why the Niqab is Religious and Not Cultural" [Video], *Ebrahim College, YouTube,* September 19, 2013, accessed November 9, 2016, https://www.youtube.com/watch?v=lhdb0-w8Rg4.
68. For review of scholars that state this view see Muḥammad ibn 'Alī al-Ḥaskafī, *al-Dur al-Mukhtār Sharḥ Tanwīr al-Abṣār wa Jāmi' al-Baḥār* (Beirut: Dār al-Kutub al-'Ilmīyah, 2002), 656; Muhammad ibn Ahmad ibn Isma'il al-Muqaddam, *al-Rad al-'Ilmī 'alā Kitāb Tadhkīr al-Aḥbāb bi-Taḥrīm al-Niqāb* (Alexandria: Dār al-Imān li-al-Ṭabi' wa-al-Nashr wa-al-Tawzī', 2003), 158-159.
69. This is most likely in regards to al-Tantawi's ban on the *niqāb* in al-Azhar; see Ahmed Al-Sayyed, "Al-Azhar Bans 'Niqab' in Classrooms, Dormitories," *Al-Arabiyya News*, October 8, 2009, accessed November 9, 2016, https://www.alarabiya.net/articles/2009/10/08/87407.html.
70. Ad Duha, "Why the Niqab is Religious."
71. "Leadership," *Darul Qasim*, accessed May 19, 2016, https://darulqasim.org/abou-tus/leadership.
72. Muhammad Taqi Usmani, *Taqleed in Shari'ah: The Legal Status of Following a Madhab* (Karachi: Zam Zam Publishers, 1999).
73. "Darul Qasim's Position on the Moral and Legal Obligations for Muslims Regarding Sexual Crimes," *Darul Qasim*, December 15, 2014, accessed November 9, 2016, https://darulqasim.org/statement.
74. Houde and Wescott, "Elgin Islamic Leader Now Accused".
75. "Darul Qasim's Position."
76. "Media (Friday Reflections & Lectures)," *Darul Qasim*, accessed April 30, 2016, https://darulqasim.org/reflections.
77. Aasim Padela et al., "Dire Necessity and Transformation: Entry-Points for Modern Science in Islamic Bioethical Assessment of Porcine Products in Vaccines." *Bioethics* 28 (2014), 59–66; Ahsan Arozullah and Mohammed Amin Kholwadia, "Wilāyah (Authority and Governance) and its Implications for Islamic Bioethics: A Sunni Māturīdi Perspective" in *Theoretical Medicine and Bioethics* 34 (2013), 95–104; Aasim Padela et al., "Brain Death: Ethico-Legal and Metaphysical Challenges for Modern Islamic Bioethics," in *Islam and Bioethics*, ed. Berna Arda and Vardit Rispler-Chaim (Ankara: Ankara Üniversitesi, 2012), 141–159; Aasim Padela et al., "Using Fatawa within Islamic and Muslim Bioethical Discourse: The Role of Doctrinal and Theological Considerations—A Case Study of Surrogate Motherhood," ibid., 160–76.
78. "Leadership," *Darul Qasim.*
79. Arozullah and Kholwadia, "Wilāyah."
80. Padela et al., "Dire Necessity."
81. Padela et al., "Brain Death."
82. Padela et al., "Using Fatawa."

NOTES ON THE CONTRIBUTORS

Christopher Pooya Razavian undertook his Ph.D. under the supervision of Professor Sajjad Rizvi at the University of Exeter. His doctoral research is focused on the relationship between autonomy and tradition in Shi'ism. He has also spent many years in Iran, at both the Islamic Seminary and the University of Tehran.

Nathan Spannaus is a graduate of McGill University's Institute of Islamic Studies and Harvard University's Department of Near Eastern Languages and Civilizations, and he has previously held positions at Princeton University and the University of Tennessee-Knoxville. He specializes in Islamic intellectual history, and his research focuses on modernity and secularization in the Islamic world and their impact on forms of religious and social thought, particularly from the mid-eighteenth through the early twentieth centuries. His work has appeared in *Arabica*, *The Journal of the Economic and Social History of the Orient* (forthcoming), *The Muslim World*, *Islamic Law and Society*, and *The Oxford Handbook of Islamic Theology*. His monograph, *Preserving Islamic Tradition: Abu Nasr Qursawi and the Beginning of Modern Reformism*, is forthcoming.

INDEX

Abbasid Caliphate, 164
Abdo, Geneive, 44
ʿAbduh, Muhammad, 129
Abd-ullah, Umar Faruq, 15
Abdulmutallab, Umar Farouk, 158
al-Abharī, Athīr al-Dīn, 58
abortion, 144, 170–1
abrogation *see naskh*
Abu Dhabi, 40
Abū Ḥanīfah, 141
Abu Nur Institute, 44
Abū Yūsuf, 195
Abul-Fadl, Mona, 102, 108, 109
AbuSulayman, AbdulHamid, 98, 101, 102, 109
Ad Duha, Shams, 24, 181–2, 192–201, 204
adab (Islamic norms of behaviour), 15, 52–3
adultery, 124
al-Afghani, Jamal al-Din, 129
Ahmed, Akbar, 108
Alalusi, Hesham, 39
alcohol, 127, 170, 174, 196, 197
Alder, Martimer J., 58
Ali, Abdullah ibn Hamid, 55–6, 73–4
Ali, Yusuf, 101
ʿAlī ibn Abī Ṭālib, 75
Allievei, Stefano, 11–12
AlMaghrib Institute, 18–19, 157–9, 174–5; *see also* Qadhi, Yasir
Alqueria de Rosales *madrasah*, 13–15
al-Alwani, Taha Jabir, 98, 99, 101, 102, 105, 106, 108–9, 110–15, 147
Alshareef, Muhammad, 158
American Islamic College, 113
American Journal of Islamic Social Sciences (*AJISS*), 101, 104, 105, 108
American Muslim Council, 113
American Muslim identity, 13, 19, 41, 45–8, 50, 51, 60, 102–3, 159
American Muslims for Constructive Engagement (AMCE), 115, 116
Amin, Hafiz, 24–5
al-ʿamr bi al-maʿrūf wa al-naḥy ʿan al-munkar (commanding good and forbidding evil), 24–5, 202–3
analogical reasoning *see qiyās*
Ankara University, 204
apostasy, 24, 56, 168–9
ʿaqīdah (Islamic creed), 15, 29, 126, 193
ʿaql (reason), 76–7, 157
Arab Spring, 145
Arabic language, 26, 28, 40, 41, 43, 72, 73, 88, 114, 181, 182
Aristotle, 58
Arozullah, Ahsan, 204
Ashʿarism, 55, 77, 156
Association of Muslim Social Sciences (AMSS), 98–9, 101, 115
astronomy, 63
atheism, 18, 56, 61, 63, 203
al-Attas, Muhammad Naguib, 21, 42, 49, 52, 53, 54, 64, 100
Auda, Jasser, 22–3, 106, 112–13, 114
Austen, Jane, 61
Australia, 5, 157
authority *see* Islamic authority; *wilāyah*
al-Awlaki, Anwar, 158
Al-Ayn, 40
al-Azhar, 8, 72, 77, 87, 98, 116, 123, 158, 164, 201

al-Bajuri, Ibrahim, 77
Bakewell, Joan, 73
balanced reason, 76–7
Bangladesh, 5, 193
al-Banna, Hassan, 77, 100, 123, 129
Barelvis, 8
al-Barzinji, Jamal, 101–2, 116
Basyouni, Waleed, 158
Bayyinah, 27
beauty, names of *see jalāl*
Bedeir, Reda, 158
Belgium, 5
Bennabi, Malek, 129

Berkeley, 16, 39, 40, 42
Bin Bayyah, Abdullah, 21, 40, 42, 56–7, 147, 163, 173
bioethics, 148, 192, 204–5
Birjas, Yaser, 158
Black Muslim culture, 7, 46
Bombing without Moonlight (Winter), 73
Bowen, John, 8, 19, 182
"Boys will be Boys" (Winter), 21–2, 79, 82
brain death, 205
British Muslim identity, 13, 19, 79, 85–7, 194, 196–201
Brothers Karamazov, The (Dostoyevsky), 61–2
Brown, James, 88
Bruinessen, Martin van, 11–12
Brussels, 5
Buddhism, 128
Buffalo, 8, 182
Bury, 8, 181
Bush, George W., 41, 47

Caesarean Moon Births (Yusuf), 63
Cairo, 43, 72, 98, 123
Cambridge Muslim College (CMC), 16–17, 87–90
Cambridge University, 72
Cameron, David, 193, 197–200
Canada, 114, 157, 182
capitalism, 80, 109, 113, 144, 145
Carlyle, Thomas, 86
Center for Islamic Legislation and Ethics (CILE), 17–18, 23, 114, 146–8; *see also* Ramadan, Tariq
Chapra, Muhammad Umer, 112
Chicago, 7, 18, 113, 153, 180, 182, 202
China, 85, 164
Chittick, William, 49, 76
Choudary, Anjum, 193
Christianity, 9, 16, 40, 43, 73, 86–7, 108, 128, 145, 163, 166–7, 169, 170–1, 199
Clergy Letter Project, 167
clothing, 41, 62, 170, 196, 200–1
colonial rule, 3, 5
common good *see maṣlaḥah*
communism, 43
companionship *see ṣuḥba*
compassion, 41, 81
Connecticut Muslim Coordinating Committee, 44
consensus, 139, 173
contingent norms, 126
converts to Islam
  "convertitis," 85
  legitimacy of, 9
  in prominent roles, 7, 9, 16, 39, 41
  socio-economic backgrounds, 9
  United States, 7, 9, 27, 47
  at Zaytuna College, 47
  see also Shakir, Zaid; Winter, Tim; Yusuf, Hamza
Cordoba University *see* Graduate School of Islamic and Social Sciences (GSISS)
Cox, Harvey, 52
creation, 166–7

Damascus, 44, 87
Danish cartoon controversy, 45
dār al-ḥarb (non-Muslim world), 57, 125–6
dār al-islām (Muslim world), 57, 125–6
dār al-shahādah (land of witness), 126
Dar' al-Ta'āruḍ (Ibn Taymīyah), 156
dār al-'ulūms (Islamic seminaries), 17, 18, 37, 87, 88, 90, 180, 181–3, 193, 206
Dars-i Nizāmī curriculum, 184, 188
Darul Ishaat, Karachi, 182
Darul Qasim
  adaptation to modern realities, 182–3, 191–2, 206
  allows study of any of the *madhhabs*, 18, 183
  connections with mainstream academia, 192
  curriculum, 18, 180–1, 183–91
  Dars-i Nizāmī curriculum, 184, 188
  degrees offered, 180–1
  and the Deobandi tradition, 18, 180, 183–91
  and educational reform, 191–2
  establishment of, 180
  and *furū'*, 183–4
  ḥadīth studies, 183–4
  and the *Ḥanafī* school, 183
  and mainstream academic structures, 182, 184–8
  and pluralism, 18
  and recitation, 188
  and responsible citizenship, 24–5, 202–3, 206
  satellite chapters, 181
  as second wave institution, 180, 181, 206
  study of foundational texts, 18
  and *taqlīd*, 153, 183
  training of *imāms*, 181, 183
  and *uṣūl al-fiqh*, 183–4
  see also Kholwadia, Mohammed Amin
Darul Uloom *madrasah*, Buffalo, 8, 182
Darul Uloom *madrasah*, Bury, 8, 181
Darul Uloom *madrasah*, Dewsbury, 8, 193
Darul Uloom *madrasah*, New York, 8, 188
Darwin, Charles, 84
deduction and inference *see qawaid al-istinbat*
deductive reasoning, 141
Deen Intensive Foundation, 41
democracy, 24, 47, 159, 160, 195

Deoband
  Dars-i Niẓāmī curriculum, 184, 188
  and the *Ḥanafī* school, 18, 183
  influence in diaspora communities, 8
  madrasahs in the U.K. and U.S., 8, 181–2, 197–200
  provision of *imāms*, 8
  and *taqlīd*, 18, 23, 153, 183, 202
  in the U.K., 8, 181–2, 192, 196–201
  in the U.S., 8, 182
  see also Darul Qasim; Ebrahim College
Dewsbury, 5, 8, 181, 193
dhikr (form of pious recitation), 51
dhimmah (agreement of protection), 197
diaspora communities
  influence of traditional centers of Islamic learning, 7–8
  labor migration, 5–7
  marginalization of, 5–7
  migration patterns linked to colonial past, 5
  as percentage of host population, 5, 6
  segregation of, 198–200
  socio-economic status of, 5–7, 9–10
  sourcing of *imāms* from home countries, 7–9
  United Kingdom, 5–8, 181, 192, 196–201
  United States, 5, 7–8, 9–10, 180–1, 182
difference feminism, 79–84
disagreement *see ikhtilāf*
diversity, 15, 46, 47, 60, 72, 85–6
divine revelation *see waḥī*
divorce, 79, 173
Diyanet, 8
Doha, 113
Dostoyevsky, Fyodor, 61–2
dress codes *see* clothing

East Meets West (Abul-Fadl), 108
Ebrahim College
  adaptation to modern realities, 182–3, 191–2, 206
  connections with mainstream academia, 192
  curriculum, 181, 183–91
  Dars-i Niẓāmī curriculum, 184, 188
  degrees awarded, 181
  and the Deobandi tradition, 18, 180
  and educational reform, 191–2
  establishment of, 181, 193
  ḥadīth studies, 184
  and the *Ḥanafī* school, 183
  and mainstream academic structures, 182, 184–8, 192
  and public engagement, 193–201
  and recitation, 188
  as second wave institution, 180, 181, 206
  and social media, 193
  and *taqlīd*, 153, 183, 194
  training of *imāms*, 181, 183
  Zaid Shakir speaks at, 26
  see also Ad Duha, Shams
economics, 108–9, 111–12, 145
education, 3, 10–12, 43, 99, 147, 191–2
Egypt, 43, 49, 72, 98, 114, 123, 163–4, 182
"Embassy Islam," 10, 11
English language, 15, 116
environment, 50, 144
Erskine, John, 58
European Council for Fatwa and Research (ECFR), 114, 125
European Muslim identity, 11–12, 13, 18, 19, 125–34
evil, forbidding of *see al-ʿamr bi al-maʿrūf wa al-nahy ʿan al-munkar*
evolution, 19, 83, 84, 163, 166–7
excommunication *see takfīr*

Fairfax Institute (TFI), 97, 103, 113–14, 116
family structures, 79
Farfour, Muhammad Salih, 87
al-Faruqi, Ismail Raji, 98–9, 100, 101, 105, 106–8, 109, 110, 113, 115, 116
fashion industry, 79
Al Fatih Islamic Institute, 87
Fātiḥah, 195
fatwās
  Bin Bayyah's, 42
  conservative, 19, 155, 163–5
  on Islamic finance, 137–8
  on the printing press, 19, 155, 163–4
  Qadhi on, 19, 23, 155, 163–5
  Ramadan on, 125, 131–2, 133–4, 137–8
  on surrogate motherhood, 205
Federal Bureau of Investigation (FBI), 103, 158
Female Eunuch, The (Greer), 79
feminism, 19, 79–84; *see also* gender debates; women
Finland, 21, 49
fiqh (jurisprudence)
  adaptation to modern realities, 3–4, 20–5, 28–30, 56–7, 110–13, 117, 124–48, 161–75
  legal theory *see uṣūl al-fiqh*
  of minorities *see fiqh al-aqallīyāt*
  of realities *see fiqh al-wāqiʿ*
  reconciliation with science, 17, 22–3, 135–43, 166–7
  schools of *see madhhabs*
  sources of, 139
fiqh al-aqallīyāt (*fiqh* of minorities), 20–2, 42, 56–7, 105, 111, 114, 117, 137, 147
fiqh al-wāqiʿ (*fiqh* of realities), 20–2, 56–7
Fiqh Council of North America, 113, 114–15

foundational texts
Darul Qasim study of, 18
direct engagement with, 23, 75–6, 161–2, 194
literal readings of, 129, 130
memorization of, 28, 48, 60, 193
Ramadan's typology of approaches to, 129–31
recitation of, 40, 60, 181, 188
study of at traditional centers of learning, 9, 26, 28
see also ḥadīth; *Qur'ān*
France, 5, 8, 123–4, 170, 200
freedom of conscience, 56, 168–9
Fromherz, Allen, 147
Furlow, Christopher, 103, 116
furū' (positive law), 141, 183–4

Gahbiche, Tijani, 16, 87
Galileo, 166–7
Gemmell, Ian, 82–3
gender debates, 21–2, 62, 79–85; *see also* feminism; women
gender segregation, 81
Geneva, 123
Germany, 5, 8, 11
Ghaly, Mohammed, 148
al-Ghazālī, Abū Ḥāmid, 12, 13, 15, 51, 76, 77
Gilligan, Carol, 83–4
Global Center for Renewal and Guidance, 42
global Islamic revival, 99–100
globalization, 7, 26–7, 126
God
attributes of, 156
as Immanence *see tashbīh*
names of, 80–1
as Transcendence *see tanzīh*
unity of *see tawḥīd*
God's Laws and Man-Made Laws (Qadhi), 170–2
Gomaa, Ali, 123
Graduate School of Islamic and Social Sciences (GSISS), 102, 103, 109, 113, 115, 116
Graduate Theological Seminary, Berkeley, 42
Great Books approach, 58
Greer, Germaine, 22, 79
Grewal, Zareena, 157, 158, 159
Gülen movement, 8
Gutenberg, Johannes, 163

Habermas, Jürgen, 84
ḥadīth
direct engagement with, 23, 161–2, 194
on the *niqāb*, 200–1
on responsibility, 24–5, 202
on seeking knowledge of creation, 139
study of at Cambridge Muslim College, 88
study of at Darul Qasim, 183–4
study of at Ebrahim College, 184
study of at IUM, 156
see also foundational texts
Hamas, 115
Hamid, Sadek, 42
Ḥanafī school, 18, 141, 183, 195, 196–7, 200–1; *see also madhhabs*
Ḥanbalī school, 156–7, 200; *see also madhhabs*
Hanson, Mark *see* Yusuf, Hamza
harm principle, 195–6, 201
Hartford Seminary, 114
Hassan II Foundation, 8
hegemony, 126, 135, 145
Henry, Virginia Gray, 47
Herndon, 98, 102, 116
Hero as Prophet, The (Carlyle), 86
Hick, John, 73
hifz (memorization of the *Qurān*), 28, 48, 60, 193
ḥijāb, 62, 200–1; *see also* clothing
ḥikmah (wisdom), 197
ḥilf al-fuḍūl (pact of the virtuous), 128
Hitler, Adolf, 159
Holocaust, 159
Holy Land Foundation, 115
home-schooling, 43
Homer, 61
homosexuality, 19, 24, 155, 157, 168, 169, 170, 173–5
human rights, 45
Huron University College, 114
Hutchins, Robert Maynard, 58

ibādāt (ritual practices), 15, 29, 126
Ibn 'Abd al-Wahhāb, 106–7
Ibn 'Arabī, 12, 15, 77
Ibn Badis, 129
Ibn Hajar Asqalani, 188
Ibn Humām, al-Kamāl, 196–7
Ibn Kamāl, 77
Ibn Taymīyah, 12, 56, 155–7, 163
Idea of Public Reason Revisited, The (Rawls), 167
ignorance *see jahilīyah*
Iḥyā' al-'Ulūm al-Dīn (al-Ghazālī), 51, 77
ijtihād (independent reasoning), 22, 105, 108–9, 110–11, 129, 130–4, 136, 137–43, 147–8
Ijtihad (al-Alwani), 105
ikhtilāf (disagreement), 24, 25, 192, 194–6, 206
al-Imam Muhammad University, 158

imāms
Netherlands cultural orientation programme for, 11
permissibility of female *imāms*, 81
provided by traditional centers of Islamic learning, 7–8
sourced from home countries, 7–9
training at Darul Qasim, 181, 183
training at Ebrahim College, 181, 183
training at The Fairfax Institute, 114
training at the Graduate School of Islamic and Social Sciences, 113
training at Zaytuna College, 39, 45
young Muslims consider becoming, 27
In the Footsteps of the Prophet (Ramadan), 128
independent reasoning *see ijtihād*
India, 180, 201–2
individualism, 29, 61
inductive reasoning, 141
industrialization, 5, 135
Institute of Islamic Education (IIE), Chicago, 182, 202
Institute of Islamic Education (IIE), Dewsbury, 181
Institute of Islamic Research, Karachi, 98
integration, 46, 127, 136
interest, 127
Interfaith Voices, 161–2
internal reform, 28, 98
International Center for Religion and Diplomacy, 115
International Fiqh Council, 114
International Institute of Islamic Thought (IIIT)
aims of, 17, 97, 104–5
American Journal of Islamic Social Sciences, 101, 104, 105, 108
and American Muslim identity, 102–3
connections with mainstream academia, 98, 104, 114–16
and creativity in Islamic thought, 104–5
educational activities, 97, 103, 113–14
engagement with Western modernity, 17, 22, 97, 102–4, 109–13
establishment and history, 98–104
failure of Khartoum conference, 101–2
Fairfax Institute, 97, 103, 113–14, 116
and *fiqh al-aqallīyāt*, 22, 105, 111, 117
funding, 115–16
and the GSISS, 102, 103, 109, 113, 115, 116
Herndon headquarters, 98, 102, 116
and the history of Islamic civilization, 105–6
and *ijtihād*, 105, 108–9, 110–11
and internal reform, 98
international branches, 22–3, 97, 101
and Islamism, 100, 115
and the Islamization of knowledge project, 22, 42, 52, 99–102, 104, 106–10, 116–17
links with the IIUM, 102, 113, 116
London branch, 22–3, 102–3, 112, 114
and *maqāṣid al-sharīʿah*, 17, 22–3, 95, 105, 106, 111–13, 117
methodology for contemporary Islam, 103–4, 110–13, 117
and the Muslim Brotherhood, 100, 115
publishing activities, 101, 102–3, 104, 105–6
Qadhi lectures at, 156
and science, 17, 22, 99, 105, 107
scrutiny of after September 11 attacks, 103, 116
and secularism, 107
significance of American setting, 116–17
and *tawḥīdic* epistemology, 22, 102, 106–10
and *tawḥīdic* methodology, 100–2
Western Thought Project, 107–8
International Islamic University of Malaysia (IIUM), 102, 113, 116
International Union of Muslim Scholars (IUMS), 147
Iqbal, Muhammad, 129
Iran, 115
Irigaray, Luce, 81
Islam, Yusuf, 16, 87
Islam and Evolution (Keller), 84
Islam and Liberal Citizenship (March), 172
Islam and the Arab Awakening (Ramadan), 145
"Islam, Irigaray, and the Retrieval of Gender" (Winter), 80
Islam, the West and the Challenges of Modernity, 135
Islamic authority, 28–30, 47–8, 50, 146; *see also* legitimacy
Islamic awakening *see Ṣaḥwah* movement
Islamic banking and finance, 113, 114, 137–8, 192
Islamic councils, 10
Islamic creed *see ʿaqīdah*
Islamic Foundation of Leicester, 124
Islamic history, 105–6, 184
Islamic hypocrisy, 174–5
Islamic Institute of Al-Ayn, 40
Islamic mysticism *see* mysticism; *taṣawwuf*
Islamic Organization for Medical Sciences (IOMS), 205
Islamic Society of North America (ISNA), 26, 41, 115, 116
Islamic State of Iraq and Syria (ISIS), 29

Islamic theology *see kalām*
Islamic University of Medina (IUM), 153, 155–6, 158
Islamic Vision of Development (Chapra), 112
Islamism
and the AlMaghrib Institute, 158
incentives for, 5
and the International Institute of Islamic Thought, 100, 115
and *'jāhilī* law, 171–2
and marginalization, 5
media focus upon, 29
and morality, 49
and Qadhi, 171–2
and Ramadan, 123
rejection of Western modernity, 29
and socio-economic status, 4–5
state efforts to eradicate, 11, 197–9
and terrorism, 9, 73, 115
in the U.K., 197–9
Yusuf on, 49
see also Islamic State of Iraq and Syria (ISIS); al-Qaida; radicalization
Islamique online magazine, 193
Islāmīyat al-Ma'rifah, 104
Islamization of knowledge project, 22, 42, 52, 99–102, 104, 106–10, 116–17
Islamophobia, 9, 161, 200
Issues in Contemporary Islamic Thought (al-Alwani), 105
istiḥālah (transformation), 205
istiṣlāḥ (public interest), 132
Italy, 5

Jackson, Sherman, 46
Jacob, James, 86
'jāhilī law, 171–2
jahilīyah (ignorance), 171–2
jalāl (names of majesty), 80–1
Jamaat-i-Islam, 8
jamāl (names of beauty), 80–1
Jawharah al-Tawḥīd (al-Laqqānī), 77
Jeddah, 72, 114, 155
jihad, 86
Jordan, 88, 162
Judaism, 49, 108, 128, 159, 170–1, 199
al-Junayd, Abū al-Qasim ibn Muḥammad, 77
jurisprudence *see fiqh*

Kaftaru, Ahmad, 44
kalām (Islamic theology), 184
Kamali, Mohammed Hashim, 113
Karachi, 98, 182
Keller, Nuh, 42, 84
Khalil, Imad al Din, 105
Khan, Nouman Ali, 27
Kharijism, 75
Khartoum, 101–2, 115
Khatab, Sayed, 171
Kholwadia, Mohammed Amin, 180, 192–3, 201–5
Kingdom Foundation, 116
Kinza Academy, 43
Knight, Faatimah, 64
knowledge
and *adab*, 52–3
al-Attas on, 52, 53, 54
Islamization of knowledge project, 22, 42, 52, 99–102, 104, 106–10, 116–17
and morality, 51, 52–3, 107, 135–6
and the *Qur'ān*, 107
Ramadan on, 135–43
and secularism, 52, 53–4, 64, 107
specialist, 2–3, 20
and spirituality, 51, 52
and Sufism, 51
tacit, 2–3, 20
*tawḥīd*ic epistemology, 20, 22, 102, 106–10
"Two Books" approach, 135–43, 147
Yusuf on, 42, 44, 51, 52–4
and Zaytuna College, 53–4, 64–5
see also science
Kuwait, 115, 157

labor migration, 5–7
language barriers, 9
Lapidus, Ira, 53
al-Laqqānī, Ibrāhīm, 77
Laurence, Jonathan, 10–11
law *see fiqh*; secular law; *sharī'ah*
legal theory *see uṣūl al-fiqh*
legitimacy, 9, 47–8, 50, 167–8; *see also* Islamic authority
liberal arts, 16, 17, 37, 39, 52, 58, 87, 90
Liberal Reformism, 129, 130
literacy, 164
literature, 60–2
literalism, 129, 130
logic, 58, 184
London, 22–3, 102–3, 112, 114, 181, 193, 196

*madhhab*s (schools of jurisprudence)
Ad Duha on, 194, 195
neo-traditional respect for, 15, 37, 55, 57–8, 72–3, 74–5
as precluding sufficient use of reason, 22, 129, 130, 131
Ramadan's rejection of as legal framework, 22, 129, 130, 131, 133
and reasonable pluralism, 194, 195
Salafi rejection of, 19, 74, 194

madhhabs (schools of jurisprudence) (*cont.*)
  study of any allowed at Darul Qasim, 18, 183
  Winter on, 72–3, 74–6
  Yusuf on, 57–8
  and Zaytuna College, 57–60
  see also Ḥanafī school; *Ḥanbalī* school; *Mālikī* school; *Shāfi'ī* school
Mahmoud, Abdullah Ali, 40
Majallat Qaḍāyā Islāmīyah, 115
majesty, names of *see jalāl*
Malaysia, 102, 113
Mālik ibn Anas, 132
Mālikī school, 40, 42, 132, 201; *see also madhhabs*
maqāṣid al-sharī'ah (principles of the *sharī'*ah), 17, 20–3, 95, 105–6, 111–13, 117, 132–3, 137, 141–7, 173
March, Andrew, 145–6, 172–3
al-Marghinānī, Burhān al-Dīn, 196
marriage, 19, 86, 112, 160
Marxism, 109
Masjid al-Islam, 43
maṣlaḥah (common good), 132, 133, 134, 136, 142
materialism, 16, 61, 80
Māturīdism, 55, 183
Mauritania, 40
Mawdudi, Abu Ala, 130, 171
Mazahirul Uloom school, 193
Mecca, 99, 102, 128
media reporting, 9, 12, 29, 47, 48, 123
medicine, 41, 144, 204–5; *see also* bioethics
memorization, 28, 48, 60, 193
mercy *see raḥmah*
metaphysics, 27, 81, 100
militant Islam *see* Islamism; radicalization
military, 43, 82–3, 113, 114
Mill, John Stuart, 195–6
mindfulness, 51, 64
Minhaj ul Quran, 8
minority status, 20–1, 22, 24, 42, 56–7, 105, 111, 127–8, 130, 168, 170
Mitchell, Ricky *see* Shakir, Zaid
Moosa, Ebrahim, 205
morality
  al-Attas on, 52
  and economics, 108–9, 111–12
  and gender, 84
  and Islamism, 49
  and knowledge, 51, 52–3, 107, 135–6
  and literature, 61–2
  and science, 62–4, 105, 107, 135–6
  and secular law, 168–75
  and secularism, 49–50, 52
  and spirituality, 51
  and Sufism, 43, 51
  and transformative reform, 127–9, 143
  and Western modernity, 50, 110–12
  and Yusuf, 40–1, 42, 43, 44, 49–51, 61–4
  and Zaytuna College, 41, 51–2
Morocco, 8
mu'āmalāt (social practices), 126
Muhammad, Prophet, 60, 86, 128
Muhammad Ali Pasha, 163–4
Mukhtaṣar (Qudūrī), 183
Murabit al-Hajj, 40
Murad, Abdal Hakim *see* Winter, Tim
Murata, Sachiko, 76, 80–1
Muslih, 103
Muslim Academic Trust, 16, 87
Muslim Brotherhood, 44, 100, 115, 123
Muslim converts *see* converts to Islam
Muslim Council of Britain (MCB), 10
Muslim Students Association (MSA), 98, 100, 115
Muslim subjectivities, 9, 12
Musulmans dans la laïcité, Les (Ramadan), 123–4
mutability *see taghayyur*
mut'ah (time-based marriage contracts), 160
mysticism, 15, 78, 100
Myth of God Incarnate, The (Hick), 73

Napoleon Bonaparte, 163
Naqshbandi-Khālidīyah, 44
naskh (abrogation), 75
Nasr, Seyyed Hossein, 99, 100, 109
Nation of Islam, 101
neo-conservatism, 13, 18–20, 23–5, 27, 153–206
neo-legalism, 13, 17–18, 20, 22–3, 95–148
neo-traditionalism, 13, 15–17, 20–2, 26, 27, 37–90
Netherlands, 6, 8, 11
New Brunswick Islamic Center, 43
New Haven, 43–4
New York, 8, 18, 188
New York Times, 47
New Zealand, 5
Newsnight (BBC), 193
niqāb, 200–1; *see also* clothing
North American Islamic Trust, 115
Northern Council of Mosques, 198
Notes from the Underground (Dostoyevsky), 61
Notre Dame University, 124
nuclear families, 79
Nursi, Said, 77, 129

Omar (television series), 164–5
On Salafi Islam (Qadhi), 162–3, 172
orthodoxy, 78
Ottoman Empire, 163, 164

al-Ouda, Salman, 163, 165
Oxford University, 18, 123, 124
Ozymandias (Shelley), 61

pact of the virtuous (*hilf al-fuḍūl*), 128
Padela, Aasim, 204
Pakistan, 98, 182
Palestine, 98
paper manufacturing, 164
parental investment, 83
Peirce, Charles, 84
Perennialist school, 100
Persian language, 72
personal piety, 48, 50, 51
philosophy, 15, 108, 128, 156–7, 184
Pius XII, Pope, 167
pluralism, 18, 24, 72, 78, 128, 194–201, 206
poetry, 60–1, 76–7
Polanyi, Michael, 2
Political Liberalism (Rawls), 167
Political Literalist Salafism, 129, 130
polygamy, 86
polytheism, 107, 160
pork products, 197, 204–5
pornography, 79
positive law *see furū'*
positivism, 107, 171
pragmatism, 46, 62, 86, 110, 165
prayer, 48, 56, 62
printing press, 19, 155, 163–4
psychology, 83–4
public engagement, 193–201, 202
public interest *see istiṣlāḥ*
public reason, 167–8
punishments, 124, 168–9
purification, 37, 44, 51
purification from evil *see tazkiyah*

Qadhi, Yasir
  on abortion, 170–1
  and adaptation to modern realities, 23–4, 153, 155, 157, 159, 161–75
  and the AlMaghrib Institute, 18–19, 157–9, 174–5
  and American Muslim identity, 159
  on apostasy, 168–9
  background, 155
  on conservatism, 19, 155, 163–5
  on democracy, 159, 160
  education, 153, 155–6
  on evolution, 84, 163, 166–7
  on *fatwās*, 19, 23, 155, 163–5
  God's Law and Man-Made Laws, 170–2
  on the Holocaust, 159
  on homosexuality, 19, 155, 157, 159, 168, 169, 170, 173–5
  on Ibn Taymīyah, 155–7
  Interfaith Voices interview, 161–2
  and Islamic hypocrisy, 174–5
  and Islamism, 171–2
  on *'jāhilī* law, 171–2
  On Salafi Islam, 162–3, 172
  and al-Ouda, 163, 165
  and reasonable citizenship, 23–4, 155, 167–75
  and reasonable Salafism, 155, 163–7
  and reciprocity, 24, 168, 170, 174–5, 201
  on revelation and reason, 156–7
  and Salafism, 19, 23, 153, 155, 159–67
  on same-sex marriage, 19, 155, 157, 159, 168, 170, 173–5
  on science, 163, 166–7
  on Shi'ism, 160–1
al-Qaida, 158
al-Qānūn al-Kulī (Universal Rule), 156
Qaradaghi, 'Ali, 147
al-Qaradawi, Yusuf, 99, 100, 113, 114–15, 147, 173
Qasid Arabic Institute, 88
Qatar, 113, 114, 123, 147
Qatar Faculty of Islamic Studies, 147
Qatar Foundation, 18, 23, 112, 147
qaṭ'ī (definitive) evidence, 134, 142
qawaid al-istinbat (deduction and inference), 22, 130
qiyās (analogical reasoning), 139
Quest for Meaning, The (Ramadan), 128
Quick, Abdullah Hakim, 158
Qur'ān
  on creation, 166
  direct engagement with, 23, 161–2
  on homosexuality, 157
  memorization of (*hifz*), 28, 48, 60, 193
  recitation of, 40, 60, 181, 188
  on seeking knowledge of creation, 139
  as source of *fiqh*, 139
  as source of knowledge, 107
  study of at Cambridge Muslim College, 88
  see also foundational texts
Qutb, Muhammad, 100
Qutb, Sayyid, 129, 171

Radical Reform (Ramadan), 128, 131, 136–7, 138–46
radicalization, 4–5, 9, 11, 77, 192–3, 197–200, 201; *see also* Islamism
raḥmah (mercy), 81
Rahman, Fazlur, 98
Ramadan, Said, 13
Ramadan, Tariq
  on abortion, 144
  and adaptation to modern realities, 124–48
  on the application of reform, 144–8

Ramadan, Tariq (*cont.*)
background, 123
on capitalism, 145
and the Center for Islamic Legislation and Ethics, 17–18, 23, 95, 123, 124, 146–8
connections in France, 123–4
connections in the U.K., 124
on context and reform, 124–9, 132, 137–43, 144
debate with Sarkozy, 124
debate with Yusuf, 48, 56
on democracy, 145
education, 123
and European Muslim identity, 11–12, 18, 125–34
on *fatwās*, 125, 131–2, 133–4, 137–8
global following, 27
and *ijtihād*, 22, 129, 130–4, 136, 137–43, 147–8
In the Footsteps of the Prophet, 128
and the International Institute of Islamic Thought, 114
Islam and the Arab Awakening, 145
Islam, the West and the Challenges of Modernity, 135
on Islamic authority, 146
and the Islamic Society of North America, 26
and Islamism, 123
on knowledge, 135–43
and *maqāṣid al-sharīah*, 95, 113, 132–3, 141, 142–3, 144–5, 146, 147
and *maṣlaḥah*, 132, 133, 134, 136
Les musulmans dans la laïcité, 123–4
popularity of, 17–18, 27
and Qaradawi, 147
and *qawaid al-istinbat*, 22, 130
The Quest for Meaning, 128
Radical Reform, 128, 131, 136–7, 138–46
reconciliation of science and Islamic law, 23, 135–43
refused entry to U.S., 123, 124
rejects the *madhhabs* as legal framework, 22, 129, 130, 131, 133
and Salafi Reformism, 22, 129–31
scrutiny of, 123, 124
on secularism, 145
on Text and Context, 140–2, 146, 147
To Be a European Muslim, 125, 130, 131, 132–3, 135
and transformative reform, 127–9, 137–9, 141, 143
"Two Books" approach, 135–43, 147
typology of approaches to reform, 129–31
Western Muslims, 125, 128, 129, 131, 133–4, 135, 136, 137, 138, 147
Rawls, John, 24, 155, 167–8, 170, 172, 173, 174, 175, 194–6
Razavian, Christopher Pooya, 24
al-Rāzī, Fakhr al-Dīn, 156
"Reason as Balance" (Winter), 76–7
reasonable citizenship, 23–4, 155, 167–75
reasonable pluralism, 24, 194–201, 206
reasonable Salafism, 155, 163–7
reciprocity, 24, 168, 170, 174–5, 201
recitation, 40, 60, 181, 188
reproductive strategies, 80, 83
responsible citizenship, 24–5, 202–3, 206
retreats, 13–15, 41
Reuther, Rosemary, 80
Rida, Rashid, 76, 129
Rihla programme, 16, 41, 44
ritual practices *see ibādāt*
Robinson, Francis, 28
Romanticism, 61
Rūmī, Jalāl ad-Dīn, 12, 15, 76–7
Rutgers University, 43

Sacred Caravan, 16
Safar Academy, 193
Ṣaḥwah movement, 100
Salafi Literalism, 129, 130
Salafi Reformism, 22, 129–31
Salafism
Ad Duha's criticism of, 194
and the AlMaghrib Institute, 157, 158–9
and democracy, 160
direct engagement with texts, 23, 75–6, 161–2, 194
influence in diaspora communities, 8
literal readings of texts, 129, 130
mainstream Salafism, 158, 159–63
and Qadhi, 153, 155, 159–63
reasonable Salfism, 155, 163–7
rejection of the *madhhabs*, 19, 74, 75–6, 194
and Shi'ism, 160–1
in Syria, 44
in the United States, 155, 157, 159
Winter's criticism of, 74, 75–6
Yusuf's criticism of, 57
see also AlMaghrib Institute; Wahhabism
Ṣalāḥ al-Dīn, 21, 49
Saleem, Mohammed Abdullah, 202
same-sex marriage, 19, 155, 157, 159, 168, 170, 173–5
Sandala Productions, 16
Sardar, Ziauddin, 100
Sarkozy, Nicolas, 124
Saudi Arabia, 8, 72, 99, 100, 114–16, 153, 155, 158, 164
Scholastic Traditionalism, 129, 130, 131
Schuon, Frithjof, 100, 109

science
  evolutionary theory, 19, 83, 84, 163, 166–7
  and gender, 79, 82–5
  and the International Institute of Islamic Thought, 17, 22, 99, 105, 107
  and morality, 62–4, 105, 107, 135–6
  Qadhi on, 163, 166–7
  Ramadan on, 23, 135–43
  reconciliation with *fiqh*, 17, 22–3, 135–43, 166–7
  Winter on, 79, 82–5
  Yusuf on, 53, 62–4
  see also knowledge
scriptural reasoning, 74
scriptural texts *see* foundational texts
Secular City, The (Cox), 52
secular law, 19, 21, 23–5, 127, 160, 168–75, 202–3, 206
secularism
  al-Attas on, 21, 49, 52, 53, 54, 64
  distinction between the secular state and secularization, 21, 49–50
  and the IIIT, 107
  and knowledge, 52, 53–4, 64, 107
  and morality, 49–50, 52, 168–75
  Ramadan on, 145
  Winter on, 72
  and women, 80
  Yusuf on, 21, 49–50
  Zaytuna College position on, 48–51
Sense and Sensibility (Austen), 61
September 11 attacks, 9, 41, 103, 116, 124
Sexism and God-Talk (Reuther), 80
sexual harassment, 24–5, 202–3
sexuality, 79–80, 83, 86, 174
Shādhilīyah order, 40, 42
al-Shāfi'ī, 75, 141
Shāfi'ī school, 57, 75, 195, 200; *see also* *madhhab*s
Shāh Walī Allāh al-Dihlawī, 77
Shakespeare, William, 61
Shakir, Zaid, 16, 26, 39, 42, 43–5, 46–7, 48, 51, 62
al-Shanqiṭi, Muḥammed al-Amin, 158
sharī'ah
  and apostasy, 168–9
  faithfulness to in Western contexts, 127, 135–43, 170–1
  and human rights, 45
  implementation of for non-Muslims, 196–7
  principles of *see maqāṣid al-sharī'ah*
  and the "Two Books" approach, 135–43
  and women, 80
sharī'ah councils, 19, 164–5, 168, 204, 205
sharī'ah patrols, 196–7
Shariati, Ali, 130
al-Shāṭibī, Abū Isḥāq, 132–3, 141
Shaw, George Bernard, 86
Shelley, Percy Bysshe, 61
Shenandoah University, 114
Shi'ism, 75, 160–1
al-Shingieti, Abubakar, 98, 115
shirk (polytheism), 107, 160
Siddiq, Abdullah Ould, 40
Smith, Wilfred Cantwell, 98
social activism, 43, 44–5, 51
social contract, 172–3
  social integration, 46, 127, 136
social media, 165, 193, 202
social practices *see mu'āmalāt*
Society for Islamic Thought and Culture, 115
socio-economic status, 4, 5–7, 9–10, 27
South Africa, 43, 188
Spain, 5, 13–15
specialist knowledge, 2–3, 20
spirituality
  and knowledge, 51, 52
  and morality, 51
  neo-traditionalist emphasis upon, 15, 37
  and Rūmī, 76–7
  and Sufism, 43, 51, 76–8
  and Western modernity, 29
  and Winter, 72, 77–8
  and Yusuf, 40–1, 42, 43, 44, 45, 49, 51–2
  and Zaytuna College, 41, 45, 51–2
stability (of states), 167–8
Stanford University, 42
states
  consultation with Muslim groups, 10, 11
  efforts to eradicate Islamism, 11, 197–200, 201
  laws of *see* secular law
  legitimacy of, 167–8
  regulation and reform of education, 10–12
  and secularism, 21, 49–50
  stability of, 167–8
Stevens, Cat *see* Islam, Yusuf
stoning, 124
Stubbe, Henry, 86
Studies in Islamic Civilization (Essa and Ali), 106
as-Sufi, Abd AlQadir, 40
Sudan, 101–2, 115
Sufism
  and al-Azhar, 77
  and feminism, 80–1
  internal focus of, 129, 130
  and knowledge, 51
  and mindfulness, 51
  and morality, 43, 51
  and neo-traditionalism, 15
  and reform, 129, 130

Sufism (*cont.*)
  and spirituality, 43, 51, 76–8
  Sufi orders, 40, 43, 44
  Sufi poetry, 61, 76–7
  in Syria, 44
  and *taṣawwuf*, 15, 78
  and Winter, 74, 76–8
  and Yusuf, 40, 43, 51, 61
  and Zaytuna College, 51
ṣuḥba (companionship), 15, 37
sunnah, 75, 78, 103, 139, 157, 194
surrogate motherhood, 205
al-Suyūṭī, Jalāl al-Dīn, 58
Sweden, 21, 49
Switzerland, 99, 123
Syria, 44, 87, 182

Tableegi Jamaat, 8
  tacit knowledge, 2–3, 20
taghayyur (mutability), 56
takfīr (excommunication), 172
Ta'leef Collective, 27
al-Talib, Hisham, 116
tanzīh (God as Transcendence), 76
Tao of Islam, The (Murata), 80–1
taqīyah (concealing faith when in mortal danger), 160
taqlīd (following of authority), 18, 23, 109, 110, 153, 183, 194, 202
taṣawwuf (Islamic mysticism), 15, 78; *see also* mysticism
tashbīh (God as Immanence), 76
tawḥīd (unity of God), 106–7, 111, 135–6, 195
Tawhid publishing house, 123–4
*tawḥīd*ic epistemology, 20, 22, 102, 106–10
*tawḥīd*ic methodology, 100–2
Taylor, Charles, 16
tazkiyah (purification from evil), 111
technology, 41, 63
television, 41, 164–5
terrorism, 9, 73, 115
Theocrats Living under Secular Law (March), 172–3
Tibi, Bassam, 11–12
To Be a European Muslim (Ramadan), 125, 130, 131, 132–3, 135
tolerance, 25, 47, 192, 197, 206
traditional centers of learning, 7–8, 9, 26, 28; *see also* al-Azhar; Deoband; Diyanet; Salafism
transcendental meditation, 43
transformation *see istiḥālah*
transformative reform, 127–9, 137–9, 141, 143
Tri-State Muslim Education Initiative, 43–4
Trivers, Robert, 83
Turkey, 8, 204
Turkish language, 72
"Two Books" approach, 135–43, 147

'Ubayd-Allāh ibn Jahsh, 169
Uddin, Hafiz Mushfiq, 181–2
'Umar ibn 'Abd al-Khattāb, 164–5
'umrān (building of civilization), 111, 112
Understanding Islam and the Muslims (Winter), 73
Understanding the Four Madhhabs (Winter), 72–3, 74–5
United Arab Emirates (U.A.E.), 40, 157
United for Change, 44
United Kingdom (U.K.)
  AlMaghrib seminars, 157
  British Muslim identity, 13, 19, 79, 85–7, 194, 196–201
  dār al-'ulūms, 17, 18, 37, 87, 88, 90
  Deoband, 8, 181–2, 192, 196–201
  diaspora community, 5–7, 181, 192, 196–201
  and diversity, 85–6
  London branch of IIIT, 22–3, 102–3, 112, 114
  madrasahs, 8, 181–2, 197–200
  military, 82–3
  Muslim Council of Britain (MCB), 10
  niqāb debate, 200–1
  and radicalization, 192–3, 197–200, 201
  Ramadan's connections in, 124
  sharī'ah councils, 19
  sharī'ah patrols, 196–7
  sourcing of *imāms* from home countries, 7–8
  suitability of Islam to, 85–7
  see also Cambridge Muslim College; Ebrahim College
United States (U.S.)
  abortion laws, 170–1
  AlMaghrib seminars, 157
  American Muslim Council, 113
  American Muslim identity, 13, 19, 41, 45–8, 50, 51, 60, 102–3, 159
  Black Muslim culture, 7, 46
  Clergy Letter Project, 167
  converts to Islam, 7, 9, 27, 39, 40, 47
  democracy, 47
  Deoband, 8, 182
  diaspora community, 5, 7, 9–10, 180–1, 182
  education, 43
  Federal Bureau of Investigation (FBI), 103, 158
  Fiqh Council of North America, 113, 114–15
  foreign policy, 41

Islamic Society of North America (ISNA), 26, 41, 115, 116
madrasahs, 8, 182
military, 43, 113, 114
popularity of Islamic institutions based in, 12–13, 27
Ramadan refused entry to, 123, 124
Salafism, 155, 157, 159
same-sex marriage laws, 19, 155, 170
September 11 attacks, 9, 41, 103, 116, 124
socio-economic status of Muslims, 7, 9–10, 27
sourcing of *imāms* from home countries, 7–8
see also AlMaghrib Institute; Darul Qasim; International Institute of Islamic Thought; Zaytuna College
unity of God *see see tawḥīd*
Universal Rule *see al-Qānūn al-Kulī*
universality, 85, 86, 108, 125, 126, 128–9
University of Science and Technology, Yemen, 114
Usmani, Taqi, 202
uṣūl al-fiqh (legal theory), 23, 75, 112–13, 131, 133, 137, 138, 141, 146, 183–4
al-Uthaymin, Muhammad ibn Salih, 158, 194
ʿUthmān, 75

Vision of Islam, The (Chittick), 49, 76
voting *see* democracy

Wadud, Amina, 48
Wahhabism, 15, 72, 77, 106–7; *see also* Salafism
waḥī (divine revelation), 203–4
waqf (religious endowments), 116
Warren, David, 147
Washington, D.C., 17, 97, 98
wealth, 111–12; *see also* socio-economic status
Weiss, Bernard, 130–1
Welt des Islams, Die, 148
Western education, 3, 99
Western modernity
critique of, 16, 29
engagement with, 16, 17, 19–20, 27–30, 60–5, 97, 102–4, 109–13, 124–43, 193–201
enrichment of, 17, 27
and hegemony, 126, 135, 145
and individualism, 29, 61
and integration, 46, 127, 136
and materialism, 16, 61, 80
and morality, 50, 110–12
and spirituality, 29
and transformative reform, 127–8, 137–9, 141, 143
and women, 79–80
Western Muslims (Ramadan), 125, 128, 129, 131, 133–4, 135, 136, 137, 138, 147
Western Thought Project, 107–8
"What is Scriptural Reasoning?" (Winter), 74
Whole Woman, The (Greer), 22, 79
wilāyah (authority and governance), 204
al-wilāyah al-takwīnīyah, 160–1
Winter, Tim
on American Muslim identity, 45–6
on balanced reason, 76–7
Bombing without Moonlight, 73
"Boys will be Boys," 21–2, 79, 82
and British Muslim identity, 79, 85–7
and Cambridge Muslim College, 16–17, 37, 72, 87–90
conversion, 73
as convert to Islam, 9, 16, 27, 73, 85
criticism of Salafism, 74, 75–6
criticism of Wahhabism, 72, 77
on diversity, 72, 85–6
education, 72
on evolution, 84, 167
on gender, 21–2, 79–85
global following, 27
"Islam, Irigaray, and the Retrieval of Gender," 80
on the *madhhabs*, 72–3, 74–6
neo-traditionalism, 16–17, 37, 72, 73–8
on orthodoxy, 78
and pluralism, 72, 78
popularity of, 27, 37
"Reason as Balance," 76–7
on science, 79, 82–5
on scriptural reasoning, 74
on secularism, 72
and spirituality, 72, 77–8
and Sufism, 74, 76–8
Understanding Islam and the Muslims, 73
Understanding the Four Madhhabs, 72–3, 74–5
visiting scholar at Alqueria de Rosales, 15
"What is Scriptural Reasoning?," 74
wisdom *see ḥikmah*
women
clothing, 62, 170, 196, 200–1
and difference, 79–85
and evolutionary biology, 83
Greer on, 22, 79
in the military, 82–3
Murata on, 80–1
and the names of God, 80–1
physical weakness of, 82–3
and psychology, 83–4
in religious roles, 48, 56, 62, 81

women (*cont.*)
and secularism, 80
segregation of, 81
and sexuality, 79–80
and *sharī'ah*, 80
and Western modernity, 79–80
Winter on, 21–2, 79–85
Yusuf on, 56, 62, 82
Zaytuna College position on, 48, 62
see also feminism; gender debates
World Congress of Muslim Philanthropists, 116
World Forum for the Proximity of Islamic Schools of Thought, 115

Yale University, 44, 153, 155–6, 172
Yemen, 114
Yusuf, Hamza
as advisor to institutions and governments, 41–2
and American Muslim identity, 41, 46–8, 60
and al-Attas, 21, 42, 49, 51, 54
background, 40
and Bin Bayyah, 21, 40, 42, 56–7
as convert to Islam, 9, 16, 27, 39, 40, 41
criticism of, 41, 47
debate with Ramadan, 48, 56
education, 40
on engagement with Western modernity, 60–5
establishes Kinza Academy, 43
establishes Zaytuna College, 16, 39, 41
on gender, 56, 62, 82
global following, 27
influences upon, 21, 42
and the Islamic Society of North America, 26, 41
on Islamism, 49
on knowledge, 42, 44, 51, 52–4
on the *madhhabs*, 57–8
on mainstream education, 43
and the *Mālikī* school, 40, 42
media representations of, 48
medical career, 41
and morality, 40–1, 42, 43, 44, 49–51, 61–4
on poetry, 60–1
popularity of, 12, 15, 27, 37, 41
on respect for secular law, 21
and the *Rihla* programme, 41, 44
on Salafism, 57
on science, 53, 62–4
on secularism, 21, 49–50
and spirituality, 40–1, 42, 43, 44, 45, 49, 51–2
and Sufism, 40, 43, 51, 61
and tradition, 40, 41, 42, 54–5, 58–60, 159
see also Zaytuna College

Zaman, Mujadad, 88
Zaman, Qasim, 28
ẓannī (conjectural) evidence, 134, 142
Zarruq, Ahmad, 51
Zaytuna College
and *adab*, 52–3
aims of, 16, 39, 45, 50
and American Muslim identity, 45–8, 50, 51, 60
and Bin Bayyah, 56–7
conservatism, 48
curriculum, 16, 39, 42, 44, 45, 46, 58–60, 188
degrees awarded, 16
dress code, 41
engagement with the Muslim community, 48
engagement with Western modernity, 16, 60–5
establishment of, 16, 39, 41, 44
and *fiqh al-wāqi'*, 56–7
and Islamic authority, 47–8, 50
and knowledge, 53–4, 64–5
legitimacy of, 47–8, 50
and the liberal arts, 16, 37, 38, 52, 58
links with other Islamic learning initiatives, 16, 41
and the *madhhabs*, 57–60
and memorization, 48, 60
and morality, 41, 51–2
numbers of native converts, 47
position on homosexuality, 48
position on secularism, 48–51
position on women's religious roles, 48, 62
and renovation of tradition, 56–7
rules and regulations, 41, 48
and spirituality, 41, 45, 51–2
and Sufism, 51
and tradition, 48, 54–7, 58–60
training of *imāms*, 39, 45
see also Shakir, Zaid; Yusuf, Hamza
Zionism, 49